Mechanical Systems

HANDBOOK
FOR HEALTH CARE FACILITIES

J. Robin Barrick, PE
Ronald G. Holdaway, PE

The American Society for Healthcare Engineering (ASHE)
of the American Hospital Association (AHA)
155 North Wacker Drive, Suite 400
Chicago, IL 60606
312-422-3800
www.ashe.org
ashe@aha.org

About the Authors

Rob Barrick has served as CEO of Smith Seckman Reid, Inc. (SSR) since 1986 and has been Chairman and CEO since 1995. Rob began his career with Smith Seckman Reid, Inc. in 1974. He held the positions of mechanical engineer, project manager, and mechanical department head before moving to Houston in 1983, where he started and managed the Houston office before returning to the Nashville office in 1986. He is a registered Professional Engineer in 16 states, a Certified Energy Manager, a Green Building Engineer, and a LEED™ Accredited Professional. Rob holds a bachelor's degree in mechanical engineering from Vanderbilt University and a master's of business administration from Vanderbilt Owen Graduate School of Management. Rob is a member of the American Council of Engineering Companies and National Society of Professional Engineers. He received the Engineer of the Year award in 2003 and the Young Engineer of the Year award in 1989 from the American Council of Engineering Companies of Tennessee. Professional contributions with American Council of Engineering Companies of Tennessee include Chairman Ethics Committee; PEPP Chairman; ACE/PAC Trustee; and President. Rob served as an adjunct professor at Vanderbilt University, teaching building systems and LEED certification preparation. Rob has lectured at national and regional ASHE meetings on mechanical systems, solar energy system design, and chiller refrigerant options, and to the Design and Construction Quality Institute, PSMA, PSMJ, and the American Council of Engineering Companies of Tennessee on management, ownership transition, team structure, and project management. ASHE published his first edition of this book in 1992.

Ron Holdaway, PE, LEEDAP, spent 39½ years in Nashville working for Smith Seckman Reid, Inc.. Ron's latest role at SSR was Senior Design Principal responsible for conceptual design, value engineering, systems coordination, and overall direction of projects. Ron is a member of ASHE and has spoken on high-performance design for hospitals at a recent ASHE PDC conference. He has been a member of ASHRAE since 1973, having joined as a student member while attending Tennessee Tech. Ron's areas of specialized knowledge include hospital mechanical systems, high-performance and sustainable design, direct digital control and energy management systems, central plant design, district chilled water and heating distribution systems, airflow analysis, smoke control systems, and acoustics. Ron now lives and works in Panama City, Florida. As RG Holdaway Consulting, LLC, he provides mechanical consulting services, including system evaluations, standards creation, design reviews, facility assessments, commissioning, high-performance design, and energy performance reporting.

ASHE Disclaimer

ISBN: 978-0-9863239-0-4

Contents

Figures

Chapter 2

Chapter 3

Chapter 4

Chapter 5

Preface

Since this book's original publication in 1993 and update in 2006, the energy consumed by mechanical systems in health care facilities has become a major focus of design engineers, contractors, and the hospital personnel who operate these systems. For too many years, the industry practice has been to simply accept the high energy consumption for which many hospitals are responsible. Commercial buildings consume 42 percent of total U.S. energy, and a relatively small number of hospitals (approximately 5,000 acute care hospitals) in the United States consume 2 percent of this total. Given our awareness of these facts, the status quo is no longer acceptable, nor should it be. The legacy mechanical systems still used in some facilities must be updated to reduce the energy consumption and carbon footprint of hospitals across the country. The designs and operating strategies of the past are no longer acceptable.

The purpose of this volume is to provide basic instruction in the fundamentals of both legacy and current HVAC systems, to increase the hospital engineer's knowledge of the design process and the rationale behind system and equipment selection, and to introduce the concept of high-performance systems. Hospital engineers must be key members of the design and construction teams. These professionals work in dynamic environments where codes, regulations, and technology constantly evolve and the expectations of those who use the facilities continue to increase. Participating in and understanding the rationale behind these decisions will increase engineers' effectiveness in operating and maintaining these systems over their 20- to 40-year lives.

While many updates to this book were needed, much of the information included in the original edition, written more than 20 years ago by Rob Barrick, PE, is still useful. Mr. Barrick acknowledges the contributors who assisted in creating this information, including: Rick Wood, Jr., PE; John Alsentzer, PE; Leo Old, PE, C.I.H., CHFM; and Spivey Lipsey, Jr., PE.

—Ronald G. Holdaway, PE

CHAPTER 1

Introduction and Overview

This book is intended to provide a basic understanding of the systems and components that make up the heating, ventilation, and air-conditioning (HVAC) systems, or mechanical systems, in health care facilities. Mechanical systems in health care facilities tend to be more complex than systems in most other buildings and need more rigid maintenance to meet the special needs and functions of the facility.

In recent years, a paradigm shift has occurred in design and operation of mechanical systems. The industry has acknowledged that we cannot continue to accept the high energy consumption of the legacy systems found in most hospitals. High-performance design and operation is the new normal. Patient outcomes are the number one priority for hospital operations. Designing and operating more efficient systems can produce exceptional patient outcomes while lowering cost, reducing noise, and maintaining better environmental conditions.

The average energy utilization index (EUI) in U.S. hospitals is one of the highest of any building type. The 24/7, 365-day operation; the high ventilation rates required for ventilation and sepsis control; and the critical nature of the procedures performed in hospitals are some of the reasons the industry has accepted these high rates of energy consumption.

Research efforts and recent hospital design and construction innovations have proven that these high consumption levels need not be tolerated. Some new hospitals have achieved EUIs approaching 100 kBTU or less. Research conducted by University of Washington Integrated Design Lab Target 100! documents that EUIs can be decreased for hospitals in every region of the United States with a focus on integrated building design. High-performance design and operation of hospitals is the new paradigm.

The HVAC system in a hospital does far more than just keep occupants comfortable. It also serves a critical role in patient health and therapy. For example, areas such as burn treatment require warmer, more humid conditions than areas dedicated to respiratory patients. These functions must be considered in hospital design, but they should not necessarily grant a pass for significantly higher energy consumption. A hospital's mechanical systems represent at least 20 percent of the initial cost of constructing the facility and up to 60 percent of the utility cost of operating the building. (The remaining utility expense is for domestic water heating; lighting; electrical plug loads; miscellaneous electrical loads for elevators, computers, and conveyor systems; and so on.) Mechanical systems present a unique challenge to the hospital engineer because he or she constantly balances the systems' performance requirements with their operating costs. The mechanical engineer is responsible for designing 70 percent of energy systems.

Hospital mechanical systems must be designed and maintained to provide the following fundamental environmental control functions:

- Temperature
- Humidity
- Air filtration
- Introduction of fresh air for the dilution of odors, bacteria, and carbon dioxide
- Proper pressure relationships between clean and dirty functions to prevent contamination and the spread of infection

- Smoke control and smoke evacuation in the event of a fire
- Proper pressurization for the entire building to prevent moisture from entering exterior wall cavities and causing moisture, mildew, and possible freezing that can damage the facade of a building
- Redundancy to provide continuous service with minimum disruption during scheduled shutdowns for maintenance and unexpected breakdowns

The industry has learned that to reduce energy consumption in health care facilities, the facility engineers must be involved in the planning, design, and construction phases of renovation and expansion projects. The industry is embracing integrated building design, which is a collaborative approach that involves all stakeholders in the performance of the building systems. Hospital engineers' understanding of the existing facility, the capabilities of local service organizations, and their own organization and staff capabilities are critical to the planning and design process and the success of the overall project. Based on the belief that a hospital engineer should be a member of the planning and design team, this book is intended to increase the hospital engineer's knowledge of the options regarding equipment and systems. The results should be better decisions made during the planning and design process and more effective operation of the mechanical systems as the hospital engineer carries forward the responsibility of operating and maintaining these systems. Hospitals are subject to unique code requirements that affect the design, operation, and maintenance of mechanical systems and equipment. Many of these codes are constantly changing and subject to interpretation by local authorities. Current code issues are addressed where they apply to various systems and components throughout this book. Each jurisdiction may also have unique codes or standards. Codes, standards, and guidelines that apply to HVAC systems include the following:

- *Guidelines for Design and Construction of Hospital and Outpatient Facilities*, 2014 edition, Facility Guidelines Institute

- *Guidelines for Design and Construction of Residential Health, Care, and Support Facilities*, 2014 edition, Facility Guidelines Institute
- ASHE Sustainability Roadmap for Hospitals (www.sustainabilityroadmap.org)
- ANSI/ASHRAE/ASHE Standard 170-2013: *Ventilation of Health Care Facilities*
- ANSI/ASHRAE/ASHE Standard 90.1-2013: *Energy Standard for Buildings Except Low-Rise Residential Buildings*
- *HVAC Design Manual for Hospitals and Clinics*, 2nd Edition, ASHRAE
- ANSI/ASHRAE Standard 62.1-2013: *Ventilation for Acceptable Indoor Air Quality*
- ASHRAE Standard 55-2010: *Thermal Environmental Conditions for Human Occupancy*
- United States Pharmacopoeia Chapter 797
- ANSI/AAMI Standard ST79: *Comprehensive Guide to Steam Sterilization and Sterility Assurance in Health Care Facilities*
- *ASHRAE Advanced Energy Design Guidelines for Large Hospitals*, 2012
- Leadership in Energy and Environmental Design (LEED®) for Healthcare, V4.0
- Model building and mechanical codes such as IBC, IEC, and IMC

The root causes of most common and recurring problems in mechanical systems in health care facilities usually are related to system controls and balances. This book addresses these problems both from the standpoint of what can be accomplished using in-house personnel and what should be expected from outside contractors performing work in these areas. Retro or continuous commissioning is the norm in hospitals today to ensure that the systems are operating efficiently and as intended in the original design. Frequent control tune-ups are necessary to maintain building performance.

Finally, this book is intended to be a reference for the hospital engineer. Additional resources are suggested throughout this book and in the appendixes. The hope is that this information will make needed information and qualified advice regarding equipment operation problems more accessible. New high-performance design and operation strategies and practices are also presented here.

CHAPTER 2

High-Performance Design and Operation

Hospitals consume large amounts of energy. They are open 24 hours a day. Thousands of employees, patients, and visitors occupy the buildings daily. Sophisticated HVAC systems control the temperatures and air flow. Many energy-intensive activities occur in these buildings: laundry, medical and lab equipment use, sterilization, computer and server use, food service, and refrigeration. The 2007 Commercial Building Energy Consumption Survey (CBECS) data showed that large hospitals (greater than 200,000 square feet), of which there were approximately 3,040 in the United States at the time data was collected, consumed 5.5 percent of the total delivered energy used by the commercial sector that year.

Many design decisions affect a building's energy use (expressed in whole-building area-weighted EUI, or kBtu/ft2/yr). The design and construction team on a new project or facility management on an existing facility needs to establish target energy goals for design and operation. Average U.S. hospital energy consumption varies between 240 and 270 kBtu/ft2/yr, even though many newer hospitals have been designed with sustainability as a goal. Sustainable best practices such as LEED standards have not achieved the desired reductions in energy consumption in hospitals. Research by University of Washington Integrated Design Lab provides the component breakdown for energy use in a hospital shown in Figure 2-1.

Figure 2-1 Hospital Energy by End Use

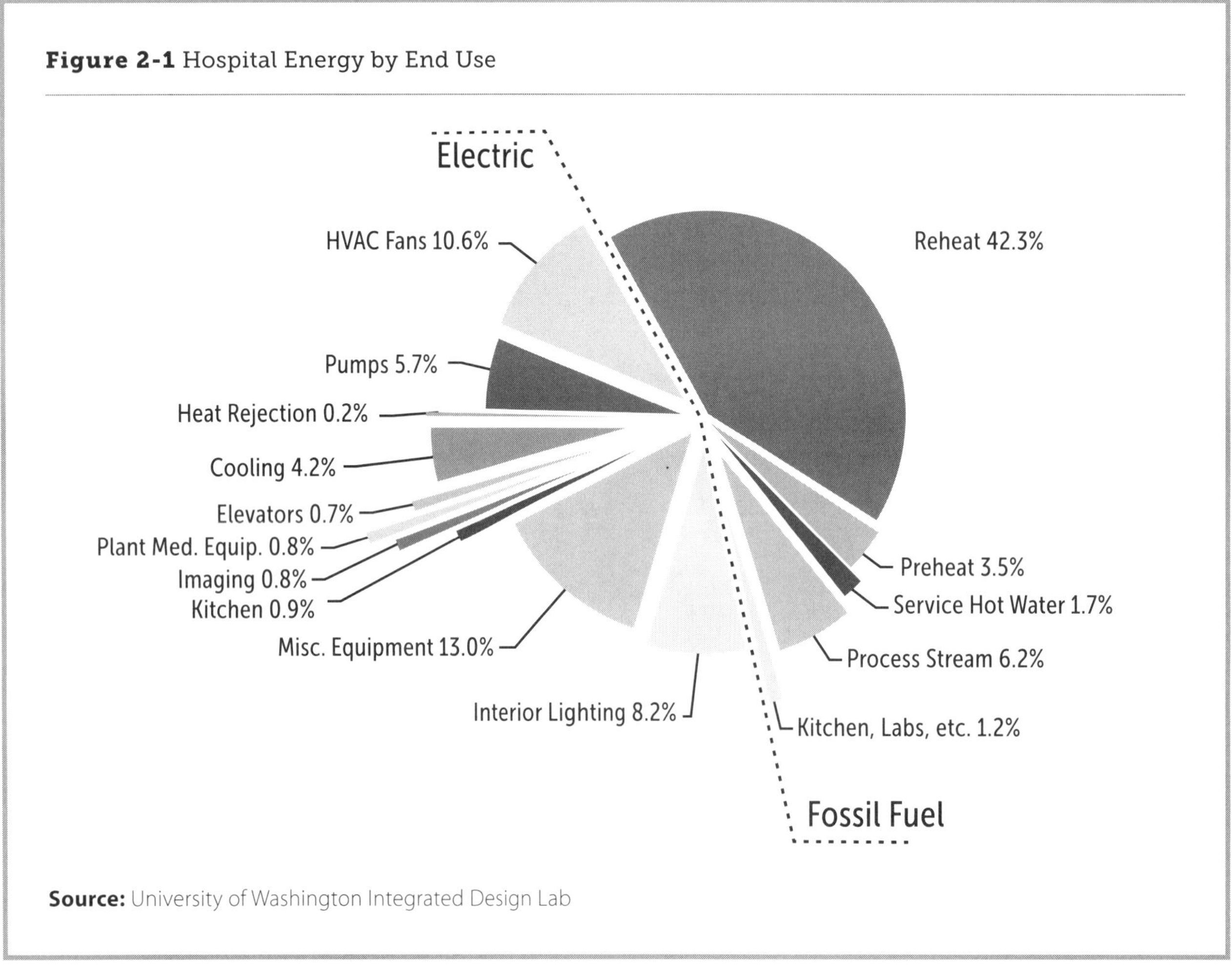

Source: University of Washington Integrated Design Lab

It is worth noting that 42 percent of the energy a hospital uses is used for reheat. This obviously needs to be a focus for the design engineer and the hospital operator. The high air change requirements in hospitals result in a greater supply of air than is needed to meet the space load. The oversupply is cooled, then reheated. One hospital engineer reported that an increase in steam use when outside air temperatures increased caused more chillers to come online. The air-handling units in most hospitals condition all of the air to 50 to 55°F, then reheat the air to maintain space temperature. Neither the designs of the past or current designs have addressed this wasteful use of energy.

In most hospitals, no synergy exists between systems. The chillers or DX units produce cold air and water, and the steam or hot water boilers produce hot Btus. The process significantly increases the facility's energy use as the boiler reheats the air and the chiller removes this heat, along with the envelope and internal loads. These are then rejected via a cooling tower to the plant.

Why is this still an acceptable practice? Reasons include that it is what has always been done in hospital design, it is how the engineer designed his or her last hospital, the architect-engineer (A/E) team does not have the resources to evaluate alternative systems, the hospital staff is only familiar with this design, and high-performance systems are frequently value engineered out of the project due to higher first cost even if the life cycle cost merits use of the more energy-efficient approach.

ASHRAE's *Advanced Energy Design Guide for Large Hospitals* is intended to educate design engineers and operators on other approaches. One method it suggests to reduce energy consumption in a hospital is to eliminate central steam boilers. To many engineers and designers, this will sound like heresy. The internal load, including equipment, lights, and people, is the cheapest energy source for space and domestic hot water heating. The systems must be designed to recover this energy. This is not feasible in every hospital design, but the engineer and operator should remain open to new ideas.

There is no single certification that inarguably designates a building as high performance, sustainable, or green. Several programs (e.g., ASHE's Energy to Care, ASHRAE BeQ, Energy Star, LEED, BOMA 360, Green Globes) attempt to designate buildings as green or sustainable. "High-performance" is simply a term that attempts to move a building a step beyond the traditional notion of green.

Energy Benchmarking

In today's environment with its focus on energy performance and costs, hospital operators will need to benchmark their facility's energy use. Energy benchmarking compares a facility to others of similar size and scope. One industry standard used for energy benchmarking is EPA's Energy Star Profile Manager. The building characteristics and billing data are entered into EPA's online tool, which provides a score based on the comparison of similar facilities in the database. A score of 75 or greater earns the Energy Star certification and indicates that the facility is in the 75th percentile or higher compared with similar facilities.

High-Performance Design Charrette

New projects should begin with documenting the owner's project requirements (OPR) for energy performance. All stakeholders should participate in a series of collaborative meetings to establish the energy performance of the project. Frequently, sustainability charrettes focus on nonenergy features and systems. This is one reason facilities are meeting sustainability guidelines but not measurably reducing energy use or carbon footprint. NREL's *Guide to Conducting a High Performance Design Charrette* can help focus the design and construction team on energy performance.

Energy Modeling

Energy modeling is a high-performance design tool that design engineers and energy consultants use to compare various energy alternatives during design and as an operational tool. The energy model is an 8,760-hour annual predication of energy use of a baseline system compared to various alternatives. Programs used by engineers include Trane Trace, Carrier HAP, eQuest, DOE-II, EnergyPlus, and IES. LEED-certified projects are required to have a baseline energy model as described in Appendix G of ASHRAE 90.1.

An energy model is not a tool to predict utility costs. The many variables make this impractical. Instead, it is a comparative tool used for early design stage climate analysis, load reduction analysis such as building envelope alternatives, and life cycle cost analysis. For new projects, various energy systems must be vetted to determine which system has the lowest life cycle cost while meeting the OPR. This decision should be made early in the design phase. An energy model has a higher potential for performance impact when it is chosen early than when it is made after the decisions on design, project, and, most important, project cost have been made. The opportunities for cost-effective, energy-saving design solutions decrease tremendously after the design team has met for the first time. Important decisions and design changes are much easier to make at the start of the project timeline. In later phases, major changes may be set aside due to the level of effort required to make them once the design has progressed too far.

Measurement and Verification

The old adage is true: You can't manage what you don't measure. Measurement of energy systems in a hospital is necessary to harness capital and human resources for improving energy performance. Adding meters to primary systems such as cooling, heating, lighting, and electrical plug loads can direct efforts to reduce energy consumption. On new projects, this is becoming the norm. Electrical loads must be designed to be divided among lighting, plug loads, process loads such as sterilizers and dietary, cooling, and heating. Energy meters for domestic hot water, chilled water, heating hot water, and steam are the standard in today's designs. The metering devices are frequently listed as possible value engineering cost savings, but this should be resisted. Measuring energy by component does not contribute to effective management of overall energy consumption in the facility. During the design phase, the energy end uses (e.g., lighting, heating, cooling, ventilation, plug loads, pumps, and motors) must be estimated and the largest end uses by type most aggressively attacked. During operation, the operator receives instant feedback allowing him or her to compare design estimates to actual use and to identify and correct discrepancies.

CHAPTER 3

Powerhouse Equipment

This chapter describes the types and functions of primary mechanical equipment traditionally found in a hospital powerhouse, or main mechanical equipment room. It also identifies high-performance design alternatives. Many combinations of equipment and systems can provide the environmental control functions listed in Chapter 1. Component and system selection depend on the size of the facility, the climate of the area where the facility is located, local practices and customs of the facility's design engineers and operating engineers, and the state of the art that existed when the facility was constructed. The original construction budget also may have a significant effect on the choice and configurations of the systems. This chapter makes general comparisons of the advantages and disadvantages of the different types of systems and components. Specific circumstances at a particular facility will influence equipment and system selection.

Powerhouse

Larger hospital facilities may have a separate powerhouse or main mechanical room that houses the primary heating and cooling equipment. Often the gas, fuel oil, water, and electric service entrances are found in this central location, along with the boilers, the chillers, and their associated equipment.

Maintaining a central plant location as the facility is expanded and renovated may have advantages. Bringing in a new electric service or adding a new chiller or boiler at another location within the hospital may reduce the cost of a single renovation project, but keeping the equipment in one place offers several advantages.

Traditionally, central plant has always been thought of as the only feasible system for larger hospitals. Recent hospital designs challenge this thought. Design teams must rethink the system choices of the past. At least, a vetting process should be used to consider all of the factors related to system choices. Table 3-1 presents the benefits and disadvantages of central plant equipment.

Table 3-1 Pros and Cons of Central Plant Equipment

Pros	Cons
Lower first cost. Larger equipment that is centrally located may result in lower per-unit capacity than smaller equipment located throughout the facility.	Decentralized equipment or a combination of centralized and decentralized equipment may result in lower first cost than central equipment.
Lower operating costs. Larger equipment may have a lower operating cost per unit of capacity. Standby losses may penalize central equipment. For example, maintaining a large steam boiler in standby mode can add significant energy consumption.	Distribution (pumping, steam distribution, fan energy) energy costs may be higher than other system alternatives. Smaller equipment such as condensing boilers is operated when the load exists.
Lower maintenance costs. Centrally located equipment of a larger size may be easier to maintain because tools, diagnostic equipment, and personnel can be located in one place without having to move throughout the facility.	Maintenance personnel frequently are not adequately trained to maintain central equipment. Smaller, incremental equipment may be more within the capabilities of the maintenance staff.
Lower life cycle costs.	Life cycle costs must be evaluated, not assumed because of past designs.
Noise and vibration control. Keeping mechanical equipment in a central location, or even away from the main hospital facility, reduces the cost of preventing noise transmission to occupied spaces within the facility.	Noise can be managed in designs not in a central plant. Distributed equipment may have lower vibration and noise generation.

Table 3-1 Pros and Cons of Central Plant Equipment (*continued*)

Pros	Cons
Pollution control. Having a pollution control device that can serve several units in one location is obviously more cost-effective than installing individual pollution control devices on units located throughout the facility.	Smaller equipment may not reach thresholds requiring complex pollution controls.
Safety. Safety procedures may be easier to control when staff and visitors are separated from the facility's major pieces of machinery. It may reduce operating costs to preserve a clean and safe environment when only one central location needs to be maintained by maintenance and operating personnel.	Smaller equipment can be easily isolated from the public. Less hazardous equipment may be possible with distributed equipment.
Centrally located equipment may or may not reduce the total space required for mechanical systems.	Many recent designs have proven that a modified design requires less equipment space.
Flexibility. Health care delivery, and therefore health care facilities, will continue to exist in a rapidly changing dynamic environment. Hospitals are continually expanding and renovating to meet changing health care technology and to improve the way health care services are provided to the public. Design and facility engineers are constantly reminded of the need to provide flexibility and expansion capability in the facility's equipment and systems.	Distributed systems may make it easier to accommodate future expansion. Frequently, first cost penalty of building in equipment or distribution cost for central plant equipment and systems can be avoided. Oversizing equipment for the future may be prohibitively expensive and wasteful.

Boilers

The American Society of Heating, Refrigerating, and Air Conditioning Engineers (ASHRAE) defines a boiler as a pressure vessel designed to transfer heat (produced by combustion) to a fluid. The National Fire Protection Association (NFPA) defines a boiler as a closed vessel in which water is heated, steam is generated, steam is superheated, or any combination thereof, by the application of heat from combustible fuels. The three most common types of boilers found in health care facilities today are large, built-in-place water tube boilers (usually constructed before 1994); packaged fire tube boilers; or water tube packaged boilers. The last two are the most common in hospitals built since 1994, but recent trends suggest this is changing to reduce energy consumption.

Newer facilities are being designed with condensing hot water boilers for heating and domestic hot water generation. These boilers operate at efficiencies between 88 and 94 percent. ASHRAE (2010) recommends as a best practice for reducing energy consumption avoiding large central steam distribution systems in favor of condensing boilers and point of use generation for sterilizers, dietary, and humidification. Boilers are usually classified into groups based on working pressure and temperature, fuel used, shape, and size. All boilers are constructed to meet the American Society of Mechanical Engineers (ASME) Pressure Vessel Code, Section 4. The type of boiler used in a facility and its working pressure depend on the facility's equipment and its steam requirements. For example, if the facility has a laundry with steam-heated flatwork ironers, 125 psi steam is required to run the flatwork ironers at an acceptable rate; however, hospitals are moving away from in-house laundries. Most sterilizers used in central sterile supplies and flash sterilizers adjacent to operating rooms require 50 to 80 psi steam for proper operation. Facilities also use steam to humidify the air supply to critical areas such as operating rooms, delivery rooms, intensive care units, and nurseries, except in tropical climates. A facility with a steam boiler also uses steam to heat the facility, either through a heat exchanger that creates hot water or by piping steam directly to heating coils in air handlers and ductwork. Steam may also be used in heat exchangers to heat domestic water and for steam kettles and other dietary equipment.

Boilers that operate above 15 psi are classified as high-pressure boilers which, under most code authorities, require a qualified boiler operator to be available on a 24-hour basis.

The Scotch or Scotch Marine boiler, which is the most common, is a packaged steel boiler designed for medium and large applications. It is a fire tube boiler with a central fluid-backed cylindrical fire box. This type of boiler is popular because of its relatively low cost and compact size.

Most boilers typically have an efficiency rating of between 75 and 85 percent. Recently, some hot water boilers have been designed to condense flue gases within the boiler and the stack, and these boilers have achieved efficiencies of between 85 and 95 percent. A boiler that is not designed to condense flue gases within the shell and the exhaust stack should never be operated at a temperature lower than 140°F, because condensing flue gases are highly corrosive and will damage the steel and cast-iron boiler components. A discussion on how to control hot water systems to save energy and protect the boiler follows in Chapter 4.

Steam boilers usually have pressure-actuated controls that vary the input fuel to the boiler. The controls should be modulating, which infinitely varies the fuel input from 100 percent down to a selected minimum point. Hot water boilers are controlled by a temperature controller that varies the input to maintain a selected water temperature leaving the boiler.

Fuel Type

Many boilers in health care facilities today are dual-fuel fired and are capable of burning natural gas and number 2 fuel oil with very minor adjustments to the burner. Because hospitals have emergency generators that often burn number 2 fuel oil, and because the storage tank and associated piping are necessary parts of this emergency power system, including a multiple fuel–burning burner for the boilers to allow the hospital to have a backup source of fuel is relatively inexpensive. Hospital codes require backup equipment for sterilization and space heating in health care facilities. An alternate fuel source provides additional redundancy to ensure continuous operating capability. On most packaged boilers, the gas and fuel oil control train are preassembled components that are specified to meet all the safety requirements of government agencies and insurance agencies. Number 2 fuel oil is usually atomized by the fuel boiler burner by introducing the oil through a nozzle at high pressure, using either a high-pressure feed pump or compressed air. This burner is a pressure-atomizing type and is the simplest and most reliable way to atomize fuel oil for proper combustion. Heavier oils, which may be available for use by health care facilities near shipping ports, are usually atomized using air or steam. Heavier oils also may require preheating to reduce the viscosity for proper combustion.

Another benefit of having a dual-fuel fired boiler is the flexibility it provides to switch from one fuel to the other when energy costs fluctuate (i.e., fuel oil versus natural gas). Additionally, many natural gas utilities offer interruptible gas rates for customers who can switch fuels during seasons of high natural gas usage.

Code and Safety Issues

The open combustion that takes place inside boilers and their high operating pressures make boilers good candidates for nasty accidents. For this reason, numerous and extensive codes govern the design, installation, and operation of boilers. NFPA requirements for boiler design, manufacture, engineering, and operation are contained under NFPA Section 85. NFPA states, "The most basic cause of furnace explosions is the ignition of accumulated combustible materials within the confined space." Interruption of the fuel supply to an operating boiler, a fuel leak into an idle furnace, or repeated unsuccessful attempts to start a boiler without appropriate purging are the most frequently cited reasons for boiler explosions. Thus, the controls that initiate the purging cycle and control the fuel flow to the boiler are subject to very strict requirements in almost all code books. The International Mechanical Code (IMC) gives the details for boiler room design, including fuel requirements, working clearances, and controls. Per the IMC, boilers shall be designed and constructed in accordance with the requirements of ASME CSD-1 and as applicable, the ASME Boiler and Pressure Vessel Code, Section I or IV; NFPA 8501; NFPA 8502; or NFPA 8504. ASHRAE Standard 15 requires a refrigerant detector to shut down the boiler in the event of refrigerant leakage. It is best practice to locate any combustion equipment and chillers in separate rooms. Most states have unique boiler inspection and operating requirements. ASME CSD-1 has several requirements that affect boiler room design, including remote emergency shutdown switches, catwalks, and ladders on boilers taller than 8 feet.

Deaerators

Functions

Deaerators are used along with water treatment to remove oxygen and other gases from boiler feed water using a reduction in pressure or heat or a combination of both. Many small- and medium-sized boiler plants do not use deaerators but instead use a feed water makeup tank with boiler feed pumps. Today, most deaerators are furnished in a package that includes boiler feed water controls and deaeration in one unit. In boiler plants that operate at a low pressure and have a very small requirement for makeup water, deaeration may not be necessary and the oxygen and carbon dioxide can be removed from the makeup water through the use of chemicals. In hospitals, boilers usually operate at either 60 psi or 125 psi (to provide steam for sterilizers and laundry equipment, respectively), and if direct steam is used for humidification the makeup water requirements can be significant during the winter.

Removing oxygen and carbon dioxide from the boiler feed water reduces the following:

- Corrosion in return condensate lines and boiler feed lines
- Repair and maintenance of steam traps
- Maintenance (by bringing feed water and boiler temperatures closer together)
- The amount of chemical treatment required to neutralize oxygen and carbon dioxide
- Energy costs (because exhaust and flash steam can be reused to preheat boiler feed water)
- Boiler blow-down requirements (because fewer chemicals are used)

Types

Deaerators can be either single-tank or two-tank construction, and can operate as a pressurized shell or an atmospheric-pressure-vented-type shell. Deaerators are rated based on their ability to remove residual oxygen from the water. Ratings are either 0.03 cc/liter or 0.005 cc/liter, which represents the remaining entrained air in a liter of feedwater. The type of deaerator required depends on the characteristics of the steam load and makeup water supply, but for hospitals a 0.005 cc/liter deaerator is almost always the recommended choice to mechanically remove as much entrained oxygen as possible from the boiler feedwater. Most 0.005 cc/liter deaerators are dual-tank type with a surge tank and a pressurized deaerating section. Some manufacturers provide the same performance with a single-tank design. Surges in makeup water requirement and the amount of makeup water necessary determine the capacity and type of deaerator needed.

Condensing Hot Water Boilers

Designing hot water systems for condensing hot water boilers requires different pumping and control arrangements than for noncondensing hot water boilers. Many facilities with condensing hot water boilers experience problems because designers are not familiar with the system differences or fail to follow the recommended piping and controls suggested by the condensing boiler manufacturer.

For condensing boilers, the key design criterion is hot water return temperature. The temperature must be between 90 and 120°F. Traditionally, hot supply temperatures for hospital systems are designed for 180°F supply and 150 to 160°F return temperature. Applying condensing hot water boilers in the traditional design would not be beneficial because maximum efficiency would be impossible with the higher return water temperature.

Most condensing boilers are low mass boilers. The pumping arrangement and controls must recognize this design difference. Some manufacturers' condensing boilers can be arranged for variable flow primary pumping; others require the boilers be arranged for primary-secondary pumping or with boiler circulating pumps for each boiler. Depending on the system capacity, the low mass design of the condensing pumps may require a buffer tank of sufficient size to prevent short-cycling.

These design differences are worth accommodating to realize the maximum efficiency of 92 to 96 percent. The condensing boilers design can be used to heat domestic hot water for the facility via double wall plate-frame heat exchangers. The low-return water from a domestic hot water system will lower the common return water temperature to the condensing boilers.

Chillers

Function

The water chiller is the heart of a centralized chilled water cooling system in which heat is transferred from the air moving across a cooling coil in an air-handling unit to the chilled water, where it is rejected to the refrigerant in the water chiller, which then rejects it through condenser water to a cooling tower outside the building.

Types

Four basic types of water chillers are traditionally used in health care facilities:

1. Reciprocating
2. Centrifugal (hermetic/open, single/multiple-stage, direct-driven/gear-driven)
3. Rotary or helical screw
4. Absorption (steam-fired absorption machines or direct, gas-fired absorption machines)

High-performance chiller options include the following:

1. Centrifugal chillers with magnetic or ceramic bearings
2. Modular chillers using scroll, screw, or centrifugal compressors

3. Central geothermal chillers
4. Adsorption chillers using low-grade heat such as heat from a microturbine

The type of water chiller used in a particular facility depends on multiple factors. For example, a required cooling load of less than 100 tons may dictate a reciprocating or helical screw water chiller. Absorption machines and centrifugal machines generally are not available in capacities smaller than 300 tons and are not economically competitive in the smaller sizes. The efficiency of the machines also may affect the decision. Electric-drive centrifugal chillers often approach efficiency ratings of 0.50 kW per ton. Helical screw machines are available in efficiencies of around 0.65 kW per ton, and reciprocating chillers are available in efficiencies of between 0.7 and 0.8 kilowatts per ton.

Single-stage steam-fired absorption chillers use approximately 19 pounds of steam per ton. With the energy rates available in most areas of the country, these machines are not competitive unless a source of waste steam is available, such as a noncondensing turbine drive on a centrifugal chiller (a Cascade system) or from a cogeneration plant where heat from a gas-fired engine is used to produce electricity and the waste heat is converted to chilled water through an absorption-cycle machine.

Two-stage absorption units that use higher-pressure steam and can approach 10 pounds of steam per ton result in a much higher efficiency than single-stage machines. Direct-fired absorption units also can compete with electric-drive central units in areas of the country where gas rates are low in comparison to electrical rates. These units also offer the advantage of allowing the chilled water system to be on emergency power without the initial expense of sizing an emergency generator large enough to drive an electric-driven water chiller. On average, a direct-fired absorption machine costs twice as much as an electric centrifugal chiller.

Some hospitals install hybrid chiller plants. A hybrid chiller plant includes at least one chiller that is electrically driven and at least one that is fueled by natural gas or fuel oil (i.e., an absorption chiller or engine-driven chiller). Besides the obvious flexibility benefits, this scenario allows for chiller optimization based on utility rate structures by peak shaving to reduce electrical demand changes.

Magnetic-lev chillers offer frictionless, high-performance chiller designs. These Energy Star–rated chillers are used in many LEED-certified buildings. They use positive pressure refrigerants and eliminate oil that can contaminate the chiller refrigerant as well as the entire oil management system, resulting in a low-maintenance chiller for reliable and high-performance operation. Some centrifugal chiller manufacturers use ceramic bearings as an option to the mag-lev design to provide some of the same benefits.

Modular chillers are excellent for new or retrofit applications. They may use scroll, screw, or mag-lev centrifugal compressors. The modular nature of these chillers produces low operating costs, provides redundancy, and offers dedicated heat recovery chillers (DHRC) to reduce the cost of new energy for reheat or heating for domestic hot water. DHRC chillers can be arranged to provide simultaneous heating and cooling by balancing the production of chiller water and hot water. Retrofit applications have shown paybacks as quick as one to two years. This heat pump chiller operates without a reversing valve to increase reliability and reduce required maintenance. Many DHRC chillers are being used in new hospital designs. Hot water temperature from DHRC can be 150°F, but many hospitals are being designed using 130°F hot water from the DHRC for space heating and reheat and for domestic hot water production.

Central geothermal chillers are being used in some hospitals that offer chilled water and hot water production and interface to a geothermal borefield.

Adsorption chillers are purely hot water driven, whereas absorption chillers are driven by hot water, steam, or combustion. Adsorption chillers work on the principle of adsorption using solid sorption materials such as silica gel and zeolites. There are no possibilities of crystallization, corrosion, or hazardous leaks, and the electricity consumption is minimal. This makes them ideal for use in commercial as well as industrial air-conditioning, process cooling, and waste heat recovery applications. Adsorption chillers range from 2 to 150 tons and are being used where a source of hot water is available, such as from a cogen microturbine.

Adsorption chillers have the following advantages:

- No crystallization, corrosion, hazardous leaks, or chemical disposal issues
- Low operational costs and maintenance
- Only minor service required (once every three years)
- More than 30 years of machine life
- Low carbon emissions; eco-friendly operations
- No vibration or noise
- Simple and continuous operation
- Operates over a wide temperature range for hot, cool, and cold water

Refrigerants

Chiller refrigerants used today are HCFC-123, HFC-134a, or HFC-410a. Production has stopped for the older refrigerants R-11, R-12, and R-22, but there is an aftermarket for them. R-11 and R-12 were used for many years in centrifugal chillers. Most of these chillers are being replaced with more efficient chillers or are retrofitted to use R-123 or R-134a. Because HCFC-123 contributes to ozone depletion and global warming, its production for new equipment will end in 2020. Currently in the United States, there are no phase-out requirements for R-134a or R-410a. However, in Europe there is already regulatory pressure to begin phase-out of HFCs because of the higher global warming potential of R-134a. (See Table 3-2.) Alternative refrigerant research is ongoing. Replacement HFOs (F-gases) have been developed to replace the HCFCs and HFCs, but in Europe the use of HFOs (F-gases) are reduced in favor of natural refrigerants such as ammonia, CO_2, and natural gas. The new HFO refrigerants are shown in Table 3-2.

Table 3-2 Global Warming Potential of HFO Refrigerants Compared to R410A and R134A

Refrigerant	GWP	Replaces	
R410A	2,880	-	
R134A	1,300	-	
R32	675	R410A	
R1234yf	4	R134A	
Solstice L-41	<500	R410A	Blend with R1234ze
DR-4 (blend)	<300	R134A	
DR-5 (blend)	<500	R410A	

Cooling Towers

Function

A cooling tower is the most commonly used device for returning heat removed from a building or an industrial process back into the environment. In the past, heat has been rejected directly into rivers and lakes. Wells also have served as heat sinks. Air-cooled heat exchangers can be used to cool the condenser water off a water chiller by rejecting heat directly into the atmosphere. However, this type of heat exchanger would be very expensive and would only be capable of cooling the water to a temperature of approximately 20 degrees above the outside air temperature. By evaporating water as it passes through, a cooling tower uses only 5 percent as much water as a direct once-through system would use, and it can cool the water to within 5 degrees of the wet-bulb temperature, or approximately 35 degrees lower than an air-cooled-type heat rejector.

As heated water passes through the cooling tower, some of the water evaporates, removing the heat of vaporization from the water that remains. Cooling towers are the least expensive major component of a facility's air-conditioning system and often the most neglected.

Types

The two basic types of evaporative cooling tower are the direct-contact tower, which is used with water chillers discussed in the previous section, and closed-circuit fluid coolers, which often are used for water-to-air heat pump systems and industrial process cooling. Most hospitals use the direct-contact tower. A third type of tower induces airflow by spraying condenser water through nozzles at relatively high pressure.

Cooling towers also are classified as natural draft and mechanical draft. Natural draft towers are usually very tall (between 350 and 500 feet) and operate on the principle of heated air within the tower rising to the top, which induces more air into the bottom of the tower. Mechanical draft towers use either a centrifugal or propeller fan to induce or force an air draft through the tower. These towers are either built in place or factory assembled and shipped as a package. Built-in-place towers are usually made of redwood or fir and treated with a waterborne preservative to prevent rot and insect damage. Most packaged towers are made of galvanized steel or fiberglass with PVC-fill material. Induced-draft towers are larger than forced-draft towers but require only about one-third as much horsepower to operate the propeller fan as most forced-draft towers. In cold climates, the design usually includes a remote sump, located inside the building so there is no water in the outside basin of the cooling tower during cold winter months. The remote sump eliminates the need to drain the tower during the winter to prevent freezing or having to maintain a temperature above freezing with basin heaters. The volume of the remote sump must accommodate the water held in the tower fill and in the condenser water piping, including the piping above the tower.

The location of a cooling tower is critically important to its performance. The tower must have adequate open area to allow air to free-flow into it, and no obstructions should be present around the top of the tower that would cause it to recirculate saturated air back into the intake. When these types of conditions occur because of either the way the tower was originally sited or new construction around the tower, the efficiencies of the tower can be decreased as much as 30 percent, causing the performance of the entire air-conditioning system to suffer greatly. The cooling tower should be located as far away from parking structures and parking areas as possible, because the chemicals used to treat cooling tower water, which can be carried a considerable distance by the wind, can damage the surface of automobiles. Cooling towers should not be located directly adjacent to emergency generator exhaust or boiler flues. If boiler flues or generator exhaust is located around the tower, the flues should be extended above the top of the cooling tower and arranged so the towers are upstream of the flues relative to the prevailing wind direction. Even with these precautions, combustion effluents can be very corrosive to the structure of the cooling towers.

Cooling tower capacity control usually is accomplished by varying fan speed with a variable frequency drive (VFD). The fans on cooling towers are large and relatively noisy. Consideration for noise transmission should be given to neighboring buildings on constricted sites, as well as to the hospital itself when the tower is located too close to occupied areas of the facility. Possible solutions include putting up barrier walls and extending the discharge stack to raise the area from which sound exits the tower. When these solutions are used, it is important to remember the open-area requirements around the tower and note that increasing the discharge stack may increase the fan horsepower.

Cooling towers need makeup water to compensate for water that is lost due to drift and evaporation and intentionally bled from the tower to reduce the concentration of minerals and salts. Cooling towers are very efficient since only 1 percent of the water is evaporated to cool the remaining 99 percent of the recirculated water. A small amount of water, 0.005 percent, is lost to drift loss, in which water droplets form on and pass through the eliminators and then are discharged with the rejected air. Water is also intentionally bled from the system at a rate necessary to maintain the cycles of concentration. This rate can vary significantly but is usually 0.3 to 0.5 percent of the total recirculated flow rate. With these three sources of water loss, the cooling tower makeup water requirement is usually between 1 and 2 percent of the total condenser water flow. Because makeup water is required, a proper chemical treatment program with a continuous feed is necessary to maintain efficiency and extend the life of the tower.

Chemicals are required to prevent corrosion, scale, and biological growth. Corrosion inhibitors are usually phosphate or nitrogen based, or molybdenum or zinc based. Scaling inhibitors are usually polymer-based chemicals or organic phosphonates, or scaling is prevented by adding acid. Tower systems will usually maintain a residual oxidizing biocide, such as bromine or chlorine. The tower makeup is controlled based on conductivity in the system. Typically, towers operate between three and eight cycles of concentration (COC). COC is calculated based on hardness in the condenser water divided by hardness in the makeup water. The higher the COC, the less makeup water used but the more potential for scaling, corrosion, and fouling of the condenser tubes. Chemical treatment is also required to minimize biological growth. Fouling of the chiller's condenser water tubes can have a significant negative impact on the system's performance. The tower basin contains warm water in a dark environment and is an excellent area for the growth of algae and fungi. These algae and fungi form an insulating coating on the surfaces of the heat transfer components in the condenser tubes and can restrict the flow through the condenser bundle. The requirements for chemical treatment can vary widely depending on where the tower is located, and a competent water treatment specialist can be invaluable in protecting the system from corrosion and fouling.

Cooling towers consume large amounts of water and discharge chemicals into both the municipal water treatment system and the environment. Over the life of the facility, these chemicals may have a greater impact on the local environment than any other building system. Chlorine and bromine added to the water as biocide agents are stripped from the water and released into the environment. The heavy metals, phosphates, and biocides are sent to the municipal treatment system. Hospitals should always be looking for ways to reduce the environmental impact of the cooling systems. The EPA website discusses these effects at *www.epa.gov/greenchemistry*. Nonchemical water treatment devices (NCDs) are being used in many facilities to reduce water consumption and the environmental impact of traditional condenser water treatment. These technologies include pulsed-electric fields, ultrasound, magnetic agitation, and ozone with inject of microwaves. Each has an active following.

Application success depends on water chemistry, operating procedures, and the hospital staff's willingness to accept and maintain these technologies.

Cooling towers must be monitored for growth of *Legionella.* Resources available for creating a risk management building water system program for *Legionella* include ASHRAE, WHO, and HACCP. The hospital staff and management must create and follow a risk management program to prevent and control *Legionella* in the facility's water systems. At time of this publication, ASHRAE Standard 188P: *Legionellosis: Risk Management for Building Water Systems, 4th Edition*, has been released for public review. This document will require hospitals and other health care facilities to have a formal program to establish minimum Legionellosis risk management requirements for the buiding water systems. The water management program must (1) identify the program team; (2) describe the buildings water system, including flow diagrams; (3) provide an analysis of the building water systems; (4) identify where control measures must be applied and maintained; (5) describe monitoring proceduces; (6) describe corrective actions/confirmation; and (7) spell out documentation and communication procedures.

The U.S. Department of Health and Human Services recommends the following periodic procedures to prevent *Legionella* bacteria growth in cooling tower water:

- Systematic use of biocides
- Monthly microbiologic analysis of cooling tower water
- Monitoring and documentation of the cooling tower water quality

If *Legionella* is found, the recommended emergency action is to hyperchlorinate the system to achieve a chlorine level of 5 parts per million.

ASHRAE Guideline 12 can provide the hospital staff and design engineers guidance to minimize *Legionella* contamination in building water systems.

Cooling towers are relatively simple pieces of equipment, and in the packaged steel version they are inexpensive compared to the other components of a mechanical system. But because of their function and location, they require constant maintenance for proper operation. To extend the life of the tower and reduce maintenance needs, the cold water basin should always be constructed of stainless steel and, if the budget permits, the hot basin, too. For coastal applications, the entire cooling tower should be constructed of stainless steel or other noncorrosive material, such as FRP. The maintenance program should include the following:

- Regular and periodic inspections of the fill tank hot and cold water basins and eliminators to ensure that they are maintained in a good state of repair
- Periodic draining and cleaning of wetted surface areas to prevent accumulation of dirt, scale, and algae where bacteria may develop
- Proper treatment of the cooling tower circulating water for bacteria and corrosion control
- Documentation of the operation and maintenance procedures to provide proof of a regularly scheduled maintenance program

When troubleshooting because of cooling system capacity problems, the cooling tower performance is a good place to start, and the tests necessary to locate the problem are relatively simple. The flow of the condenser water can be determined using the pump curve, motor amp measurements, and the pressure difference on the entering and leaving side of the pump. If flow appears to be a problem, the strainer at the top inlet and the screen in the cooling tower basin are likely locations of water flow restriction. Condenser tube fouling can be readily observed by measuring the water temperature rise across the condenser of the chiller and the approach to saturated condenser temperature. If the machine was selected for a 10 degree rise and the condenser water temperature is only rising at 8 degrees at a 100 percent demand, fouled condenser tubes are the likely cause.

Cooling tower recirculation can be easily confirmed using a sling psychrometer. Measure the wet-bulb temperature away from the cooling tower inlet and then measure at the cooling tower inlet louvers. A 1 or 2 degree increase in wet-bulb temperature at the inlet indicates that the discharge off the cooling tower is likely recirculating back through the cooling tower inlets. Steam vents, laundry exhaust fans, recirculation from an adjacent cooling tower or restricted inlet air configuration, or other sources of moisture may be discharged near the cooling tower inlets and raise the apparent wet-bulb temperature. The cooling tower manufacturers can assist with derating the cooling tower capacity based on adjacent buildings or walls that may obstruct free airflow into the cooling tower. A good rule of thumb is that the distance between the obstruction of the cooling tower inlet should be equal to the height of the cooling tower. Another rule of thumb is that there should be no wall higher than the cooling tower discharge within 30 feet of the cooling tower. These rules can be adjusted based on prevailing wind conditions and louvered walls.

A cooling tower should not be located near outside air intake louvers in a hospital. Not only would this increase the possibility of airborne microbial contaminants entering the hospital, but the added moisture in the airstream would likely contribute to a much higher latent load on the air handlers than anticipated during design. Cooling towers should not be located so that flue gas from the boilers or exhaust from emergency generators is drawn into the cooling tower fans. Check prevailing wind direction and extend stacks above the tower fan deck to prevent reentrainment of the effluent gases.

Cooling Tower Energy Management Opportunities

In new installations, consideration should be given to slightly oversizing the cooling tower. Packaged steel towers cost in the range of $100 per ton, and the slight additional expense of oversizing the cooling towers by 10 to 15 percent can be made up in reduction of fan horsepower requirements and operating time. Also, because wet-bulb temperatures significantly affect the performance of the tower, sizing the tower to handle a one-degree-higher-than-design wet bulb will ensure that the tower has the capacity to operate effectively on those 5 or 10 days a year when the wet bulb may be higher than design.

Consideration can be given to allowing the cooling tower to operate on a free cooling cycle either using a heat exchanger to directly transfer heat to the chilled water loop, or using a sand filter and pumping cooling tower water through air-handling unit cooling coils. Generally, using the condenser water directly in air-handling unit cooling coils should be avoided. Most air-handling units are not designed to be easily cleaned, as the condenser tubes are located in a chiller.

Pumps

Although there are many different types of pumps, the centrifugal type is the most commonly used in hospital mechanical systems. Centrifugal pumps recirculate hot water for heating, chilled water for cooling, and condenser water for cooling towers and are used for boiler feed and condensate return. They operate by using a rotating impeller. Water enters the pump casing at the center of the impeller, and the impeller hurls the water toward the outer casing, where the discharge is located.

Centrifugal pumps may have a single- or double-entry impeller, depending on the flow characteristics. The pumps may be single stage or two stage, depending on the pressure needed to overcome the resistance in the system. The pumps are classified by how they are connected to the electric motor and the location of the suction connection to the pump casing. Figure 3-1 shows the types of centrifugal pump normally used in hydronic systems, and Figure 3-2 shows a cross section of an end suction pump.

The mechanical systems pump provides the motive force that distributes heating or cooling throughout the hospital. After chillers and boilers, they usually are the equipment that consumes the most energy in the hospital. Each centrifugal pump has a

Figure 3-1 Centrifugal Pumps Used in Hydronic Systems

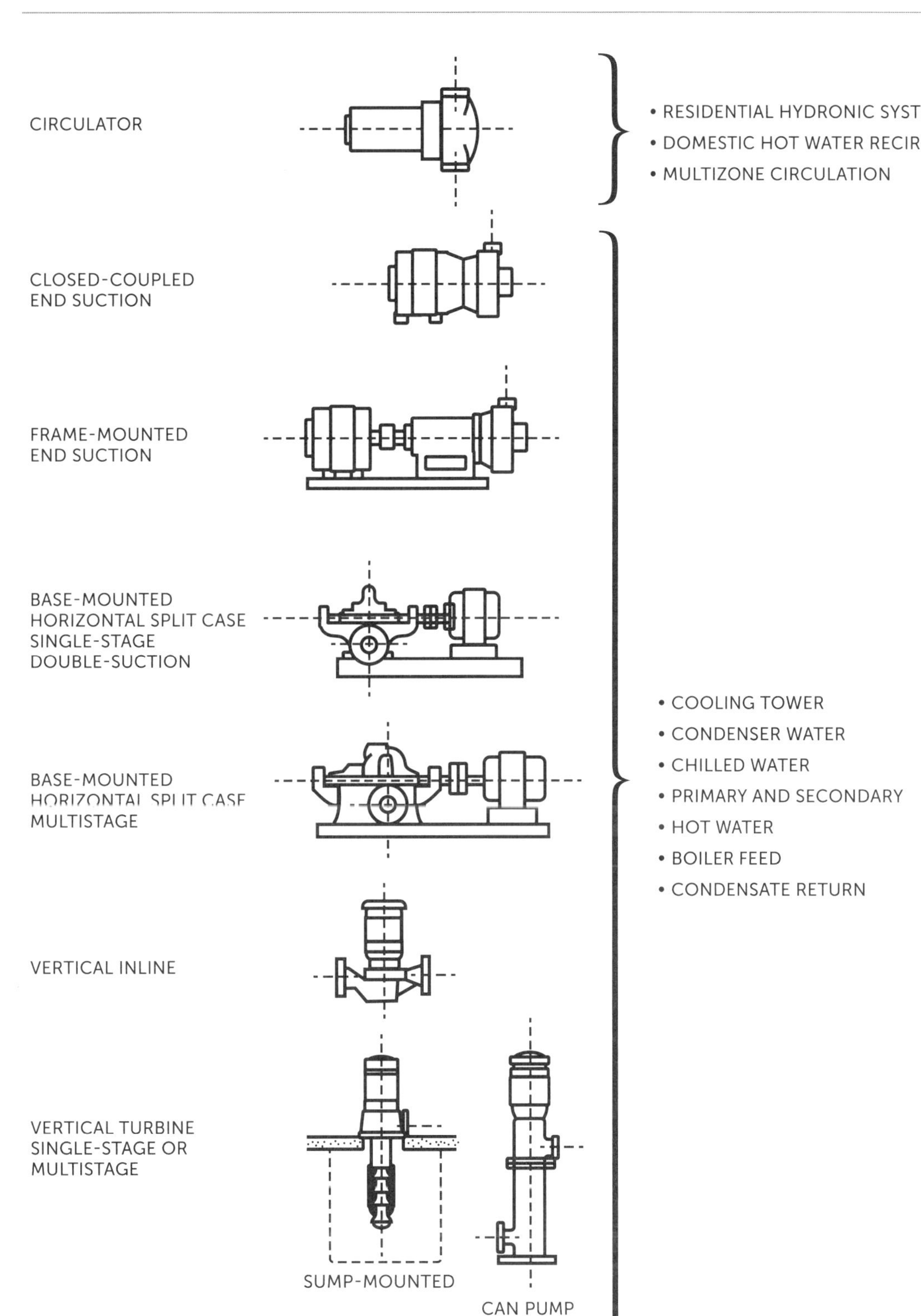

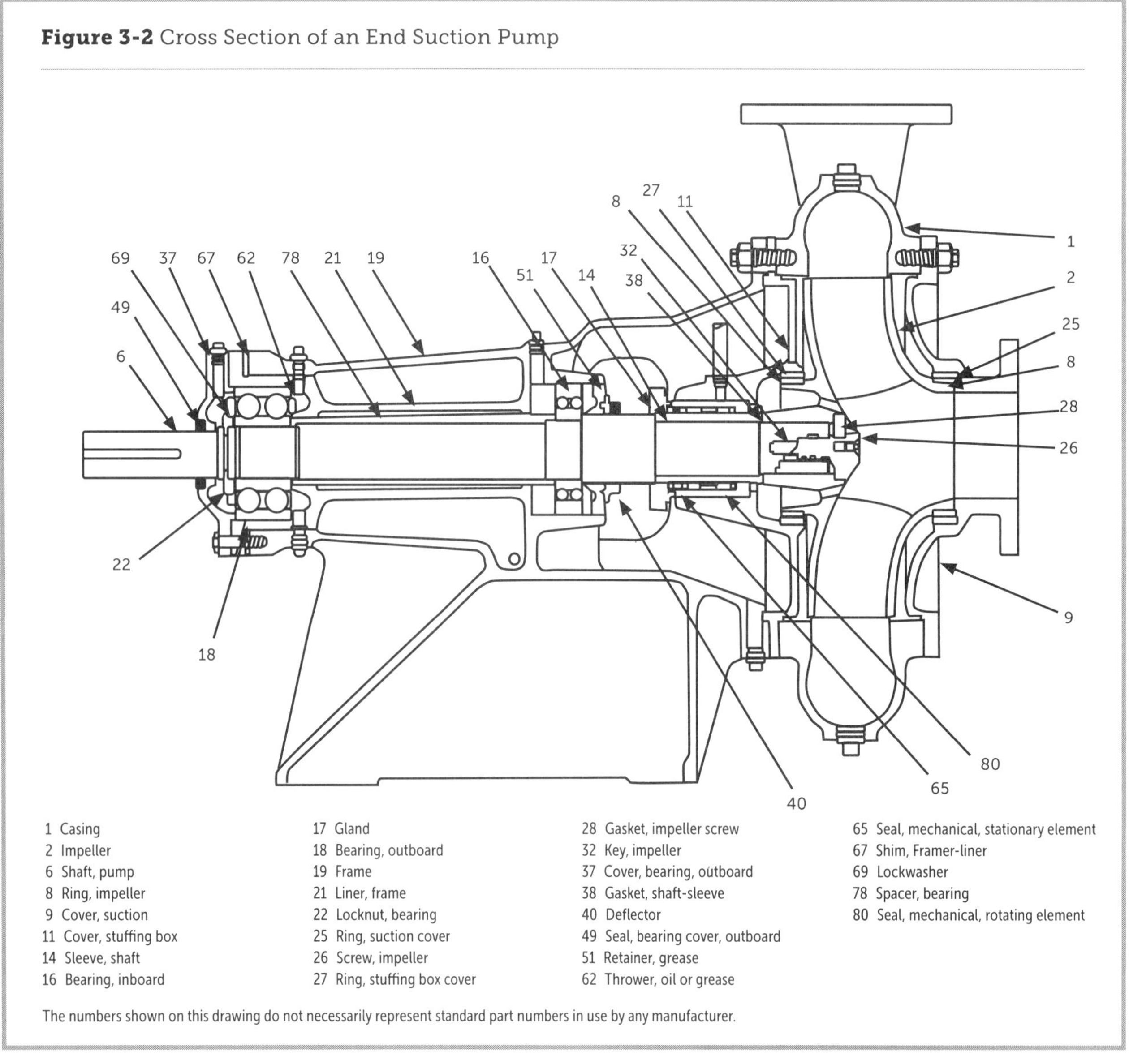

Figure 3-2 Cross Section of an End Suction Pump

The numbers shown on this drawing do not necessarily represent standard part numbers in use by any manufacturer.

performance curve that defines the flow and pressure produced by a given pump based on the diameter of the impeller and the rotation speed. Changing either the impeller diameter or the rotation speed changes the entire pump curve and the pump's operating characteristics.

Centrifugal pumps usually are not self-priming; that is, they are not capable of removing air from the pump casing to begin pumping water. For that reason, care must be taken to keep air from entering the circulating systems, and provisions for removing air need to be incorporated in the pumping and piping system. Vents at the highest point of the piping where air can be removed should be installed and, if they are not automatic, should be manually checked to prevent air-locking a portion of the circulating system.

Each centrifugal pump has a unique minimum net positive suction head requirement, depending on the type of pump and its operating characteristics. The liquid enters the impeller at a very low pressure, and this pressure must stay high enough to prevent vapor pockets from forming. These vapor pockets will form if the absolute pressure on the liquid approaches the vapor pressure of the liquid. This leads to pump cavitation, which results in reduced capacity, noisy operation, and over an extended period, damage to the pump impeller and bearings. Hot water and chilled water systems that are closed systems and are pressurized by city water makeup connections usually are not subject to this problem. However, cooling tower condenser water pumps and boiler feed pumps that are open to atmospheric pressure can be plagued by cavitation, if the pump is located incorrectly with respect to the cooling tower basin or if the pump strainer is not cleaned on a regular basis.

In most hospitals, pumps are piped in parallel to provide redundancy for the heating and cooling systems. When pumps are piped parallel and both are running, the total flow rate can be increased, although the total maximum pressure or head of the pump is not increased.

In most heating and cooling applications, a common way to conserve water flow and reduce energy consumption is to use two-way control valves as heating and cooling valves that vary the total flow of the water in the circulating system. Centrifugal pumps respond to this variable flow very well. At reduced flows, they may show only a very slight increase in total system pressure or head but produce a significant reduction in energy used at the pump motor.

Use of variable-speed drives in piping systems with two-way valves is a common design approach to increase the energy-saving characteristics of centrifugal pumps. Motor speed can be reduced as a response to pressure out in the system, or the pressure setpoint can be reset based on the control valve with the most demand, resulting in energy savings in the ratio of the cube of the flow reduction.

VFDs can be retrofitted on existing pumps to reduce energy consumption if the system is a variable flow system (i.e., coils have two-way control valves, not three-way valves). If VFDs are added to existing motors, the motors may need to be changed to inverter duty motors.

The standard VFDs for the HVAC industry are six-pulse drives. These drives can cause harmonic distortion in the electrical distribution system. As the percentage of nonlinear loads such as VFDs and electronic lighting ballasts has increased, a harmonic analysis is mandatory for today's hospitals. IEEE-519 defines the maximum allowable voltage and current distortion in various facilities. For hospitals and other critical spaces, this is a limit of 1 percent total harmonic distortion (THD) and 2 percent total demand distortion (TDD). At a minimum, VFDs must be provided with line reactors or other means to mitigate the harmonic distortion. VFDs for larger motors need to be 18-pulse drives or active fronts to eliminate any harmonic distortion from the drive. The VFD manufacturer should perform the harmonic analysis based on the details of the electrical distribution system and the specific harmonic content generated from the VFDs. VFDs should also include RFI filters to prevent electromagnetic interference, which can disturb imaging selector and other electronic diagnostic equipment. If the pumps are not selected for adequate redundancy, the VFD should be provided with a bypass contactor to allow for constant speed operation. The control system should be designed with means to prevent overpressurization of the hydronic system when operating at constant speed.

Heat Exchangers and Converters

By definition, heat exchangers are devices that allow heat to be transferred from one fluid to another. Cooling coils and heating coils as well as the evaporator and condensing sections of chillers all are heat exchangers, which are used primarily to convert steam to hot water or to transfer heat from one water system to another.

The most commonly used heat exchangers in mechanical systems are shell-and-tube-type or plate-frame heat exchangers (see Figures 3-3 and 3-4). The basic equation that governs the capacity of heat exchangers is Q = UA ΔT. Q is the heat flow rate, U is the conductance of the material through which heat is being passed, and A is the area over which the exchange takes place. ΔT is the difference in temperature between the two fluids. Therefore, the rate of heat transfer between two fluids can be increased by (1) reducing the resistance to heat flow of the material separating the fluids, (2) increasing the surface area where the heat flow takes place, and (3) increasing the difference in temperature between the two fluids. Shell-and-tube heat exchangers generally have a steel shell that surrounds a copper tube bundle. One fluid is circulated within the shell and the other within the tube bundle inside the shell. In a steam converter, the steam usually is introduced into the shell of the heat exchanger and water circulates in the tube bundle contained within.

Heat exchangers may be one, two, three, or four pass, denoting how many times the fluid in the tube passes through the heat exchanger before leaving the tube bundle. Because the phase change from steam to condensate releases so much heat (1,000 Btu per pound

Figure 3-3 Shell-and-Tube Heat Exchanger

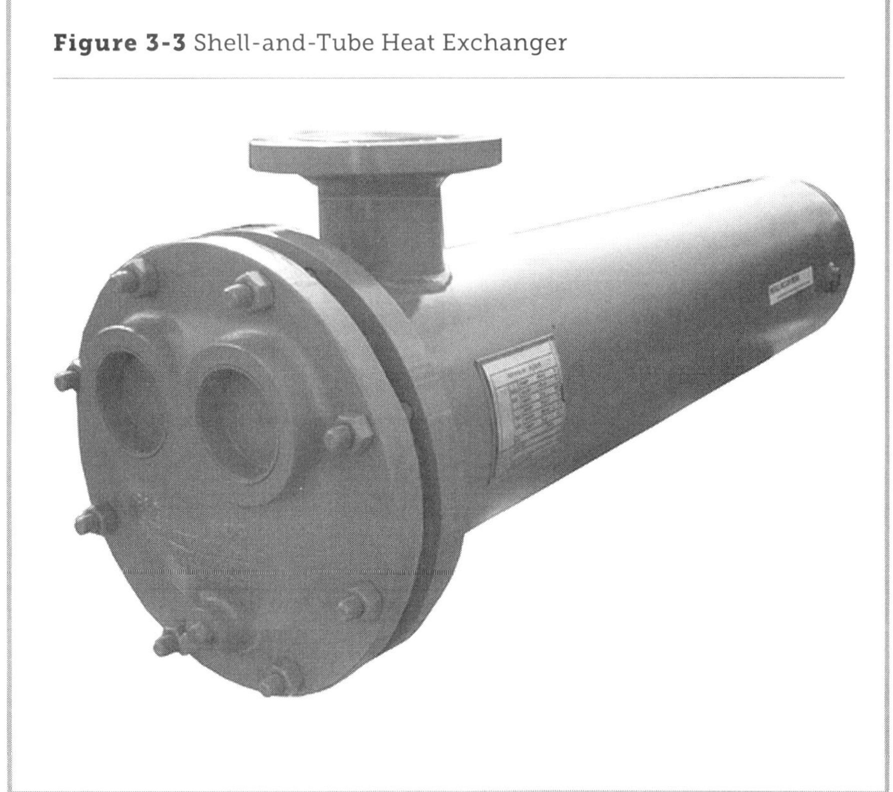

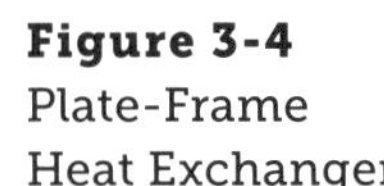

Figure 3-4
Plate-Frame Heat Exchanger

of steam) and less surface area is required to provide adequate heat transfer, shell-and-tube heat exchangers can be relatively small. Steam to hot water converters are most often used for space-heating hot water applications and increasingly for instantaneous domestic hot water heating applications.

Plate-frame heat exchangers are used when the temperature difference between the two fluids is small. These heat exchangers have a great amount of surface area to facilitate heat transfer and often are used to transfer heat from condenser water to chilled water to allow a free cooling cycle during an intermediate season when the water chilling equipment is turned off.

Heat exchangers obviously are very simple and have no moving parts. No maintenance is required other than inspecting and cleaning the heat exchanger surfaces to remove silt and corrosion deposits that would interfere with efficient heat transfer.

CHAPTER 4

Piped Distribution Systems

This chapter addresses the piping distribution systems that transfer heated and cooled fluids through the building.

Generally, health care facilities use four types of piping material. The manufacture of these materials is governed by several code authorities and agencies. The American Society of Mechanical Engineers (ASME), the American Society for Testing Materials (ASTM), the American National Standards Institute (ANSI), and the Manufacturer's Standardization Society of Valve and Fitting Industry, Inc. (MSS) provide the most widely recognized standards for the manufacture of pipe and pipe fittings.

Steel pipe is most often used on sizes 2½-inch and larger throughout the mechanical systems. The pipe may be seamless, or it may have a longitudinal seam that is welded by furnace butt welding or electric current weld. Steel pipe comes in a standard weight, or schedule 40 pipe, extra strong, or schedule 80 pipe, which has a greater wall thickness. The joints in steel pipe may be welded, threaded, or flanged, or may use a flexible neoprene grooved coupling or a mechanical joint such as Victaulic couplings.

Copper tubing is used in the smaller sizes (up to 2½-inch). Copper has the advantage of being corrosion resistant and easy to install. It is not often used on larger-size pipe because the material is more expensive than steel piping. Copper tubing comes in three thicknesses: type K, type L, and type M. Type K has the greatest wall thickness and is used for very high-pressure applications or when the pipe is buried, especially below slabs. Type L is most often used in above-ground applications for mechanical systems.

Ductile iron pipe is commonly used for buried water lines and in locations where internal or external corrosion may be a problem. Ductile iron has largely replaced cast iron in installations because it is stronger and less brittle. This pipe usually is joined with bell and spigot or mechanical joint fittings.

Thermoplastic pipe, often called PVC (polyvinyl chloride), is used in many HVAC and plumbing applications in commercial buildings. The pipe is lightweight, corrosion resistant, and inexpensive to install. However, plastic piping gives off poisonous fumes when burned, and for this reason some codes do not allow its use in health care facilities except where it is buried below ground. The Centers for Disease Control (CDC) recommend PVC for dialysis-unit deionized water systems. Plastic piping is joined with threaded joints or by solvent connections. Chlorinated PVC (CPVC) piping is used for condenser water piping.

Valves

Listed below are the various types of valves normally found in mechanical systems in hospitals:

- **Gate valves.** These valves are used to open and close a service connection. They have a very low resistance to flow. They should not be used for throttling applications. Gate valves are used almost exclusively for steam service.
- **Globe valves.** These valves are specifically designed for throttling service and have a high resistance to flow or a large pressure drop passing through the valve.
- **Check valves.** Check valves prevent the reversal of flow in a piping system. A check valve may be a flapper type or a spring-loaded ball valve, depending on size and application.
- **Plug valves.** Plug valves operate from fully open to fully

closed in a one-quarter turn. These valves may be used for throttling. They are most often found on gas and fuel oil services because the position of the actuator indicates whether the valve is open or closed.

- **Butterfly valves.** These valves can be used for throttling and have a low resistance to flow when fully opened. They are also inexpensive in the larger sizes (4 inches and larger) and thus are commonly found throughout mechanical systems.
- **Ball valves.** Like plug valves, ball valves operate from fully open to fully closed with a one-quarter turn. They have a low resistance to flow and also may be used for throttling control. These valves are often found on heating and cooling coils and are used to balance the system because they can be set to the proper position and the operator removed. Balancing valves that have pressure ports to measure pressure drop across the valve are ball-type valves.
- **Pressure-reducing valves.** These valves control downstream pressure to a constant level. Usually, they are operated by a spring and diaphragm connected by a small tube to the downstream side of the valve. The pressure in the tube moves the diaphragm to open and close the valve to maintain pressure downstream.
- **Pressure relief valves.** Relief valves open when the system pressure reaches a preset level to prevent overpressurizing the system. They usually are spring operated and set for the desired maximum pressure by adjusting the tension of the spring.

Piping Systems

Steam Piping

Steam piping may be arranged as a one- or two-pipe system. A one-pipe system uses a single pipe to carry the steam out to the load and the condensate back to the boiler, flowing against the steam flow. This system was commonly used in older buildings with steam radiators, but today almost all steam systems are two-pipe systems that carry steam in one pipe and return condensate to the boiler through another. Steam piping systems are designed to carry steam and condensate and air. The piping should be sloped to ensure the condensate flows with the steam (preferably) or against the steam flow (requiring oversized piping), depending on the applications.

Drip legs must be installed at low points in the piping to allow the condensate to be collected and passed into the condensate return piping through steam traps. Steam piping is sized according to the pressure of the steam being carried in the pipe and the allowable pressure drop over the length of the piping system. Higher-pressure steam can be carried in smaller pipes because higher-pressure drops are perfectly acceptable, and a pound of steam occupies less space at higher pressures. Low-pressure steam lines generally operate at lower velocities with pressure drops in the range of ¼ to ½ pound per 100 feet, whereas the pressure drop in high-pressure lines may be greater than 2 pounds per 100 feet.

Because steam piping is subject to temperatures ranging from ambient temperatures to over 250°F, it should be installed to allow expansion and contraction and flexibility within the system. This is less critical in hot water systems and not necessary at all in most chilled water systems because of the lower temperature swings and the typically high number of offsets in these systems. However, expansion joints or expansion loops are critical to the satisfactory operation of steam systems.

Figure 4-1 shows a typical pressure-reducing station for a steam system found in a health care facility. Most often in a hospital, steam is produced at more than 60 psi (125 psi if a laundry with a flatwork ironer is present) and this pressure is reduced for service entering humidifiers, heat exchangers, and domestic water heaters. Depending on the pressure drop involved, pressure-reducing stations may have one or more stages of reduction, for instance, from 125 psi to 60 psi and a second stage of 60 psi to 15 psi. In each stage, larger pressure-reducing stations usually have two valves sized in a 33 to 66 percent arrangement to provide adequate pressure control at low-flow conditions. Smaller stations have only one valve.

Figure 4-1 Pressure-Reducing Station for a Steam System in a Health Care Facility

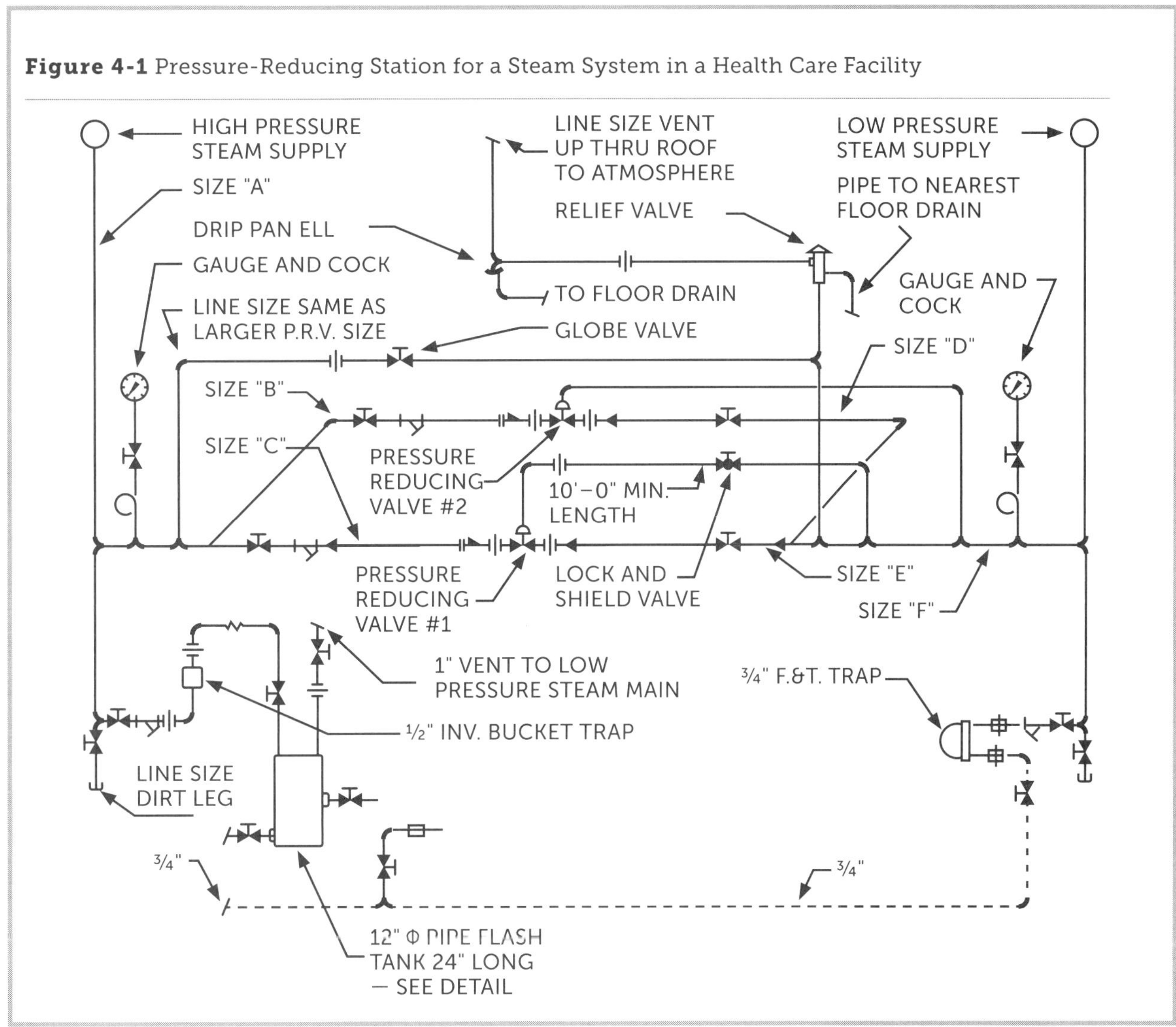

Steam Condensate Piping

The condensate return piping that returns the steam condensate back to the boiler feed unit may be either gravity or flow, or it may be pumped. Where it is not possible to return the steam to the boiler room by gravity flow, the condensate is collected in a condensate receiver and pumped back to the boiler feed unit or deaerator. Condensate piping usually is made of schedule 80 pipe because it is subject to a great deal of corrosion. The high-temperature condensate tends to release oxygen and carbon dioxide, which accelerates the internal corrosion of the piping. The thicker walls of the schedule 80 pipe provide longer piping life.

Figure 4-2 shows the various types of traps used to return condensate from the various steam-consuming equipment. The selection of the proper kind of trap, the proper trap size, and periodic

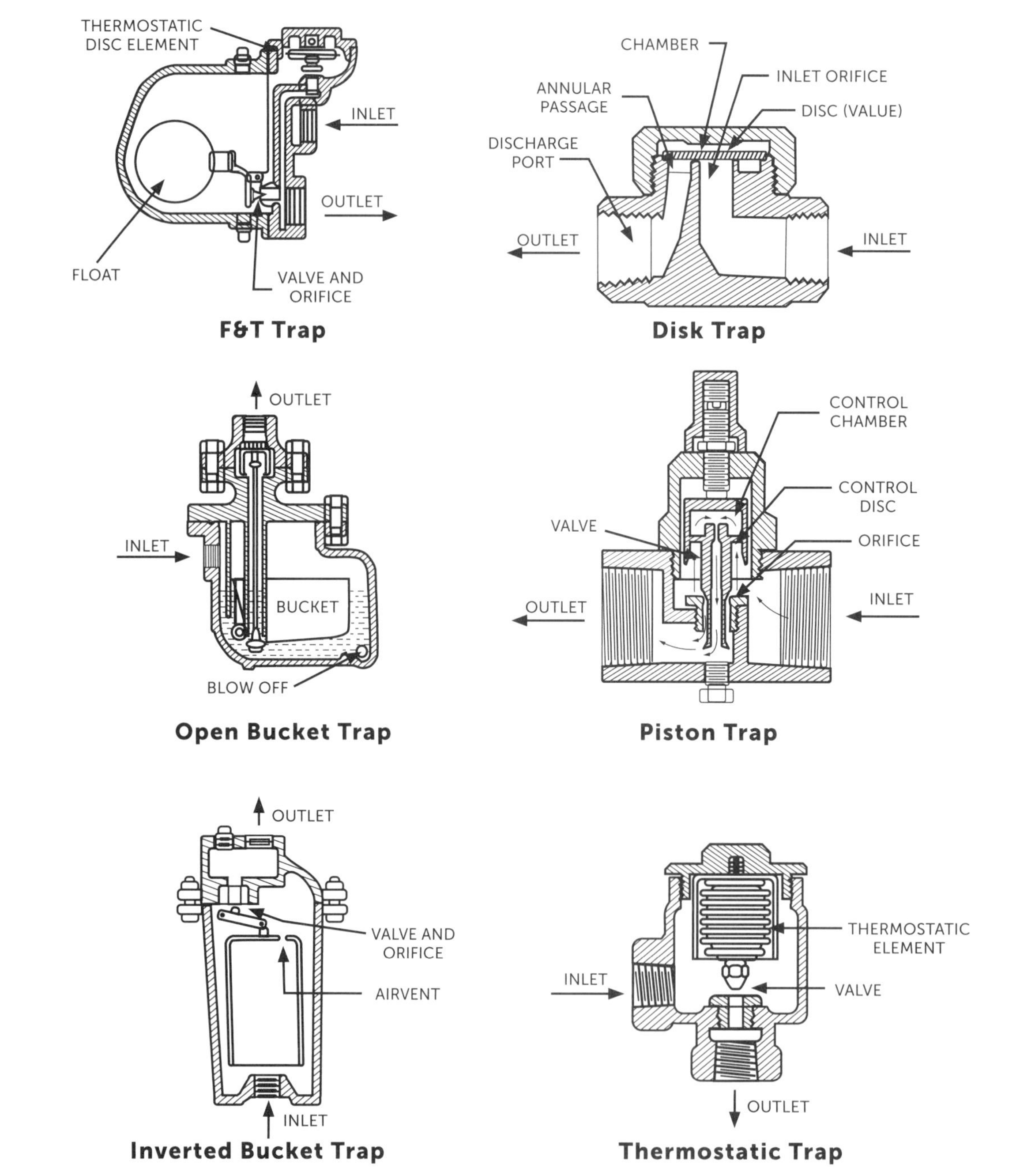

Figure 4-2 Types of Traps and Urns Used to Return Condensate from Steam-Consuming Equipment

inspection and maintenance of traps are key to an efficient steam distribution system.

Traps are designed to remove air and liquid condensate to the condensate return. A leaking trap will allow steam to pass into the condensate system, wasting energy and creating noise. A trap that is not properly sized may seriously reduce the capacity of the heat exchanger or the heating coils it serves.

Inverted-bucket, float, and thermostatic traps are the types most commonly used for equipment in a health care facility. Inverted-bucket traps are particularly well suited for draining condensate from steam lines or where a large amount of air may be present. They also are good choices where dirt may drain into the trap.

The float and thermostatic trap is a combination trap that is used where a large volume of condensate may need to be handled, such as steam heating coils, heat exchangers, and unit heaters. Float and thermostatic traps are particularly well suited for low-pressure heating systems up to a maximum pressure of 30 psi.

Steam Piping System Operation and Maintenance

Over the past 30 years, most other building types have moved away from steam heating systems. Steam generation and distribution is now being challenged in hospitals. Central steam systems require extensive maintenance and water treatment. There will always be a need for steam in hospitals for sterilization and humidification, but space heating and domestic hot water generation may be more efficiently produced with condensing boilers. This is a huge paradigm shift for hospital design engineers and for maintenance personnel, but the energy required to produce high-pressure steam may not be energy efficient compared to other alternatives.

Pound for pound, steam is 50 times more efficient in transferring heat than water. A pound of steam transfers 1,000 Btu of heat, whereas a pound of water cooling 40°F, typical for a hot water heating system, transfers only 40 Btu. Most other facility types have moved to hot water or electricity for heating because steam requires constant maintenance, damage can result if the system is not maintained properly, steam flows are difficult to control in small coils, and steam is associated with condensate trapping and return problems.

Proper boiler water treatment is critical to maintaining the life of the steam and condensate piping in the steam distribution system. Using point-of-use steam generators for sterilizers, humidification, and dietary equipment significantly reduces the cost of steam generation. The steam load may not merit a large central steam system. The amount of makeup water can be reduced with smaller, decentralized systems. The high percentage of makeup water required for central steam systems increases the need for oxygen removal via a deaerator and proper chemical treatment to maintain system reliability. Improper chemical treatment shortens the life of the piping system and increases the frequency of trap failures that waste energy by bypassing steam or causing condensate to back up in the heat exchangers, which in turn reduces the capacity of the heating equipment.

Hot Water Piping Systems

Hot water systems for heating have largely replaced steam space-heating systems because relative to steam systems, they are

- significantly cheaper to maintain,
- less expensive to install, and
- easier to control.

Hot water systems require initial balancing; steam piping systems do not. But because hot water systems are closed systems, corrosion-inhibiting chemicals can be added at start-up and do not need to be replaced unless the system leaks or is drained for maintenance or to connect additional piping to expand the system. Hot water systems usually are a mixture of steel piping with copper piping runouts to the heating coils and/or convectors. Most design engineers use dielectric unions or brass unions where steel and copper pipe are joined to prevent galvanic or electrolysis corrosion from attacking the piping where dissimilar metals are joined. Dielectric unions are a must in areas with highly active city water. Even though dielectric unions eliminate galvanic corrosion, they still require maintenance and are subject to leaking.

Proper pipe cleaning and start-up procedures are necessary to ensure headache-free operation of the hot water system. Once this is accomplished, the system should remain nearly maintenance free. However, the water should be tested periodically to ensure that the proper chemical levels are maintained to prevent algae formation and corrosion. If the system is leaking, the chemical treatment concentration will be diluted by makeup water.

All control valves in the hot water system are two-way valves. Three-way valves should not be used unless this is the only way to ensure some minimum flow in the system. Since the system is all variable flow, fixed balancing valves are not needed at each coil. Reverse return risers in multiple-story buildings may be designed to balance the pressure at each floor, and then each floor may be piped as direct return to the risers. Automatic pressure-compensating flow control valves can be used at each floor to avoid over-pumping floors closest to the pumps. Flow rates to VAV or CAV terminals can be very low, 0.5 to 1.0 gpm. Manual balancing valves may not be beneficial.

Some engineers, control manufacturers, and others advocate pressure-independent control valves (PICV). These valves make the system pressure independent regardless of pressure variation in the system. Opinions vary on whether PICV are needed and what type.

If VFDs are added to an existing system, manual balancing valves or circuit setters at the pump should be removed or, at a minimum, be fully open. Removing the circuit setter reduces the system's pressure drop. All new systems will have VFDs on the pumps controlled by a differential pressure transmitter located across the coil and valve near the most remote coil in the system. To ensure a minimum flow through the pump and hot water heat exchanger, several three-way valves may be installed at the most remote heating coils in relation to the pump, or a bypass line at a remote location with a balancing plug cock may be installed between the supply and return piping to allow the minimum flow when the system has very low-heat or no-heat requirements.

Care must be taken that all air is removed from the system at start-up, and the system should be checked periodically to ensure that air has not entered the system when it is shut down or drained for any reason. Entrained air in the system will cause the pump to cavitate, which may damage the impeller. If hot water coils near the highest point in the system become air-locked, they will lose most of their heating capacity. Manual air vents should be installed at each heating coil and in the high parts of the heating system. Some designers use automatic vents rather than manual. These devices tend to drip small amounts of water as they operate, and after several years they often fail to operate properly. The outlet of an automatic air vent should be piped to an area where leaking water will not damage ceilings or walls. The outlet also should be easily observable so that maintenance personnel will notice a water flow if the automatic vent sticks in the open position.

Air and dirt separators are used in hot water systems to remove air released during heating. They are located on the leaving side of the heat exchanger or hot water boiler and on the entering side of the pump. This is the location of highest temperature and lowest pressure, where air is most likely to be released from the water.

Hot water systems must be equipped with expansion or compression tanks that allow the volume of the water in the system to fluctuate as the temperature fluctuates. Today, full acceptance bladder tanks are used for air elimination, not just management of the air. Air and dirt separators are used to clean the system and remove debris. The location of the expansion tank and air separator is on the suction side of the pump. This is known as the point of zero pressure change in the system. The domestic water make-up valve must be set at a pressure equal to the static height of the building plus a cushion of 5 to 7 psi. Many closed systems are operating without sufficient fill pressure. The system should be periodically monitored to ensure that it is statically filled.

Chilled Water Piping

The characteristics of chilled water piping are very similar to those previously described for hot water piping systems. The issues concerning keeping air out of the system, initial start-up, chemical treatment, and balancing are the same. Two-way control valves and variable-flow loops through the cooling coil are best practice for chilled water piping systems for the same reasons described in the hot water piping section. Minimum-flow requirements through water chiller evaporators and the various options available for chiller piping configuration are discussed in this section.

Nearly all hospital chilled water systems have multiple chillers for redundancy and part-load operating efficiency. These chillers may be connected in either a series piping arrangement or a parallel piping arrangement. In the case of three or more chillers, the piping arrangement may include a combination of series and parallel connections.

Many chilled water systems are piped in a primary/secondary pumping arrangement. For many years, this was necessary to ensure constant flow through the chillers, which chiller manufacturers demand to avoid operating problems and potential damage to the chillers. Today, the adaptive controls on the chiller can handle or adapt to variations in flow, so the preferred pumping arrangement is a variable flow primary. Chiller plants are now designed as all variable speed plants, meaning the chillers, cooling tower fans, and chilled water and condenser water pumps are controlled via variable frequency drives.

Many articles have been written describing the demise of primary/secondary pumping arrangements. The primary/secondary pumping scheme contributes to low ΔT in the plant, causing more chillers to operate than is necessary to meet the load. Converting an existing primary/secondary pumping arrangement to variable flow primary may yield 10 to 20 percent energy savings. The first cost of converting from P/S to VFP can vary widely from one chiller plant to another.

Series-counterflow piping arrangements are common on large chilled water plants. In some situations, chiller efficiencies can be significantly improved with this arrangement. Series-counterflow piping should be vetted on all new projects or major central plant renovations.

At partial loads, one chiller can carry the entire building cooling load, providing redundancy in that one chiller is able to provide cooling when the other is shut down for maintenance.

The chilled water temperature control can be set so that both chillers produce the desired final chilled water temperature of 42°F. The lead chiller produces chilled water at a much higher efficiency because it is operating at much higher chilled water temperatures. When the building load decreases and the return chilled water temperature falls, one chiller can be shut down to conserve energy.

Another temperature control scheme for series chillers is to provide the temperature control sensors for both chillers downstream of the last chiller. This loads both chillers equally and, again, the upstream chiller operates at a higher efficiency due to higher entering and leaving chilled water temperature.

A third control sequence is to stagger the chiller setpoints so that the downstream chiller is loaded first to maintain a chilled water temperature of 42°F, and when the load exceeds the capacity of the downstream chiller, the upstream chiller picks up the additional load.

However, series piping for chillers can have disadvantages:

- The flow rate through each chiller is the entire system flow, and therefore the system has higher pressure drops and requires higher pumping horsepower. Because of the high-pressure drops, it is difficult to have more than two chillers in series. Adding a third chiller requires a significant increase in pumping head needed to pump the entire system's chilled water through each of the three chillers.
- Series-flow chillers usually have single-pass coolers to keep the pressure drop down, which are less efficient than the two- or three-pass coolers used on parallel-flow chillers.

- When using high system temperature differential (to reduce chilled water flow rates), cooling coils have to be sized to provide more air contact area to achieve a higher ΔT. These cooling coils have more rows (depth) and more fins per inch, which increases the static pressure drop and the fan horsepower required to overcome the increased airflow resistance.

In the common, legacy schematic of a parallel chiller sequencing piping arrangement, each chiller has a dedicated pump, and at partial loads, one pump and chiller can shut down. The characteristics of this arrangement are as follows:

- Each chiller is added with a dedicated pump; the system offers flexibility when additional chiller capacity is added.
- Loading one chiller fully before bringing the other chiller on maintains higher efficiencies because chillers reach their optimum kilowatt per ton rating at full load.
- Because each chiller has a dedicated pump, the chilled water does not flow through an inactive chiller, which reduces pumping horsepower at partial loads.

This arrangement presents flow problems. If one chiller and pump are shut down, some coils in the building may be starved. To overcome this problem, most cooling coils in the facility should be piped with two-way valves, with only enough three-way valves to ensure minimum flow through a single chiller. The flow rate can then vary at the cooling coils and more closely match the variable-flow rate, which will occur as one pump is shut down when the load is less than 50 percent of the total plant. Any existing plant with this arrangement is a candidate for retrofit by changing all three-way valves and converting to a variable flow primary.

A common legacy primary/secondary system is shown in Figure 4-3. The chillers are piped in parallel with a dedicated pump for each. The secondary pump takes water from the primary loop and pumps it to the cooling coils. The cooling coils can all have two-way valves and the secondary pump can be furnished with a VFD to further reduce pumping horsepower during low-load conditions. There should always be more flow in the primary loop than in the secondary loop; otherwise, return water from the system will be pumped out to the coils again without passing through the chillers. But the surplus chilled water flow in the primary loop acts to reduce the return temperature entering the chiller, which lowers

Figure 4-3 Legacy Parallel Sequencing Piping Arrangement

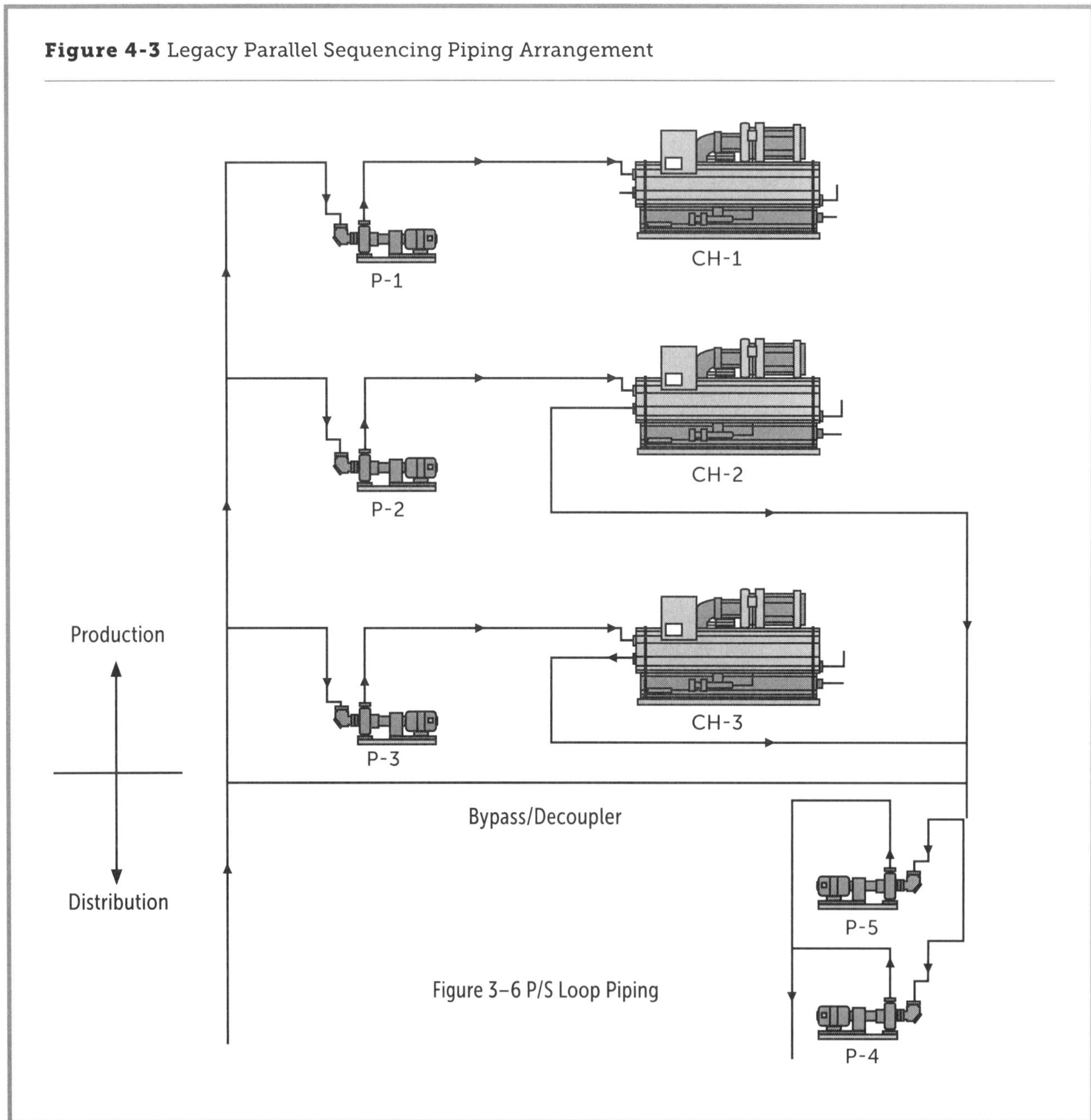

efficiency and frequently causes additional chillers to operate to meet the system flow rather than the system load.

In Figure 4-3, chilled water should always flow to the left along the bypass line. Whenever the flow stops or the flow is to the right, another chiller and pump are started to ensure an adequate supply of chilled water for the zone (secondary) pump. To avoid deficit flow in the primary loop and the corresponding higher secondary chilled water temperature, a check valve may be installed.

Figure 4-4 shows a schematic of a variable flow primary chilled water system. Each pump's speed is controlled with a VFD to maintain differential pressure at the most remote coil. Minimum flow through the chillers is maintained by a differential pressure transmitter across the chilled water. The bypass control valve is modulated to maintain differential pressure based on minimum recommended flow through the chiller. Each chiller leaving water sensor is set to 2 to 3°F cooler than design leaving water temperature. The chiller is enabled based on TS-1, the common chilled water supply temperature. As load is satisfied, chillers are staged off based on ΔT (load), chiller demand (kW), and system flow with an adjustable time period to avoid short cycling chiller on-off status. When using variable flow primary, air-handling unit control valves must have a characteristic of high rangeability (turn down) because valves nearer the primary pumps will experience much higher pressure than those farther away from the pumps. The segment ball valve has a rangeability of 300:1. If other valve types are used, excessive flow may occur at valves closest to the pumps.

Figure 4-4 Variable Flow Primary Chilled Water System

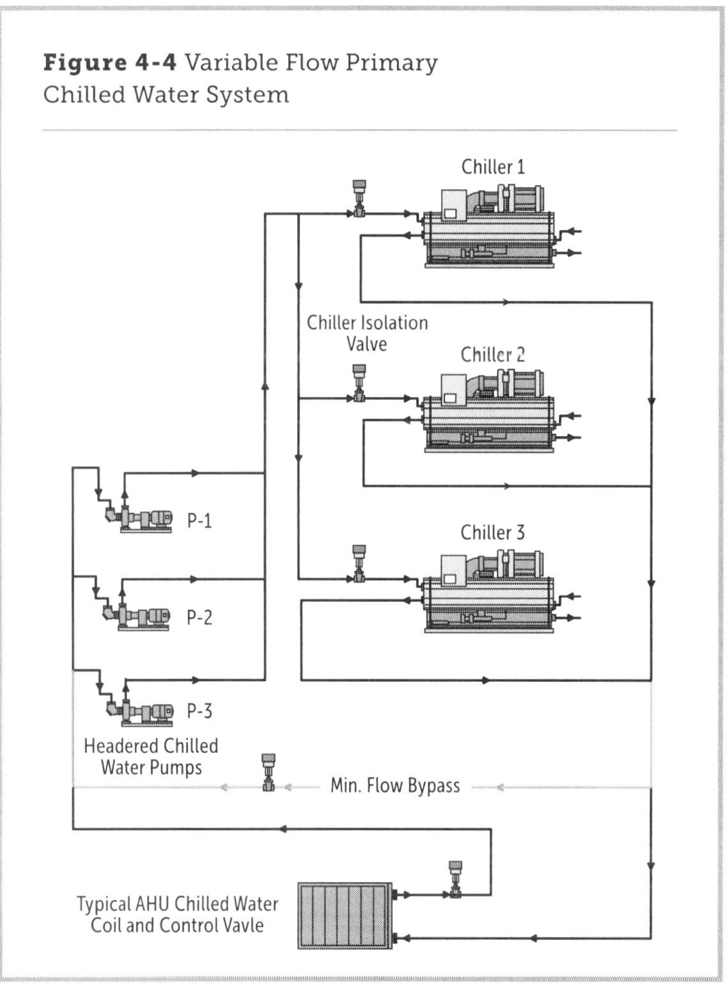

CHAPTER 5

Heating, Ventilation, and Air-Conditioning Systems and Air-Handling Equipment and Systems

Fundamentals

The laws of thermodynamics are the basis for the analysis and design of HVAC systems. This section briefly summarizes the first and second laws. This is not intended as an engineering textbook, but a basic understanding of thermodynamics is important.

There are two types of energy: stored (potential) energy and the energy of motion (kinetic energy). Regardless of the form, the first law of thermodynamics applies:

Energy cannot be created or destroyed.

The first law illustrates why energy efficiency and high-performance, sustainable design are necessary. If we could create energy, we would have no need to conserve it. But because the energy sources we use are finite, we need to conserve energy as we move to more renewable sources.

The first law of thermodynamics is captured in the following equation:

$$Q - (W_{flow} + W_{shaft}) = \Delta U + \Delta E_{potentitial} + \Delta E_{kinetic}$$

For a system in steady state, substituting for the internal, potential, and kinetic energy terms leads to the following (ASHRAE 2103a; Swift and Lawrence 2011):

$$Q - W = \dot{m}\,((u_2 - u_1) + (p_2v_2 - p_1v_1) + (V^2{}_2 - V^{21})/2 + g(z_2 - z_1))$$

where

Q = heat transferred to or from the system

E = energy contained in the system

W = work produced or required

u = internal energy of the fluid per unit of mass

$\dot{m}$ = mass of fluid

pv = product of the pressure and specific volume of the fluid

V = velocity of the fluid in the system

h = enthalpy of the fluid per unit of mass, expressed as (u + pv)

z = height of potential energy of the fluid

The internal energy (u) and flow energy (pv) terms can be combined into the fluid enthalpy:

$$h = u + pv$$

One common application of the first-law equation for a building's HVAC system is the process of generating heat to raise the temperature of a fluid to heat the building. The terms for work (W), changes in kinetic energy $(V^2{}_2 - V^2{}_1)/2$, and potential energy $(z_2 - z_1)$ are small compared to the enthalpy difference, so the first law becomes:

$$Q \cong \dot{m}\,(h_2 - h_1)$$

Energy is the ability to do work. Tapping that potential has three results: work, heat, and entropy. Work is transfer of energy via mechanical means such as a fan or pump. Heat is a form of energy transferred through temperature difference. Entropy is the indicator of the state of disorder of a system.

The second law of thermodynamics states:

> *All processes irreversibly increase the entropy of a system and its environment.*

The second law of thermodynamics is expressed in equations involving the change in entropy of the fluid. For this brief introduction and for high-performance energy decisions, studying the Carnot cycle on the temperature-entropy chart is useful.

The first and second laws of thermodynamics explain why we must conserve the finite, usable energy to which we have access. This energy will eventually and irreversibly be converted into unusable energy (the second law). Sustainable, highly efficient design and operation enable us to use our finite energy sources more judiciously and effectively.

Heat Transfer

Heat travels in three ways:

- Conduction—Heat transfer by molecular motion within a material or between materials in direct contact
- Convection—Energy exchange via contact between a fluid in motion and a solid
- Radiation—Heat transfer by electromagnetic waves; no contact required

Conduction

An example of conduction heat transfer is through the building envelope (roof, wall, window, or floor). Conduction is represented by the equation

$$Q = UA\Delta T$$

where Q is the heat transferred, A is the surface area, Δ is the temperature difference across the area, and U is the overall heat transfer coefficient.

$$U = 1/\Sigma R$$

where R is the thermal resistance for materials of the system.

The conduction equation indicates where building heating and cooling loads can be reduced. Conduction through the building envelope can be limited by using insulation materials to increase the R value of the materials used in the wall or roof.

Convection

The *ASHRAE Handbook: Fundamentals* provides many equations for calculating convection heat transfer coefficients and forced convection heat transfer. For building systems, examples of natural versus forced convection can be readily seen. Natural convection occurs due to differences in density and the action of gravity. An example of natural convection is baseboard heating. As air naturally rises it contacts the hot water or steam tube. Forced convection occurs when air or water is moved via a fan or pump.

Radiation

Radiant heat transfer is represented by the equation

$$Q = \varepsilon\sigma A({T^4}_1 - {T^4}_2)$$

where ε is emissivity, σ is the Stefan-Boltzman constant, A is area of the surface, and the temperature difference is the absolute difference between the radiant object and its surroundings.

Emissivity is a material's ability to emit thermal energy. Higher emissivity surfaces will absorb and emit more thermal energy. The rate of radiant heat transfer is proportional to the fourth power of the absolute temperature difference between an object and its surroundings.

Many building design choices can limit radiant heat transfer:

- Limited glass on east and west exposures, where radiant energy from the sun is highest
- Low-emissivity glass
- Shading or overhangs to reduce the areas exposed to the radiant source of the sun
- Cool roof designs that enhance the emissivity and absorptivity of the roof surfaces to reduce solar heat gain
- Radiant cooling in the floor of a large lobby or atrium to offset the radiant gains from the glass envelope

Forced Convection and Mass Transfer

Mass transfer by forced convection in hospital HVAC systems is primarily achieved using water and air. The energy required for a load is proportional to the fluid mass flow rate, *m*, and the temperature difference of the system's fluid, expressed as

$$Q = mc_p\Delta T$$

where c_p is the fluid's specific heat. For HVAC applications, c_p is 1.0 for water and 0.244 for air.

Two useful equations for sensible heat transfer using air and water are

$$\text{For water: } Q = (\text{gpm})(500)\Delta T$$

$$\text{For air: } Q = (\text{cfm})\ (1.09)\Delta T$$

For moist air, the equation for the latent heat transfer is

$$Q_L = (cfm)(0.68)\Delta W_{grains/lb}$$

Total heat transfer is represented by

$$QT = (cfm)(4.45)\Delta h$$

where Δh is the enthalpy difference.

Two useful equations for input energy required for forced convection and mass transfer of water or air are

$$\text{For pumps: mhp} = \frac{(gpm)(\Delta P\ ft\text{–}hd)(sg)}{(3960)\ E_{pump}\ E_{motor}}$$

where E_{Pump} is the pump effieciency; sg is specific gravity

$$\text{For air: mhp} = \frac{(cfm)(\Delta P\ in.w.g.)(sg)}{(6356)\ E_{fan}\ E_{motor}}$$

where E_{Fan} is the fan efficiency and sg is specific gravity.

To reduce fan or pump energy:

- Minimize pressure losses by increasing duct or pipe, limiting the number of fittings, or using fittings with lower losses.
- Reduce maximum duct or pipe velocities.
- Use premium efficiency motors.
- Select fans or pumps for maximum efficiency by choosing the most appropriate type of equipment for the system.

To promote efficiency in air distribution systems, ASHRAE Standard 90.1 has requirements limiting bhp/fan cfm. Any new system should comply with these limitations. For piping distribution, 90.1 limits pipe velocities to reduce system pressure losses. Design engineers frequently overlook these requirements and limitations.

Psychrometrics

Before discussing the various types of air-handling system configurations, an overview of the fundamentals of psychrometrics is in order. Psychrometrics is the dynamics of moist air. To diagnose problems in an HVAC system, a basic understanding of how air and water vapor react when heated and cooled is helpful.

Publications on psychrometrics and psychrometrics software are available that may allow the hospital engineer to better understand some of the principles discussed in this section.

Air is dry and is composed mostly of nitrogen and oxygen, with small amounts of carbon dioxide and hydrogen. It also includes water vapor in varying amounts. The amount of water vapor that air is able to hold in suspension depends on the pressure and temperature of the air. Low-temperature air has a lower water vapor capacity than does high-temperature air.

A sling psychrometer can determine the dry-bulb temperature of air, which is the temperature of air registered by an ordinary thermometer, and the wet-bulb temperature of air, which is the temperature registered by a thermometer whose bulb is covered with a wetted wick. The drier the air, the more evaporation will occur on the wick and the lower the wet-bulb temperature will be. The psychrometer is slung in a circular pattern, simulating a wind blowing across the bulb with the wetted wick. For moisture (i.e., water) to evaporate, it must absorb heat from a source. In this case, the wick draws heat out of the thermometer. The same phenomenon occurs when a person's body feels cooler after stepping out of a swimming pool when the wind is blowing. Heat is drawn out of the body as water on the skin evaporates. The difference between the wet-bulb temperature and the dry-bulb temperature can be used to determine the relative humidity of the air. If the air is 100 percent saturated, or at 100 percent relative humidity, the dry-bulb temperature and the wet-bulb temperature will be the same, because no net moisture will be evaporated from the wick when saturated air is blown across the wick-covered bulb.

Relative humidity refers to the ratio of the actual water vapor in the air compared to the amount of water vapor the air could hold at that particular temperature.

Specific humidity refers to the absolute amount of water vapor in the air expressed in pounds of water vapor or grains of water vapor per pound of dry air. (See paragraph below on specific humidity.) One pound equals 7,000 grains.

Enthalpy refers to the measurement of the total heat contained in the air–water vapor mixture. It has an arbitrary zero point, which is listed as 0°F at sea level atmospheric pressure. Enthalpy is used to measure the amount of heat energy contained in the air–water vapor mixture. Enthalpy is measured in Btu/LB dry air.

Sensible heat refers to the addition of heat to or deletion of heat from the air with no change in the amount of water vapor, or moisture, in the air. This process is represented by a horizontal line on the psychrometric chart. Latent heating or cooling, measured at Btu per hour, or Btuh, occurs when moisture is either added to or taken away from the air–water vapor mixture. A person at rest produces approximately 250 (Btuh) of sensible heat, or dry heat, which leaves the body because body temperature is higher than surrounding air temperature. People also produce 200 Btuh of latent heat, or moisture, which is added to the air in the form of evaporated perspiration. The psychrometric chart (see Figure 5-1) shows process lines representing the condition of air and what happens to it when either heat or moisture is added or taken away.

Dewpoint temperature, or saturation temperature, is the temperature at which the air is fully saturated, or at 100 percent relative humidity. This is also the temperature at which moisture will begin to condense out of the air. For example, if the space conditions were 75°F dry-bulb and 60 percent relative humidity, the corresponding dewpoint would be slightly above 59°F. This means that if any surface in the room (e.g., supply diffusers, microscope lenses, metal tables) has a temperature lower than 59°F, moisture from the air will begin to condense on this surface.

Dry-bulb temperature, wet-bulb temperature, dewpoint temperature, and relative humidity are all related, so if only two designated

Figure 5-1 Psychrometric Chart

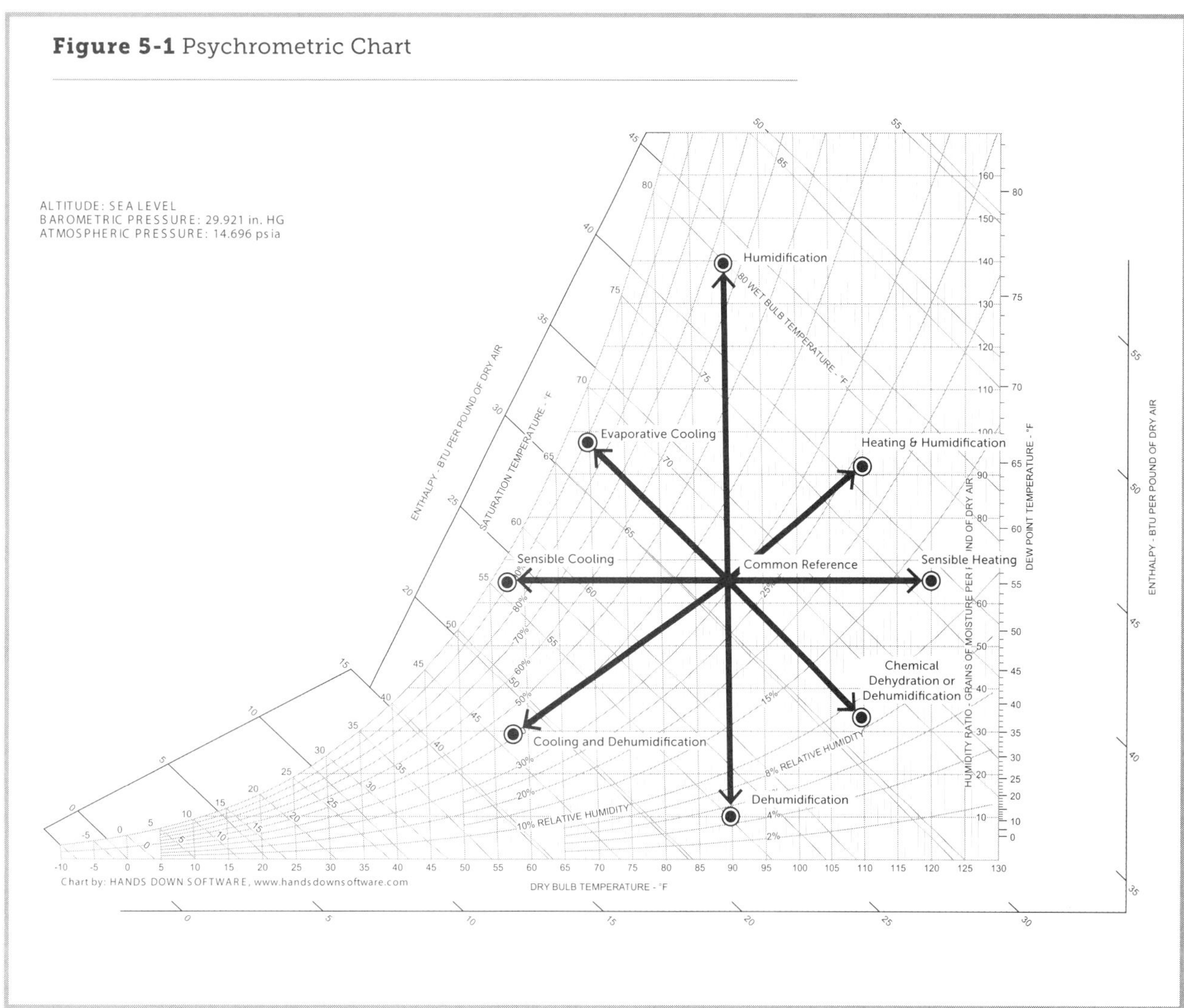

properties are known, all the other properties may be read from the psychrometric chart. The curved line, number 1 in Figure 5-2, is a saturation line. In all conditions occurring along this line, the air is fully saturated. If saturated air is further cooled, the water vapor in it begins to condense and tiny droplets form. These droplets create fog or clouds.

The psychrometric chart shows the air temperatures normally encountered in buildings. Psychrometric charts also exist for very high-temperature and very low-temperature air, but for most cases, the chart in Figure 5-1 will cover points normally encountered in a building environment. Figure 5-2 shows a skeleton chart with the location of the various characteristics of moist air. Many software

Figure 5-2 Skeleton Psychrometric Chart

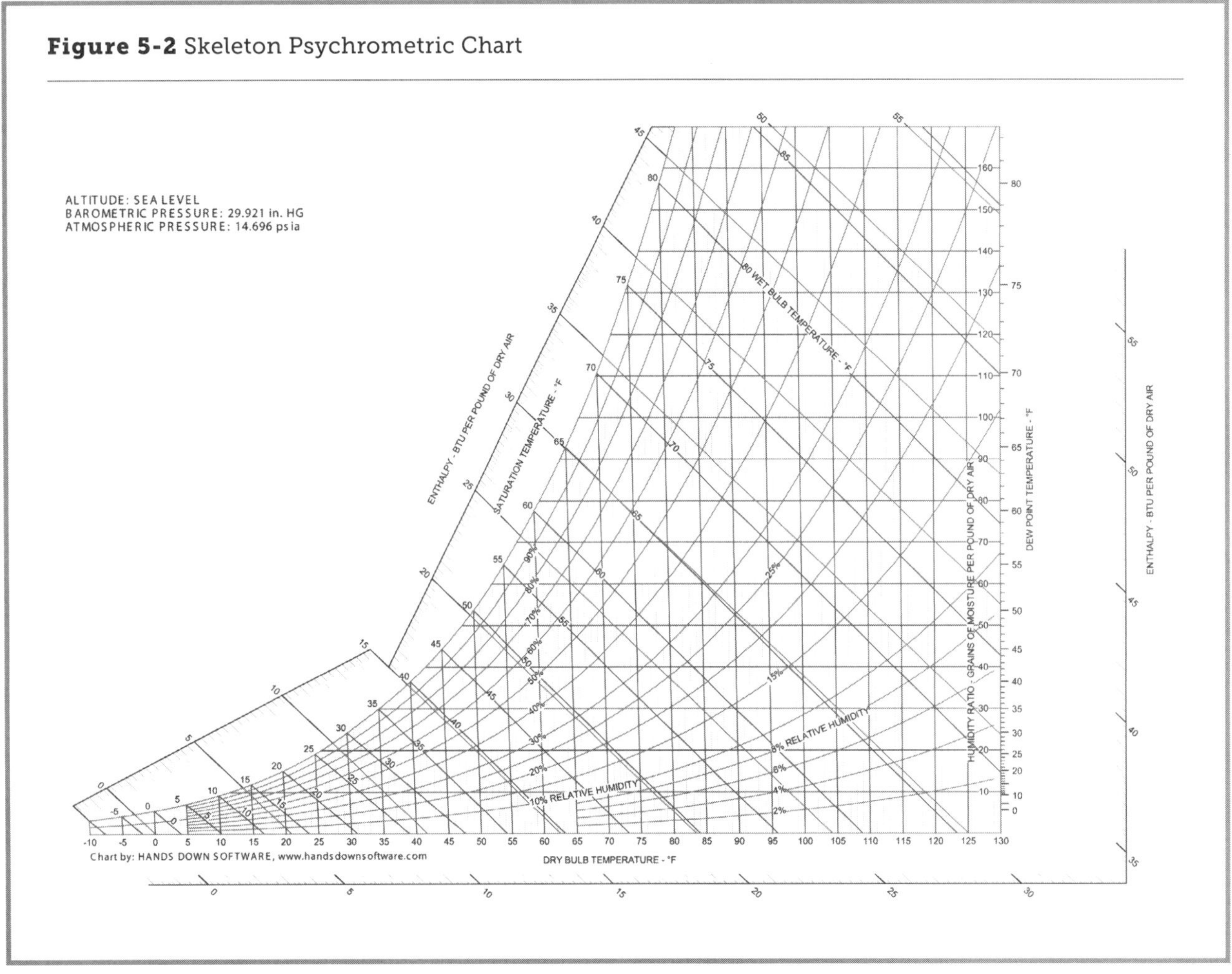

programs exist to help maintenance personnel learn the psychrometric chart and the processes. Appendix A-3 explains how to use the psychrometric chart.

Understanding the relationships of the data conveyed on the psychrometric chart helps hospital personnel see how changes made to systems can have negative effects. Many times in the quest to reduce energy consumption, hospital engineers raise air-handling unit discharge air temperature to lighten the load on the chillers. This may be fine in dry climates or when the relative humidity outside is relatively low, but once the temperature of the discharge air rises above 55°F, very little dehumidification will occur. Consequently, humidity in occupied spaces will rise. This is particularly critical in operating rooms and other sensitive areas of the hospital. It becomes even more critical if the room must be maintained at a lower temperature than 75°F, as is the case in operating rooms.

Using chilled water air-handling units with 42°F chilled water temperature and supplying 50°F leaving air temperature, many operating rooms are designed to maintain room temperatures between 70 and 74°F, with a relative humidity range of 30 to 60 percent, typically at 50 percent. When surgeons request lower temperatures, the relative humidity cannot be maintained below the 60 percent limit. This is easy to see when these conditions are plotted on the psychrometric chart. As the temperature in the space is lowered to 65°F, the relative humidity in the space will exceed 60 percent. If the temperature is lowered even further to 60°F, the space relative humidity will exceed 75 percent. An understanding of the properties of moist air and the air-conditioning process can demonstrate to maintenance personnel and surgeons why relative humidity cannot be maintained as temperatures are lowered unless the air-handling system is designed to deliver low dew point supply air temperature.

For various reasons, hospital surgeons request very low temperatures in operating rooms. Common requested design conditions are 60 to 62°F and 50 percent relative humidity. This is a dew point temperature of 41°F. Normal chilled water supply temperature of 42°F cannot produce supply air at this dew point temperature. Chilled water coils must be enhanced to provide dew point temperature of 41°F or cooler. There are two common approaches to maintaining low dew points in ORs:

- A low-temp, glycol chiller, either air or water cooled, to produce chilled water supply temperature of 34 to 35°F
- A desiccant wheel to dehumidify the supply air

Indoor Air Quality for Health Care Facilities

A building's HVAC system is designed to perform several tasks: filter, cool, heat, humidify, dehumidify, pressurize, and/or exhaust. Each of these tasks affects indoor air quality. For example, if incoming air is not properly filtered, excessive dust from the outdoors is drawn into the building. If supplied air is not conditioned or heated satisfactorily, occupants may experience thermal discomfort. If supplied air is not dehumidified appropriately, excessive relative humidity levels may promote microbial growth. If patient isolation rooms are not properly pressurized, unwanted airborne transmission of pathogenic bacteria may occur. If airborne chemicals are not properly exhausted from laboratories, these chemicals may migrate into nonlaboratory spaces. These are just a few examples of how the performance of the HVAC system can affect indoor air quality.

To effectively address mechanical system concerns, health care engineers should be aware of the corresponding indoor air quality (IAQ) issues. This chapter provides basic information regarding several key indoor air quality issues for the health care engineer. Several common mechanical systems concepts (such as building pressurization, moisture, filtration, and local exhaust) are reviewed from an IAQ perspective. By studying this chapter, the health care engineer should better understand how mechanical systems can affect indoor air quality.

IAQ Issues for Health Care Facilities

Building Pressurization

Untreated outdoor air leaks or infiltrates into a building when indoor pressure is less than the pressure outside. Buildings historically have been positively pressurized at all times with respect to the outdoors. Positive pressure forces all incoming air to enter a building through the HVAC system. Without positive pressure, outdoor contaminants, moisture, and unconditioned air enter the building through open exterior doors, open windows, and penetrations in the building envelope. Building pressurization may be checked by narrowly opening an exterior door and monitoring the direction of air flow through the door: negatively pressurized buildings pull outdoor air through the door into the building, and positively pressurized buildings push indoor air through the door out of the building. However, infiltration isn't always bad. During the heating season, a small amount of dry outdoor air leaking into the building envelope discourages moisture from condensing in the wall cavity.

During building cooling periods (such as a building located in the south during the summer), a negatively pressurized building allows hot, humid air to enter the building through open exterior doors and penetrations in the building envelope. These hot, humid air masses collide with cooler, drier air within the building. This produces an increase in humidity in localized areas and condensation on cold surfaces exposed to hot, humid air. This is also the primary cause of mold growth in damp wall cavities and behind vinyl wall coverings on exterior walls.

Causes of negative pressurization include fully or partially closed outside air dampers, blocked outdoor air intakes, an unbalanced HVAC system, and malfunctioning HVAC equipment.

When outside air dampers are closed, the HVAC system may be exhausting more air from the building than outside air is being pulled into the building. This produces a negative building pressure with respect to the outdoors. Exhaust fans and fume hoods pull air through penetrations in the building envelope and open exterior doors compensate for the loss of filtered, conditioned outdoor air supplied by the HVAC system.

Outside air intakes should be cleaned periodically to remove excessive dirt, trash, and debris that may collect on their grilles. Blocked outside air intakes prevent adequate fresh air from reaching the HVAC system.

During renovations, additional exhaust fans or fume hoods may be permanently added to a building. Fresh air supply rates should be increased to compensate for the additional exhaust. If fresh air supply rates are not increased, the additional exhaust fans or fume hoods may cause the building to become negatively pressurized with respect to the outdoors.

Room Pressurization

Certain rooms within a health care building should be positively or negatively pressurized with respect to surrounding areas. Positively pressurized rooms are usually designed to protect a patient, clean supplies, or equipment within the room. Negative pressure is used to contain airborne contaminants within a room. The 2014 FGI *Guidelines*/Standard 170-2013 provide lists of rooms that should be positively or negatively pressurized with respect to surrounding areas. The following are examples:

- Operating rooms
- Delivery rooms
- Trauma rooms
- Newborn intensive care
- Laser eye rooms
- Protective environment rooms
- Pharmacy
- Laboratory, media transfer
- Clean central medical and surgical supply rooms

A room may be pressurized so that it is positive with respect to adjacent areas for several reasons. It may be done to protect patients in operating rooms and protective environment rooms from airborne pathogens that may be present in adjacent areas. It may be done to protect sterile medical and surgical supplies in supply rooms from airborne contaminants that may be present in adjacent rooms. If these rooms are not properly pressurized, airborne contaminants from adjacent areas may be pulled into them. Increased concentrations of airborne bacteria, fungi, and viruses within these rooms may contaminate clean equipment or promote increases in nosocomial infections. Positively pressurized rooms are usually the cleanest environments in a hospital. Loss of positive pressure compromises the aseptic environment within the room.

According to the FGI *Guidelines*, the following are examples of rooms in hospitals and outpatient facilities that should be negatively pressurized with respect to adjacent areas:

- ER waiting rooms
- Radiology waiting rooms

- Triage
- Toilet rooms
- Airborne infection isolation (AII) rooms
- Darkrooms
- Cytology, glass washing, histology, microbiology, nuclear medicine, pathology, and sterilizing laboratories
- Autopsy rooms
- Soiled workrooms or holding rooms
- Soiled or decontamination room for central medical and surgical supply
- Soiled linen and trash chute rooms
- Janitors' closets

Rooms such as airborne infection isolation rooms are negatively pressurized with respect to adjacent areas to prevent airborne contaminants (e.g., microbial pathogens, chemicals) from drifting to other areas. Loss of negative pressure within these rooms allows unpleasant odors to migrate through the building and may promote the spread of airborne contaminants. One common use of airborne infection isolation rooms is for patients with active tuberculosis, a disease caused by the bacteria *Mycobacterium tuberculosis*. The bacteria are spread in the air from one person to another. A patient with active tuberculosis releases *M. tuberculosis* into the air when he or she sneezes or coughs. Other people may become infected if they inhale the airborne bacteria. Pathology and histology laboratories use substantial amounts of chemicals, including formaldehyde. If formaldehyde or other airborne chemicals are allowed to drift from these laboratories, building occupants may complain of unpleasant odors. Exposure to these airborne chemicals may also cause adverse health effects (see page 80).

If rooms are not properly pressurized (positive or negative), several causes are possible. An imbalance may exist between the supply and exhaust rates for the room. Supply and exhaust fans may not be operating properly. Supply diffusers and return grilles within the room should be checked for blockages; occupants may block them in an effort to improve their thermal comfort. Operation of fume hoods and biological safety cabinets within the room and in adjacent rooms should be checked, as poor performance of these units affects air balance within nearby rooms. Lastly, recent renovations may have altered the HVAC system in a manner that impacts the air balance among nearby rooms.

Outdoor Air Supply

Adequate amounts of outdoor air should be supplied to the indoor occupied spaces to promote acceptable indoor air quality. ASHRAE Standard 170-2013: *Ventilation of Health Care Facilities* and ASHRAE Standard 62.1-2013: *Ventilation for Acceptable Indoor Air Quality* (ASHRAE 62.1-2013) provide common standards for outdoor air ventilation rates in hospitals. Table 7-1 of ASHRAE Standard 170 lists minimum outside and total air change rates for various hospital spaces. For hospital spaces not listed in Standard 170, Standard 62.1 is used to determine the required outside air for the space. According to ASHRAE Standard 170, 7.1,6, for air-handling systems serving multiple spaces, the system minimum outside air shall be calculated using one of the following methods:

1. System minimum outdoor air quantity for an air-handling system shall be calculated as the sum of the individual space requirements as defined by the standard.
2. System minimum outdoor air quantity shall be calculated by the Ventilation Rate Procedure (multiple zone formula) of ASHRAE Standard 62.1. The minimum outdoor air change rate listed in this standard shall be interpreted as V_{oz} (zone outdoor airflow) for purposes of this calculation.

This is a significant new addition to the ASHRAE standard. Previous editions and iterations implied that the ratio of outside air to total was required. The newer procedure will result in lower, more reasonable outside air flow rates for health care facilities.

Without adequate outdoor air, indoor airborne contaminants may rise to uncomfortable or unhealthy concentrations. ASHRAE 62.1-2013 specifies two means of achieving acceptable indoor air quality from a ventilation standpoint: ventilation rate procedure and indoor air quality procedure. The ventilation rate procedure specifies outdoor air requirements for certain applications. The ASHRAE outdoor air requirements are designed to keep human body odors, carbon dioxide concentrations, and other human bioeffluent concentrations to levels acceptable to a substantial majority (approximately 80 percent) of the building population. Carbon dioxide concentrations are often measured within a building as an indicator of concentrations of other human bioeffluents. Ambient outdoor air contains approximately 370 ppm (parts per million by volume) of carbon dioxide. ASHRAE 62.1-2013 states that if indoor carbon dioxide concentrations are less than 700 ppm above ambient concentrations, human body odors and other bioeffluents are likely to be at levels acceptable to a majority of the building population.

The second method of achieving acceptable indoor air quality in ASHRAE 62.1-2013 is the indoor air quality procedure. For hospitals, the IAQ method is not acceptable to Standard 170. This procedure restricts the airborne concentration of all known contaminants to acceptable levels. These acceptable levels are established by the Occupational Safety and Health Administration (OSHA), the Environmental Protection Agency (EPA), and other agencies and organizations.

Placement of Air Intakes and Exhausts

Air intakes should not be located near vehicle loading zones, loading docks, emergency generator exhausts, kitchen exhausts, fume hood exhausts, or other locations where contaminant sources may be present. The potential for entry of contaminants from these sources into the building increases as the distances between the air intakes and contaminant sources decrease. The potential for entry of contaminants into the air intakes is also affected by the spatial arrangement of air intakes and contaminant sources. Eddies and multidirectional currents are created around a building as the wind blows toward the building. Eddies and currents may push contaminants from their sources toward air intakes. Contaminant sources and building exhausts should be located in a manner that minimizes the potential for entry of contaminants into the building.

NFPA 45: *Fire Protection for Laboratories Using Chemicals* (2011 edition) and ANSI Standard Z9.5: *American National Standard for Laboratory Ventilation* (2012 edition) require that fume hood exhausts and other potentially contaminated exhausts be discharged from the building in a manner that minimizes reentry of contaminants into the building. The locations, heights, and exhaust velocities of roof stacks affect the reentry potential for contaminants. Both standards require that roof stacks extend at least 10 feet above adjacent roof lines. The 2011 *ASHRAE Handbook: HVAC Applications* contains additional information on flow patterns around buildings and optimal design of stack sizes and locations.

Air Filtration

Appropriate air filters should be used and maintained within HVAC systems, biological safety cabinets, horizontal laminar flow benches, and pathology workstations. Filters are selected based on the type of contaminants they are designed to trap. Filters within HVAC systems are usually designed to trap particulates. In special exhaust systems and fume hoods, filters may be installed to trap gases, vapors, and particulates. Filters within biological safety cabinets and horizontal laminar flow benches are designed to trap fumes, mists, and particulates. Filters in pathology workstations are usually designed to trap formaldehyde vapors.

Minimum filter efficiencies are specified in Table 6-4 of ASHRAE Standard 170-2013. Minimum efficiency reporting values (MERV) are based on the method of testing described in ANSI/ASHRAE Standard 52.2: *Method of Testing General Ventilation Air-Cleaning Devices for Removal Efficiency by Particle Size*. MERV-A ratings are based on a test described in Appendix J of Standard 52.2. The MERV-A ratings more accurately predict filter efficiency over time so hospitals and design engineers should require MERV-A ratings when ordering or specifying filters.

Table 5-1 Minimum Filter Efficiencies

Space Designation (According to Function)	Filter Bank No.1 (MERV)	Filter Bank No.2 (MERV)
Operating rooms (Class B and C surgery); inpatient and ambulatory diagnostic and therapeutic radiology; inpatient delivery and recovery spaces	7	14
Inpatient care, treatment, and diagnosis and those spaces providing direct service or clean supplies and clean processing (except as noted below); All (rooms)	7	14
Protective environment (PE) rooms	7	HEPA
Laboratories; procedure rooms (Class A surgery) and associated semirestriced spaces	13	NR
Administrative; bulk storage; soiled holding spaces; food preparation spaces; and laundries	7	NR
All other outpatient spaces	7	NR
Nursing facilities	13	NR
Psychiatric hospitals	7	NR
Resident care, treatment, and support areas in inpatient hospice facilities	13	NR
Resident care, treatment, and support areas in assisted living facilities	7	NR

HEPA filters are designed to filter 99.97 percent of particles with a diameter of 0.3 microns. The size of 0.3 microns is the most evasive for a particulate filter. A HEPA filter is more efficient in trapping particles with larger or smaller diameters. When HEPA filters are installed within HVAC systems, they should be challenged with a testing agent to ensure that they are meeting their designed efficiency. Dioctyl phthalate (DOP) is usually used as the challenging agent.

A DOP generator creates aerosols with a mass median diameter of 0.27 microns that are injected into the HVAC system's airstream, upstream from the filter bank. A light-scattering photometer then determines the penetration of DOP aerosols that occurs through the filter and around its gasket.

HEPA filters are also placed within biological safety cabinets, horizontal laminar flow benches, and some exhaust ducts. One or two HEPA filters are placed within biological safety cabinets, depending on the type of cabinet. Biological safety cabinets should be tested and certified annually per the National Sanitation Foundation International Standard Number 49: *Class II (Laminar Flow Biohazard Cabinetry* (NSF 49). Certification of biological safety cabinets includes challenging HEPA filters with DOP aerosols. A biological safety cabinet may exhaust into its room or outdoors, depending on its design and the pathogens used within the unit.

Filtration performance may affect IAQ in several ways. Poorly maintained filters with inadequate seals and breaches in the filter media promote the passage of contaminants into occupied spaces. This seriously affects IAQ in critical areas where clean environments are needed. Particulate filters with MERVs of 14 (90 to 95 percent dust spot efficiency) or HEPA filters may be needed for critical patient areas to protect patients from airborne pathogens that may cause infections.

Severely occluded particulate filters increase the resistance of airflow through the filters, affecting air supply rates. When filters are not changed according to the manufacturer's instructions, the performance of the HVAC system is compromised.

When HEPA filters are not properly maintained and tested regularly in biological safety cabinets, there is risk of contamination of the product within the unit or release of airborne pathogens into the occupied environments. Some types of biological safety cabinets are designed to supply HEPA filtered air over the work surface to protect the product on the work surface from contamination. HEPA filters are used within all biological safety cabinets to prevent airborne pathogens released at the work surface from entering the occupied environment. When the HEPA filters within a biological safety cabinet are not performing as intended, products on the work surface may be contaminated, or pathogens used within the biological safety cabinet may be exhausted into the room.

For pathology workstations, permanganate filters are used for removal of formaldehyde vapors in air. This type of filter works differently than particulate filters. As the formaldehyde vapor–laden air passes through the filter, the vapors are absorbed onto the filter media. When the filters experience their full absorption capacity, formaldehyde vapors are not absorbed onto the media and pass through the filter. This results in formaldehyde vapors escaping into the occupied environment.

To ensure that appropriate filters are being used and maintained in accordance with the manufacturer's instructions, maintenance and laboratory personnel should be trained on the features of filters. Personnel should know the capabilities of the filters and when they should be changed. Filter inspections and testing (HEPA filters) should be included in preventive maintenance plans.

Thermal Conditions

Thermal conditions play an important role in building occupants' comfort and perception of IAQ. If occupants feel too hot or cold, occupants' perception of other IAQ problems is exacerbated.

ASHRAE Standard 55-2013: *Thermal Environmental Conditions for Human Occupancy* contains recommended temperature and humidity ranges for indoor environments. The FGI *Guidelines* also contain recommended temperature and relative humidity ranges for specific areas within hospitals. ASHRAE 55-2010 states that six primary factors must be addressed when assessing overall conditions for thermal comfort:

- Metabolic rate
- Clothing insulation
- Air temperature
- Radiant temperature

- Air speed
- Humidity

These factors should be considered together when assessing occupant thermal comfort.

Low relative humidity (<30 percent) within an indoor environment may cause occupants to experience drying of the mucous membranes and skin. Some occupants are more susceptible to these symptoms than others.

ASHRAE Standard 170 now lists design relative humidity for operating rooms (anesthetizing locations) as 20 to 60 percent. Centers for Medicare and Medicaid Services (CMS) has also approved a 20 to 60 percent relative humidity range.

Previous editions of NFPA 99: *Health Care Facilities* required smoke purge for anesthetizing locations. The smoke purge/venting requirement has been eliminated in NFPA 99-2012.

Excessive relative humidity (>60 percent) in a building promotes microbial growth. Fungi and bacteria are ubiquitous in the indoor environment. Once a material becomes wet or relative humidity exceeds 60 percent, conditions are favorable for enhanced microbial growth. (See page 82.)

Laboratories

Laboratory conditions and personnel work practices may impact IAQ within a building. In health care facilities, laboratories are often located near nonlaboratory occupied areas. Laboratories tend to contain more hazardous chemicals than other areas. Many of these chemicals have the potential to become airborne. Engineering controls and work practices are used to minimize exposure to these airborne chemicals and prevent them from migrating to other nonhazardous areas.

The FGI *Guidelines* recommend that most laboratories be kept under negative pressure with respect to surrounding areas. Negative pressure is accomplished through the use of exhaust fans, fume hoods, and biological safety cabinets. NFPA 99 requires that air exhausted from laboratories may not be returned to nonlaboratory spaces. Laboratory air should be exhausted from the building or returned to an air-handling unit dedicated to serving laboratory areas.

Laboratory employee work practices influence the amount of hazardous chemicals that are released into the indoor environment. These work practices include storage procedures, handling procedures, and fume hood and biological safety cabinet operating procedures. Hazardous chemicals should be stored in sealed containers (e.g., bottles, safety cans, drums). Containers of chemicals should not be permanently stored on the work surfaces within fume hoods or biological safety cabinets. These work surfaces are not designed for storage; storage impedes proper airflow into these units. Where large quantities of chemicals are stored, local fire prevention codes may require storage within dedicated storage rooms or storage cabinets. Storage rooms and cabinets are vented or exhausted to the outdoors to reduce the amount of airborne chemicals released into adjacent indoor areas.

Hazardous chemicals should be handled in a manner that minimizes occupants' exposure to them. When feasible, hazardous chemicals should be opened and used only in fume hoods or other hoods. Containers of hazardous chemicals should only be opened when they are needed. OSHA regulations require that laboratory personnel receive periodic training addressing chemical safety issues. (See OSHA Standard 29 CFR 1910.1450: *Occupational Exposure to Hazardous Chemicals in Laboratories*.)

If airborne hazardous chemicals are not being properly contained within a laboratory, the following issues should be examined to determine their effect on the indoor air quality. Exhaust from laboratories should be directed to the outdoors or recirculated only to other laboratory spaces. The FGI *Guidelines* recommend at least six air changes per hour within most laboratories. In areas where large amounts of chemicals are handled, a higher air exchange rate may be needed. Fume hoods and total exhaust biological safety cabinets should be functioning properly. Lastly, laboratory personnel should be using proper work practices regarding the storage and handling of hazardous chemicals.

Fume Hoods and Biological Safety Cabinets

Operation and use of fume hoods, biological safety cabinets, and other hoods affects the quality of indoor air. Fume hoods and other hoods are designed to capture and exhaust airborne contaminants generated within or directly in front of the units. Fume hoods come in a variety of sizes, configurations (e.g., horizontally or vertically sliding sashes), and specialties (e.g., perchloric acid hood).

All biological safety cabinets are designed to protect personnel and the environment from exposure to potentially harmful airborne pathogens. Class II and III biological safety cabinets are also designed to protect the product on its work surface. Biological safety cabinets are capable of protecting personnel and the environment from airborne pathogens by allowing only HEPA-filtered air to be exhausted from the cabinet. HEPA filters only remove airborne pathogens, particulates, mists, aerosols, and fumes from the air; they do not remove vapors or gases. All exhausted air from a biological safety cabinet passes through a HEPA filter before leaving the cabinet. Some biological safety cabinets are exhausted directly to the outdoors, and some are exhausted into the room.

Biological safety cabinets should not be confused with horizontal laminar flow benches. Horizontal laminar flow benches look similar to some biological safety cabinets, but they are designed to protect only the product on the work surface.

NFPA 45: *Fire Protection for Laboratories Using Chemicals* (2011 edition) requires that fume hoods be inspected and tested annually. Elements of the annual inspection and test include review of the following: physical condition of the unit, alarms for low airflow, airflow patterns, and face velocity. The average face velocity should be 80 to 120 feet per minute (fpm). Large variations (plus or minus 20 percent) from the average face velocity should be avoided. Face velocities should not exceed 125 fpm, because eddies may be created between the operator and fume hood that draw contaminants into the operator's breathing zone.

Biological safety cabinets should be certified annually and whenever HEPA filters are changed or the cabinet is relocated. The National Sanitation Foundation International Standard Number

49: *Class II (Laminar Flow) Biohazard Cabinetry* (NSF 49) contains procedures for certifying biological safety cabinets. During certification, the following elements, among others, are tested: face velocity, downward airflow velocity, HEPA filter integrity, cabinet integrity, and airflow patterns at the face and work surface. One of the major components of the biological safety cabinet certification is the DOP challenge of the HEPA filters. During this challenge, the filter's efficiency of 99.97 percent is verified. If a HEPA filter's efficiency decreases, there is a risk of contaminating the product or environment and exposing personnel to harmful pathogens.

Laboratory personnel should be knowledgeable about the hoods and biological safety cabinets with which they work. Personnel should be aware of the design, capabilities, and operational procedures regarding the units. Inappropriate work practices with a fume hood or biological safety cabinet may result in reduction of the unit's ability to properly capture, contain, or exhaust airborne contaminants.

Fume hoods and biological safety cabinets should be placed in locations with minimum air turbulence (i.e., away from doors, walkways, windows, air supply diffusers, and air return vents). Doors being opened and people walking in front of biological safety cabinets or fume hoods can disrupt the airflow pattern at the face of the unit.

Equipment should not be stored in a fume hood or biological safety cabinet. Equipment within the unit may impede airflow into the unit or create eddies that pull contaminants out of the unit into the operator's breathing zone.

Biological safety cabinets and fume hoods should be used for appropriate purposes. Pathogenic biological agents should not be handled in fume hoods. Hazardous chemicals should not be handled in biological safety cabinets, unless they are exhausted directly to the outdoors.

Failure to follow proper work practices with biological safety cabinets and fume hoods may contribute to poor indoor air quality. The best ways to prevent this are to educate the operators of this equipment and perform regular inspections, tests, and maintenance.

Exposure to Chemicals

Building occupants may be exposed to a variety of chemicals within the building. Exposure is dependent on the design of the HVAC system, the chemicals used within the building and the work practices associated with them, and employees' job tasks.

The following sections discuss some of the more commonly encountered chemicals in health care institutions and their associated health effects.

Asbestos

Asbestos is a natural, fibrous mineral that is found in building materials. Asbestos fibers are added to some building materials to increase their heat resistance. Its inclusion in buildings in the United States is now prohibited; however, many U.S. buildings have asbestos-containing materials (ACM) that were installed many years ago.

Asbestos fibers pose health risks when occupants inhale them. Renovations and maintenance operations may disturb ACM and cause asbestos fibers to become airborne. Exposure to asbestos fibers may cause several diseases, including lung cancer, asbestosis (scarring of the lung tissue), and mesothelioma (cancer of the chest cavity lining). Asbestos-related diseases usually have a latency period of 10 years or more after exposure. There are no known acute health effects from asbestos exposure.

Governmental standards (including OSHA and EPA) regulate the removal and disposal of ACM. These standards include engineering controls and work practices during removal operations. Adherence to these standards during renovation and construction activities minimizes building occupants' exposure potential to asbestos fibers.

Carbon Dioxide

Carbon dioxide is a colorless, odorless gas that is present in ambient air. Outdoor air contains approximately 0.037 percent carbon dioxide by volume (370 ppm). Carbon dioxide concentrations are often used as an indicator of the overall indoor air quality of an environment. Human occupants produce bioeffluents such as carbon dioxide, water vapor, particulates, biological aerosols, and volatile organic compounds. ASHRAE 62-2002 states that occupants' comfort level associated with exposure to these bioeffluents is satisfactory if indoor carbon dioxide concentrations do not exceed 700 ppm above the outdoor carbon dioxide concentration. If carbon dioxide concentrations rise above this level, ventilation within the building may be inadequate and occupants may experience symptoms such as headaches and fatigue.

Carbon Monoxide

Carbon monoxide is a colorless, odorless gas. It is a product of combustion (as is produced by internal combustion engines and gas-fired heaters). Carbon monoxide is a chemical asphyxiant. Inhalation of carbon monoxide reduces the blood's ability to deliver oxygen to body tissues. Symptoms of inhalation include headaches, nausea, dizziness, unconsciousness, and death. The severity of the symptoms depends on the exposure concentration, the exposure duration, and the individual's sensitivity to the effects of carbon monoxide.

Formaldehyde

Formaldehyde is a colorless gas that has a pungent, disagreeable odor at room temperature. Formaldehyde is used in many building products, including plywood, particleboard, adhesives, and wallboard. In health care facilities, it is used as an aqueous solution (formalin) in morgues and pathology laboratories. Human response to formaldehyde exposure varies greatly. Acute symptoms include nausea, headaches, and irritation of the eyes, nose, throat, and skin. The severity of the symptoms is highly dependent on the individual's sensitivity to formaldehyde.

Volatile Organic Compounds (VOCs)

Volatile organic compounds (VOCs) include a variety of chemicals that exist as a gas or vapor at room temperature or are emitted from building materials, equipment, or products. Common sources of VOCs include copy machines, photographic development equipment, paints, adhesives, cleaning solutions, carpets, pesticides, and cosmetic products. Human response to VOC exposure varies greatly. As with carbon monoxide and formaldehyde, symptoms of exposure to VOCs are dependent on the exposure concentration, the exposure duration, and the individual's sensitivity to the chemicals.

Microbiological Contamination

Exposure to microorganisms, such as fungi, bacteria, viruses, and their biological by-products, may cause disease and allergic responses in building occupants. Human exposure to pathogenic microorganisms and their by-products in an indoor environment usually occurs by inhalation and contact with the mucous membranes. In order to achieve acceptable indoor air quality, airborne exposure to fungi and other pathogens should be minimized.

For airborne exposures to microorganisms to occur, several events must happen. First, there must be a reservoir (i.e., a location where an unusually high concentration of microorganisms is present). Second, the microorganisms must be allowed to reproduce. Favorable conditions are needed for reproduction to occur. For example, fungal growth is usually optimized when moisture levels are high. Last, the microorganisms must be released into the air. For example, *Legionella* is released into the environment when cooling tower fans blow contaminated water mist into the air. Since all three steps are needed for exposure to occur, prevention of one or more of the steps from occurring will minimize airborne exposures to microorganisms.

Certain conditions contribute to microbial contamination in an indoor environment:

- Location of fresh air intakes adjacent to outdoor microbial reservoirs
- Excessive indoor relative humidity levels (greater than 60 percent)
- Stagnant water in air-handling units or other HVAC components

- Wet building materials such as carpet, gypsum board, insulation, or ceiling tiles
- Wet furniture
- Recent flooding within a building
- Inadequate building vapor barriers that allow entry of moisture into the building
- Voids in exterior insulation or cracks in buildings that allow cold outdoor air to enter the building and cool interior surfaces, which create condensation and promote microbial growth

Several controls are needed to minimize microbial contamination within a building. The HVAC system should be properly sized and installed. The system should be capable of handling the cooling and heating loads within the building. The building should be positively pressurized with respect to the outdoors to prevent the uncontrolled infiltration of moisture and airborne contaminants into the building. A preventive maintenance program should be implemented that provides regular inspections of HVAC components and prompt response to faulty equipment. All moisture leaks should be repaired immediately. Moisture should not be allowed to accumulate within wall cavities. The EPA recommends that water-damaged items should be discarded or dried within 24 to 48 hours to prevent mold growth.

Fungi

Fungi include yeasts, molds, and mushrooms. Molds are ubiquitous organisms; their most common source is the outdoor environment. Building occupants are exposed to airborne molds outdoors and indoors. Indoor air quality complaints increase when mold growth proliferates in an indoor environment. Mold can cause discoloration and degradation of building materials, odor problems, and allergic reactions in building occupants. Some building occupants may be hypersensitive to certain species of fungi. The key to minimizing indoor exposure to airborne molds is to prevent the amplification and dissemination of the organisms.

Some patients in hospitals are highly susceptible to developing infections from airborne microorganisms. One such infection is aspergillosis, which is caused by several species of the fungus *Aspergillus. Aspergillus* is a ubiquitous organism in the indoor and outdoor environments. Aspergillosis is a fungal infection of the tissue in the lungs and respiratory tract. Patients with suppressed immune systems (e.g., bone marrow transplant and organ transplant recipients) are at increased risk of developing aspergillosis. Aspergillosis can be fatal in immunocompromised patients. It may be associated with dust exposure from renovation and construction activities within hospitals; consequently, engineering and administrative controls should be in place to prevent patient dust exposure (see page 86).

Legionnella

Another potentially pathogenic microbial agent is *Legionella. Legionella pneumophila* is capable of causing legionellosis. Legionellosis has two distinct forms: Legionnaires' disease and Pontiac fever. Symptoms for Legionnaire's disease range from a mild cough and low fever to pneumonia and death. Pontiac fever produces flu-like symptoms, including fever and muscle aches. Legionellosis is usually contracted by inhalation of aerosolized water contaminated with *Legionella*. The likelihood of contracting the disease depends on the concentration of the bacteria in the water source, the susceptibility of the exposed occupants, and the duration of exposure.

Legionella bacteria are commonly found in natural water sources. Under the right conditions, *Legionella* can proliferate in domestic water systems used for heating, cooling, and drinking. According to the *OSHA Technical Manual*, several conditions may be attributed to promoting the growth of *Legionella* in water systems:

- Stagnation
- Water temperatures between 68°F and 122°F
- pH between 5.0 and 8.5

- Presence of other microorganisms that supply nutrients or harbor *Legionella*
- Presence of sediment that promotes the growth of other micro flora

Water sources that may provide optimal growth conditions for *Legionella* include cooling towers, evaporative condensers, humidifiers, decorative fountains, spas, whirlpools, and domestic hot water systems. All of these sources are capable of releasing aerosolized water into an occupied environment. To minimize the chance of disease, HVAC equipment should be cleaned periodically and maintained. Domestic water temperatures should be within acceptable temperature ranges. Water stagnation should be avoided. ASHRAE Guideline 12-2000: *Minimizing the Risk of Legionellosis Associated with Building Water Systems* provides detailed information regarding the treatment of contaminated systems, periodic cleaning procedures for equipment, and water sampling guidelines.

Proposed ASHRAE Standard 188P (4th Edition): *Legionellosis: Risk Management for Building Water Systems*, outlines the minimum legionellosis risk management requirements for the construction, commissioning, operation, maintenance, repair, replacement, and expansion of new and existing buildings and their associated water systems and components. The standard outlines the principles of a water management program utilizing various risk management principles. Hospital managers and directors must actively participate in the creation and operation of a legionellosis water risk management plan. Elements of a water management plan include the following:

- Program team: Identfiy persons responsible for the program development and implementation
- Description of water system and flow diagrams
- Analysis of building water systems
- Control measures: Determine locations where control measures must be applied and maintanined to stay within established limits

- Monitoring: Establish procedures for monitoring whether control measures are operating within established limits and if not, take corrective actions
- Corrective actions/documents
- Documentation

Renovation and Construction Activities

Maintaining acceptable indoor air quality during renovation and construction activities can be a challenge. Renovation and construction activities generate dust and odors that may contaminate the normally acceptable indoor air environment. To maintain acceptable indoor air quality during renovation and construction activities, coordination among contractors, building engineers, safety personnel, and building occupants is critical.

Renovation of occupied buildings may introduce contaminants that are not normally present into occupied spaces. One common pollutant generated during renovations is dust. Dust may be generated during demolition of drywall, plaster, and concrete. Dust exposure is usually more of a nuisance than a health hazard.

However, dust exposure may be harmful to patients with suppressed immune systems. Since *Aspergillus* is a ubiquitous organism, it can be present in drywall, building materials, and dust. Demolition of building materials releases dust that may contain *Aspergillus* spores.

FGI requires an infection control risk assessment (ICRA) document to proactively manage elements to minimize risk to building occupants during new construction and renovations to existing systems. Design recommendations and infection control risk mitigation recommendations must be submitted to health care authorities prior to a new or renovation project. Refer to FGI and other industry resources on creating and maintaining an ICRA document.

Other contaminants that may be generated during renovations include asbestos, volatile organic compounds, and products of combustion. Asbestos is a mineral that was added to certain building materials for its fire resistance. Demolition and disposal of asbestos-containing materials must follow OSHA and EPA regulations. Volatile organic compounds are generated from several types of new building products, including paints, sealants, adhesives, caulks, carpeting, pressed wood products, and cleaning agents. Combustion products and nuisance odors are generated from use of gasoline- or diesel-powered equipment, welding and cutting torch operations, and soldering guns.

Several control measures can be implemented to reduce or eliminate building occupant exposures to airborne contaminants from renovation activities. One of the best is to maintain the renovation area under negative pressure with respect to surrounding areas. This can be accomplished by use of exhaust fans or manipulation of the present HVAC system. If exhaust fans are used, the exhaust should be directed away from occupied areas and outdoor air intakes. In some situations, such as renovations near critical areas, HEPA-filtered exhaust fans may be necessary. A pressure monitor with alarm capability should be used to ensure that renovation areas are kept under negative pressure.

Another key control measure is erection of a barrier separating the occupied areas from the renovation areas. The barrier may include self-standing panels, tarpaulins, flexible plastic sheeting, or gypsum board. The type of barrier erected depends on the nature of the renovation work, duration of job, and criticality of adjoining areas. For most renovation projects, sealed barriers from floor to deck and a means of providing negative pressure within the renovation area are needed to adequately contain the particulates, vapors, gases, and microbial agents generated. Local fire prevention codes may require barriers to be constructed of materials with fire-retardant characteristics. NFPA 241: *Safeguarding Construction, Alteration, and Demolition Operations* (2000 edition) requires that only noncombustible materials be used for temporary construction enclosures. In some circumstances it also requires that walls with a one-hour fire resistance rating be used to separate renovation areas from occupied areas. Erection of construction barriers should be coordinated with the local fire department.

Other control measures include use of low-emitting building products, such as carpets, adhesives, paints, caulks, and cleaning solutions. Work activities may need to be scheduled during non-peak times. A prudent housekeeping plan should be implemented for all renovation projects. Construction debris should be removed from the site frequently. Construction debris and construction personnel should not be allowed to enter occupied patient care areas because they may spread potentially harmful dust into these areas.

Management Issues

In addition to HVAC issues and the presence of airborne contaminants, several other factors influence occupants' perceptions of IAQ. These include lighting, ergonomic issues, work-related stress, workplace morale, psychosocial issues, and the building management's approach to improving the IAQ. One of the most important aspects of an IAQ improvement project is communication between the building managers and occupants.

If a building is experiencing an IAQ problem or if several occupants have complained about the air quality, management should take certain steps to expedite resolution. Management should be forthcoming about the nature of the problem, investigative plan, results of any testing or sampling, and remediation plan. Management should provide regular updates on the status of the project through written notices and group meetings. If management has hired professional help to perform part of the investigation, the occupants should be informed. The more information occupants have about their IAQ concerns, the more patient they will likely be as the problem is resolved.

Humidity Control Issues

Indoor air quality is poor in too many buildings. Inadequate ventilation is one cause of poor indoor air quality. Another cause is excessive moisture. This moisture could come from water damage within the building (e.g., leaking pipes, water spills) or through issues in the building envelope (e.g., improper vapor retarders on the outside walls, leaks in the building envelope, roof leaks). On the other hand, the moisture damage could be from the lack of moisture control by the building's HVAC system. Unfortunately, many buildings suffer from a combination of both of these contributors.

As mentioned in the previous section, ventilation standards have been changed to increase the amount of outside air delivered into our buildings. However, simply adding more air into our buildings isn't necessarily the cure, especially in hot and humid climate zones. We must make certain we are not just trading one problem for another. In much of the country, such as in the southeast, ventilation air must be properly conditioned to ensure the building will not suffer from excessively high humidity. Without a doubt, the majority of the moisture (latent gain) inside a typical building comes from the ventilation air. It makes sense to actively control the absolute moisture level of this ventilation air. Far too often, we have only passively controlled the moisture (i.e., humidity) within the space by controlling the air temperature (i.e., cooling).

The following paragraphs and figures will illustrate this point. Let's assume, for the sake of discussion, that the summer design condition for a space within a hospital is to be 75°F dry-bulb and 50 percent relative humidity. Considering patients and employees are occupying the building, we cannot simply supply air at 75°F dry-bulb. The supply air would need to be considerably cooler than 75°F dry-bulb to absorb the sensible heat generated by the occupants, the lights, and the solar gain. However, if we are to maintain the space at an absolute moisture level of 55°F dew point (corresponding dew point temperature for 75°F db/50% rh; see Figure 5-1), air must be supplied at a dew point temperature less than 55° F to account for the moisture gain (i.e., latent gain) from the space. When conventional packaged direct expansion (DX) or chilled water cooling equipment is installed, the average supply air dew point is approximately 55°F. The engineering staff must consider calculating the absolute moisture level of the supply air to *prevent* any moisture-related problems from occurring as a result of the introduction of ventilation air. This is extremely critical in the operating suites, where the conditions are much more demanding.

Moisture can be taken out of the air by one of two methods. It must either be condensed out of the airstream, or it must be absorbed out of the airstream. When conventional cooling coils are being used to remove moisture, as with the use of the central station, factory-packaged and built-up air handling units described in the next few sections, moisture is removed by condensation. With a desiccant-based dehumidification system, moisture is being absorbed/adsorbed out of the air. This technology will be discussed further in later sections.

Today, the preferred method to properly condition outside, ventilation air to the proper dew point temperature is by separating the sensible and latent cooling processes with a dedicated outside air system (DOAS). The high latent load in the outside air is conditioned separately from the space sensible load. DOAS systems are being applied to not only provide better control but also to reduce energy consumption.

Air-Handling Equipment and Systems

Factory-Assembled Air-Handling Units

Air-handling units are almost always factory built, even if the systems dictated a custom air handling. Air-handling units are applied when a conditioned air system is either a necessary or desired component of an HVAC system. The application of air-handling units involves a variety of heating and cooling systems, including variable-air volume, constant volume, dual-duct systems, or multizone systems.

Air-handling units fall into one of two categories: cataloged air handlers or custom air handlers (also known as "engineered systems").

Cataloged Air-Handling Units

Cataloged air handling units are manufacturers' standard product offerings. Many options and features in cataloged units blur the difference between them and a true custom air handling unit. Features of cataloged units include many options that until recently were only available in custom AHUs. Figure 5-3 shows a representative factory-assembled, catalog unit. The rotary desiccant wheel is just one of the many options available in the cataloged units. Catalog units usually range from 3,000 cfm in capacity to over 100,000 cfm.

Figure 5-3 Modular Air-Handling Unit

Photo courtesy of Trane.

The unit capacity usually is limited by the face area of the cooling coil that can be effectively manufactured and shipped to a job site. Most manufacturers can produce units with up to 200 square feet of cooling coil face area. Because prudent design limits the face velocity across a coil to approximately 500 feet per minute to control moisture carryover, the airflow limit for a cooling unit is approximately 100,000 cfm. Cataloged units can include economizer sections and fans requiring only field connections supply, return, relief, and outside air ductwork or plenums.

Factory-packaged air handlers have the following advantages:

- Lower cost
- Fast delivery from the manufacturer
- Numerous plenum options for accessories such as ultravoliet lights, rotary entalphy, and desiccant wheels
- Variable aspect ratios for a given CFM to accommodating equipment space
- Spray foam insulation for superior thermal performance
- Numerous fan options including fan arrays
- Matched components
- Factory tested for capacity and performance
- Reduced shipping and installation

The disadvantages of factory packaged air handlers are as follows:

- Static pressure is limited to 8 to 10 inches
- Cabinet air leakage may be less than in a custom unit
- CFM capacity is limited to approximately 100,000 CFM
- Less flexibility than custom units for a limited number of configurations
- Usually tight clearances around components to be maintained

Factory Custom AHUs

Custom air-handling units offer virtually unlimited options and configurations. In the past, large air-handling units with unique configurations had to always be field built, but with the increase in size and options in the catalog units, custom units are used for fewer projects. The reasons for designing around custom units vary but include larger CFM capacities, static pressure ratings greater than available with cataloged units, reduced air leakage requirement, specific construction techniques (such as all-welded frames or all stainless-steel construction), or requirements for integral service vestibules.

Fans in air-handling units, cataloged or custom, can be single or dual, belt drive or direct drive. Advances in variable frequency drive (VFD) technology mean almost all new projects use direct drive fans with VFDs. A common practice, even the preferred practice today, is to use fan wall or fan array technology that incorporates multiple plenum fans in the fan section of the AHU. Fan arrays can use twenty or more smaller fans to meet CFM capacity. However, some manufacturers advocate limiting fan arrays to 4 to 6 fans. Both practices have advantages and disadvantages. The small fans are limited to a maximum horsepower (now 15 HP), which may result in quieter fan selections, small physical space for the AHU, and easier fan replacement compared to larger fans.

Desiccant-Based Dehumidification Technologies

Long gone are the days when satisfactory space conditions for the operating rooms were around 68°F to 72°F and 50 percent relative humidity. Today, due to heavy, multiple-layered gowning and long procedures, most hospitals require that their surgical suites be maintained at 60°F to 65°F or lower during the procedures. In addition to the concern for the surgeon's comfort, lower temperatures are often necessary in the operating rooms for therapeutic reasons or to keep the adhesive cements used in orthopedics from setting too quickly. Even at these lower temperatures, the relative humidity in the space is still expected to be maintained near 50 percent. With conventional HVAC systems (i.e., chilled water or DX-based), relative humidity is typically higher than 60 percent. These conditions result in a less than desirable operating room environment.

Incorporating a desiccant-based dehumidification system into the mechanical design for the hospital's operating suite allows for optimal and *active* humidity control for the overall system. No longer does the surgical staff have to tolerate unsatisfactory space conditions. The threat of "raining" in the operating room during surgeries (i.e., condensate forming and dripping from the metal fixtures on the ceiling) no longer exists. The common problem of microscope lenses fogging is also eliminated by lowering the dew point in operating rooms. Incorporating a desiccant system into the mechanical design allows the *absolute* humidity levels to be dropped much lower than chilled water (or DX) coils are capable of achieving, regardless of the temperature desired in the space. A desiccant system can be added to strictly condition the outside air requirements of the surgery suite, or it can be sized to treat the entire supply air requirements of the suite.

A desiccant is any material that has a great affinity to moisture. In the majority of the commercially available desiccant-based dehumidification systems, silica gel desiccant is impregnated onto the substrate material of the rotor (or wheel). This desiccant rotor removes moisture in the vapor stage from the process airstream by adsorption. This is the airstream that is to be dehumidified, whether it is all outside air or a mixture of outside air and return air. As the rotor rotates, it collects moisture. The moisture-laden rotor then rotates through a section of the air handler known as the regeneration section. In this section, the rotor is dried with heat from a gas-fired burner, a steam coil, or even an electric resistance heater. This process operates continuously as long as dehumidification is needed.

Installation of desiccant-based dehumidification equipment has many benefits, including the following:

- Greater comfort for physicians during surgical procedures
- Independent humidity and temperature control
- Removal of moisture upstream of any air handlers, allowing for operation of dry cooling coils
- Surgical suite ductwork stays dry to prevent mold growth
- Desiccant dehumidifiers can be added to hospital's existing mechanical system
- Allows for hospital's chiller(s) to operate at higher, more efficient temperatures

- Can accommodate additional chilled water requirements without adding chillers
- Makes efficient use of wasted excess boiler capacity during summer and off-peak seasons when using steam for desiccant regeneration
- Controlling latent loads with the desiccant system allows for precise and quick temperature changes (i.e., shorter cool down and recovery times)
- No more fogging of microscope lenses or surgeons' eyeglasses
- No more "raining" from the operating room ceilings and fixtures

Many health care engineers and plant operations managers mistakenly think a desiccant system is the same as an energy recovery (i.e., enthalpy wheel) system. Both systems include a rotor (or wheel) with a coating of desiccant material, but the similarities stop there.

A true desiccant system is *actively* regenerated, as opposed to *passively* regenerated by the requirement of cooler, drier exhaust air. The actively regenerated system does *not* require exhaust air to function; however, energy can be recovered from the hospital's exhaust air if desired and practical. The actively regenerated desiccant system also includes two or three times the amount of desiccant material, as does an enthalpy or energy recovery rotor.

A desiccant-based dehumidification and cooling unit can be designed for 100 percent outside air, 100 percent recirculated air, or a combination of both. It can also be designed with any type of filters required, such as HEPA filters.

Fan Types

Central station air-handling equipment can use several different fan types. Built-up units offer more flexibility than a factory-packaged unit, but the fans are generally classified in two categories—centrifugal or axial.

Centrifugal Fans

Generally, centrifugal fans come in three types for air-handling equipment: airfoil, backward inclined, and forward curve. These are schematically shown in Figure 5-4.

Figure 5-4 Types of Fan Wheels

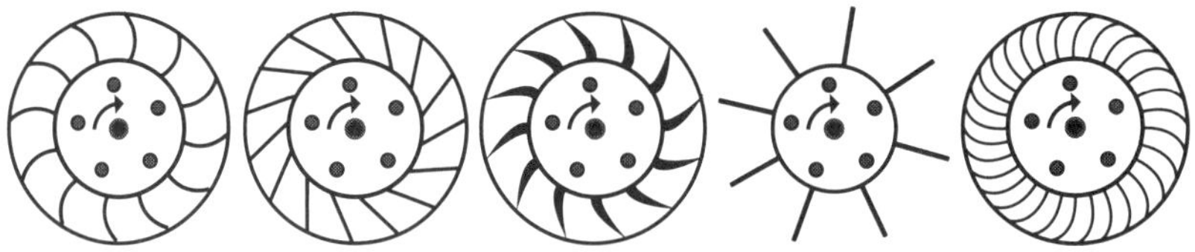

Backward curved blades
Backward inclined blades
Backward curved aerofoil blades
Radial blades
Forward curved blades

Figure 5-5 Airfoil Centrifugal Fan

Airfoil Fans

Airfoil is derived from the shape of the blade on the fan wheel. This fan type is the most efficient of all the fan designs. Airfoil fans are generally applied to HVAC systems in the higher capacity range. (See Figure 5-5.)

Backward-Inclined Fans

Generally, backward-inclined fans approach the efficiency and performance of an airfoil fan and usually are applied to smaller-capacity systems. The shape of a backward-inclined fan wheel is similar to an airfoil, except that it has a single-thickness blade.

Forward-Curved Fans

Forward-curved fans are the least efficient centrifugal fan type. These are usually reserved for use only in small-capacity, low-pressure applications.

Axial Fans

The second type of fan used is an axial flow fan. In this fan design, the airflow is straight through (see Figure 5-6). These are generally used in built-up systems, but they are often used for return fans in combination with central station air-handling units. The two axial fan types most commonly used in HVAC applications are the tube-axial and the vane-axial. The main difference is that a vane-axial fan has guide vanes upstream or downstream from the impeller, which increases the pressure capability and efficiency of the system. Both fans are used in general HVAC applications, especially where space is at a premium, due to their compact design. Axial fans also are very adaptable to parallel installation, which is the typical arrangement for a built-up central station unit with multiple fans.

Plenum fans are widely used in air handling units for supply and return air fans. The plenum fan is an unhoused centrifugal fan.

Figure 5-6 Axial Fan

Fan/Coil Configuration

Air-handling units with cooling coils can be configured in one of two ways—either a draw through or a blow through arrangement. With a draw-through unit, the cooling coil is located on the suction or upstream side of the supply fan. The supply fan therefore draws the air to be cooled across the cooling coil, and then discharges the air to some form of air-distribution system ductwork. The other unit configuration available in both factory-fabricated units and built-up units is the blow-through unit. With the blow-through configuration, the cooling coil is located between the fan discharge and the air-distribution system. Thus, the fan blows the air through the cooling coil.

The difference between a blow-through unit and a draw-through unit is the energy removal from the air by the cooling coil. With a draw-through unit, the fan energy or heat is introduced into the airstream after the air has passed through the cooling coil. With this arrangement, the cooling coil must subcool the air prior to passing over the fan wheel to achieve the required discharge air temperature. For example, if a 55°F discharge temperature is desired and the fan heat added to the cooling coil is 3°F, the cooling coil must subcool the air to 52°F before it passes over the fan wheel, at which point 3 degrees of fan heat is transmitted to the airstream, resulting in a 55°F discharge temperature.

With a blow-through unit, the fan heat is added to the airstream prior to passing through the cooling coil. Therefore, a cooling coil only cools the air to the desired discharge air temperature. For example, if the mixed air condition entering the supply fan is 80°F, the air leaving the supply fan (with fan heat) under the same conditions as in the previous example would be 83°F. The cooling coil then cools this 83°F to 55°F.

Although the effect of the sensible cooling seen by the cooling coil is the same in both examples, the difference comes in the latent heat that must be removed by the cooling coil. With the draw-through arrangement, the cooling coil sees an additional 3°F (from 55°F to 52°F) of latent cooling (assuming the air is saturated upon leaving the coil). This results in a higher total load for the draw-through unit.

Air Filtration

All air-handling systems serving hospital occupancies are required to have some level of air filtration. The level of air filtration is determined by the functions occurring within the spaces served by the air-handling equipment, the model building codes, and good engineering practice. In general, the more susceptible the patients being treated in the area are to infection or transmittal of disease, the higher the level of filtration required. Most states have adopted some form of guidelines mandating the level of filtration required. One common standard that has been adopted by many states is the 2014 FGI *Guidelines for Design and Construction of Hospital and Outpatient Facilities.*

Filters are rated according to their ability to remove contaminants from the airstream. ASHRAE Standard 52.2-2012 is the industry standard for rating filters according to their arrestance capacity, dust spot efficiency, and dust-holding capacity. This standard applies to filters up to 90 percent. Some states require 95 percent and even 99.9 percent HEPA filters for systems serving areas such as surgery, intensive care, and bone marrow transplants. These filters are rated according to the dioctal phthalic, or DOP, test developed and standardized by the U.S. military.

FGI and ASHRAE Standard 170 recommend minimum filtration levels for various hospital areas. Depending on the level of filtration, one- or two-filter beds may be required. When two-filter beds are required, the primary filters or "roughing filters" generally are located upstream of the components of the air-handling system. This arrangement removes the major dirt and other contaminants in the airstream that would adversely affect equipment performance. The secondary or higher-efficiency filters are generally located downstream of the air-handling apparatus, thus removing the remaining contaminants in the air after the air has passed through the mechanical systems. Final filters usually range between 90 and 99 percent for the more acute areas of the hospital, such as surgery, intensive care, isolation, and recovery, depending on the authority having jurisdiction. All filters must be inspected periodically and replaced as needed. The frequency of this change-out is dictated by the level of dirt loading of the filters.

The rate of dirt loading in the system generally depends on the quality of the air entering the system from the outdoors and returning from the hospital spaces. The best indication of the degree of dirt loading of a filter is to measure the air pressure drop across the filter. The level of dirt loading is generally proportional to the air pressure drop that occurs as the air passes through the filter. The dirtier a filter is, the higher the pressure drop through it will be. The filter system should be equipped with a gauge that readily indicates the filter dirt loading. This can be either in the form of a mechanical gauge mounted to the side of the filter housing that simply indicates the pressure drop in inches by the height of a water column in the gauge, or a building automation system (BAS) with replacement conditions set to indicate filter replacement due at the operator's workstation. Depending on a given facility's routine, the pressure drop realized also can be tied into an alarm system to give a local, visual, or audible indication when the filter drop has exceeded some maximum setpoint.

Generally, filters are housed in a manufactured frame that accepts the filter holding frame in some manner. Typically, these systems are set up so that various manufacturers' replaceable filter cartridges will adapt to the holding frames of other manufacturers. Filter holding frames or housings must be suited to the type of filter used. Frames and housings must provide gaskets, clips, and levels to ensure the filters are securely fitted in the frames to prevent leakage between the frames and the filters. Generally, it is advantageous for a hospital to contract with one filter manufacturer to supply all of the facility's filter media. For this reason, some form of standardization generally is helpful in planning construction or upgrade projects.

Humidification

One of the main functions of an HVAC system is humidity control, as described in the earlier section on psychrometrics. Humidity control in a hospital is important for comfort, static electricity control, and prevention of disease. Germicidal agents are more effective in controlled humidity environments.

Minimum humidity levels for various spaces in a hospital are listed in ASHRAE Standard 170-2013. The minimum humidity requirement in operating rooms, delivery rooms, and a few other spaces is now 20 percent.

Building humidity can be lowered by dehumidifying the air supply in the air-handling unit.

If, because of climate or environmental requirements, a high level of humidification is required, several types of humidifiers can be used to introduce it into the air. Humidification is accomplished by introducing steam or water vapor into the airstream, where it is absorbed by the air, and thus the humidity level is maintained in the space supplied by the system.

Many HVAC systems are set up for economizer operation or have sufficient quantities of outside air that in the wintertime, especially in colder climates, when the air does not contain sufficient moisture, the air-conditioning unit is left to maintain the required comfort levels in the hospital. This is the most critical time for humidification. Thus, a humidifier may be required.

Humidifiers in health care facilities must be steam injection type; water reservoir type humidifiers are not appropriate or acceptable. Steam for humidification is typically provided with either central boiler plant steam or a packaged electric steam humidifier that uses electricity to generate steam from domestic water at the point of use.

The most common method of humidification is the direct-injection steam humidifier, which historically has used central plant steam as a source. In accordance with Standard 170, chemical additives used for steam humidifiers serving health care facilities shall comply with FDA requirements. Some engineers and owners believe chemical additives present indoor air quality concerns to patients and hospital staff. In these cases, steam-to-steam heat exchanges are used to supply chemical-free steam to the humidifiers.

Maintenance is critical. Of all the components of the HVAC system, humidifiers have some of the highest potential for causing building damage. If the humidifier control sensors, the condensate removal traps, or the steam control valves should malfunction, the result would be excess steam entering the ductwork. Steam that cannot be absorbed by the air condenses into water, creating a wet condition in the ductwork. If the condition continues unchecked, water can drain down through the ductwork into the building. This is especially important for trim humidifiers, which are often located above the ceilings of critical areas that may house expensive diagnostic or treatment equipment. Even small amounts of water dripping from ductwork can cause significant damage to this equipment, as well as to building surfaces. Periodic checks of the traps, confirmation of the control valve operation, and calibration of the control points are all important to maintaining humidifier operation.

Economizer Operation

By nature of their design, all-air systems offer the opportunity to use economizer or "free cooling" during certain times of the year. The economizer operation is the use of outside air for building cooling whenever the heat contained by the outside air is lower than the heat contained by the indoor or return air. Usually, this function is automatic and is controlled by either a sensible temperature sensor or an enthalpy sensor via the temperature control system, or BAS. Whenever the temperature of the outdoor air drops below the setpoint (usually in the 55°F to 60°F range), the system changes over the air handler system to relief all of the building air and draw in 100 percent of the supply air from the outdoors. As the outside air temperature drops further below the supply air setpoint, the system will begin to modulate this function and mix sufficient quantities of outside air and return air to maintain the supply air setpoint temperature. Although this can result in significant savings through reduced chiller usage, it also has several disadvantages.

One disadvantage of an economizer is that it requires the use of either a return air fan or a relief air fan. With a return/relief fan, the system changes to economizer—the fan can exhaust the return air and attempt to match the building pressure that was created under normal operation. This is a difficult process to track exactly. Engineers have various opinions on how to control economizer dampers and return/relief fans. ASHRAE Guideline 16-2014: *Selecting Outdoor, Return, and Relief Dampers for Air-Side Economizer Systems*, provides guidance on sizing dampers for economizer systems and for controlling the dampers and fans. There are two predominant control strategies to control the return/relief fans and the economizer dampers: (1) airflow tracking and (2) direct pressure control. Airflow tracking requires airflow measurement of the supply and return air paths, which requires airflow measurement devices and transmitters. These devices need periodic maintenance and calibration. Many feel this maintenance is often overlooked, leading to loss of control of the system. Direct pressure measurement requires building pressure measurement as well as pressure measurement outside the building. Locating sensors in the building is a challenge. Locating an outdoor pressure sensor requires a sensor that can accommodate the fluctuating wind pressures and turbulence introduced from wind around the building. Both strategies, when properly installed, commissioned, and maintained, will control the fans and dampers to maintain the required outside air and to ensure the building is maintained at a positive pressure.

Another disadvantage of the economizer operation is the potential for system freeze-up. Outside air quantities for a central system unit with economizer will vary and at times will match the supply air quantity. This increases the size of the outdoor air louvers and dampers and makes balancing of the outdoor air quantity much more difficult. The potential for introducing excess outside air into the system is therefore greater in the event of damper malfunction. For this reason, all-air systems with economizer capability should be set up with two outside air damper sections. The first damper section is used to introduce the minimum amount of outside air required for the building occupancy. Usually, this damper is small and preferably fitted with its own damper actuator. The second damper is a larger economizer damper and is used to introduce the additional outdoor air whenever the unit is operating in the economizer mode.

With a prudent design that addresses the building pressurization and freeze protection measures, economizer operation may result in a substantial savings when applied in the right climates. Frequently, a life cycle cost analysis may indicate that a water-side economizer is more economical than air-side economizer.

Smoke Control

When an air-handling system is set up for economizer operation, the unit can also be used for smoke removal. Smoke removal is accomplished by forcing the unit into 100 percent outside air mode, thus purging a building when smoke occurs.

In addition to smoke removal, an economizer cycle also can accomplish smoke control by pressurizing and evacuating different areas or floors of the building. If an air-handling unit is put into the 100 percent outside air mode and the return air or relief air fan is stopped, the result is pressurization of the area served by the air-handling unit. If the return air or relief air fan is turned on for 100 percent relief and the supply air fan is turned off, the result is a negative pressure in that space served by the unit. With both fans running, a neutral or close-to-neutral pressure will be applied to the space and the smoke will be purged.

Packaged Direct-Expansion Equipment

Packaged direct-expansion (DX) equipment, as the name implies, refers to equipment that has the refrigeration cycle as an integral part of the equipment package. DX equipment includes a wide range of applications, from window air conditioners to computer room air conditioners to rooftop air-conditioning units in excess of 100 tons. DX equipment is typically air-cooled and in general has an application for just about every area of a hospital, although it is most typically applied to buildings with limited mechanical space and that require low initial cost, have less demanding performance requirements, and need limited equipment life. Of the variety of DX packaged systems, those most commonly found in hospitals are rooftop air-conditioning systems.

The rooftop unit generally consists of a refrigeration section, a return section, a mixing section, a prefilter section, a coil section, a fan section, and a final filter section (see Figure 5-7). Usually, the equipment is located on a roof (although it can be slab-mounted) and is ducted down into the building. In a multiple-story building, the ductwork is introduced into a shaft and ducted down to lower levels. Some of the advantages of packaged DX equipment are as follows:

- Less equipment room space required
- Lower initial installed cost and a relatively low life cycle cost

Some of the disadvantages are as follows:

- Relatively short equipment life
- Lower operating efficiency compared with other systems

Figure 5-7 Packaged Rooftop Unit

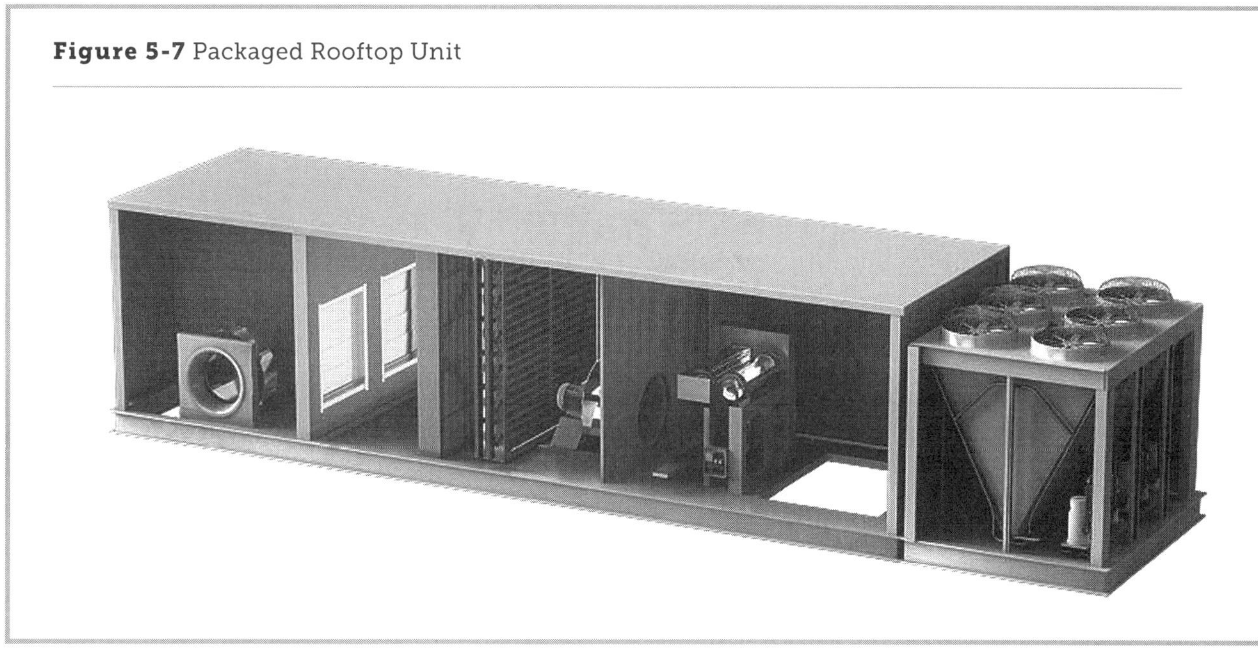

Photo courtesy of Trane.

- Poor humidity control relative to chilled water systems because small DX systems do not have modulating control
- Equipment/maintenance staff exposure to the elements
- Poor noise/vibration control

In hospitals, packaged DX equipment typically is applied to all air systems, either constant volume, constant volume with reheat, variable volume, variable volume with reheat, or multizone systems. (These systems will be described later.) For the systems listed, packaged DX equipment performs as well as any other central air distribution system with the exception of the disadvantages in the previous list; in particular, exposure to the elements does not lend the equipment to the type of maintenance generally required for hospital service, such as inspection, cleaning, filter removal and replacement, and other routine maintenance.

Natural Draft Convectors

Convectors are equipment used to heat buildings and supplement other HVAC systems. The name "convector" is derived from the fact that the equipment uses a natural convection or upward flow of relatively warm, dry air to heat spaces in a building. It is given to a group of equipment that includes baseboard heating, wall fin-tube, and wall cabinet convectors.

Typically, convectors are used to heat areas such as stairwells and building entrances or to counter the effects of cold drafts created by large expanses of wall or windows. Convectors have the advantage of being virtually maintenance free, with the exception of occasional cleaning. They consist of a carrier pipe in which the heated medium is transferred. Heat transfer is enhanced by a fin that is mechanically attached to the carrier pipe. Usually, the carrier pipe is black steel or copper and the fin can be constructed of either aluminum or copper. The fin is used to increase the heat transfer area of the convector and thereby enhances the warming effect on the air. Convectors are an excellent way to provide constant heat to cold surfaces in the building and are especially effective in colder climates.

As described previously, convectors typically are used in conjunction with some other type of HVAC system, such as an all-air system with baseboard heat. The reason for coupling the convectors with other systems is increased occupant comfort. A waiting room is a good illustration of the application of a convection system. Many waiting rooms have some glass exposure. In northern climates, this glass will almost always result in a cold surface on the interior of the room during the heating season. When the room air comes in contact with this cold surface, a reverse convection effect, or downdraft, occurs because as the air is cooled, it becomes denser and thus heavier than the surrounding air. This cold air then falls and can be felt by the room occupants.

In waiting rooms, chairs are often placed next to windows and the result is a cold, drafty feeling for their occupants. Often this draft cannot be effectively overcome by ceiling air terminals. A hot water convector can be placed next to the window and used to offset the draft. As the convector warms the room air, the natural convection or rising of the warmed air will counteract the falling action of the cold air. In addition, the convector will also warm the inside surface of the exterior wall or window and minimize the draft caused by the surface. This same theory can be applied to all areas of the hospital with exterior exposures. This is quite often necessary in the main entrance of a hospital, administration offices, the cafeteria, and other places where occupants are located on exterior exposures of the building.

Chilled Beams

Chilled beams have emerged as an attractive alternative to all-air, variable systems and have proven effective in conditioning new and existing buildings. Chilled beams must be properly applied. There are some limitations to applying chilled beams to meet or exceed the performance of a high performance variable air volume system. Chilled beams are available in three types: passive, active, and multi-function.

Conceptually, passive chilled beams are similar to finned-tube radiators, except that the passive beam is positioned in the ceiling. Passive beams operate purely from free convection. They are typically used to offset perimeter heat gains. Active chilled beams incorporate conditioned ventilation air supplied through induction nozzles in the beam. The pressure difference created by nozzles induces room air across the coil. The resulting cooled air enters the room through slots in the chilled beam. Because forced air is used in active chilled beams, the active beam can also be used for heating by supplying hot air to the coil. Multi-function chilled beams are similar to active beams but can be used to integrate lighting, sprinklers, speakers, or other building services that are typically located in the ceiling.

Chilled beams can provide energy reductions from 20 to 50 percent. To accomplish this, the chilled beams must be properly designed and appropriately applied to the building spaces. Chilled water supply to the beams is usually between 59° and 65°F. This allows chillers to operate more efficiently and promotes use of water-side economizers. Conditioned air is supplied to the active chilled beams at 68°F, well above the room dew point temperature. Airflow to the spaces with active chilled beam is significantly reduced because airflow rates needed are only for occupancy ventilation not to offset heat gains. Reheat energy may be significant with chilled beam systems.

Humidity contol is critical with chilled beams. Internal humidity in the beams must always be above the room dew point temperature. Room dew points should be maintained at between 50°F and 55°F. If this is not possible with the ventilation air due to high latent loads, chilled beams may not be appropriate for the space.

Recent studies have shown installation cost for chilled beam systems less than traditional VAV systems but this must be verified for every project. With less air supply distributed to the space, air-handling units, exhaust fans, chillers, and boilers are all smaller sizes. The savings from small equipment have been found to offset any first cost premium associated with active chilled beam systems.

Fan Coil Systems

Fan coils derive their name from the components that make up the unit. The unit is basically composed of a fan or supply air in a coil for heating and/or cooling the air. Although many HVAC systems have as their basic component a fan and a coil, the term *fan coil unit* is typically applied to units that supply from 200 to 1,200 cfm. Fan coils are one of several decentralized-type systems that, rather than having one large air-handling unit and cooling coil, have several units distributed throughout the building to serve the individual spaces. With a fan-coil-type system, each fan coil constitutes one temperature zone. Though the fan coil's principal application is a unit for each occupied space, it is possible to set the fan coils up so that they serve multiple rooms using ductwork.

The fundamental difference between a fan coil system and a typical all-air system is that water is the primary heat transfer medium instead of air. Rather than having large ductwork routed through the building for supply and return air, a set of supply and return water mains is routed through the building with branches to each of the fan coils. Typically, fan coils are applied to non-critical-type occupancies that have relatively low heat loads and do not require excessive amounts of outside air. Generally, fan coils are reserved for use in general patient rooms or possibly in some administrative areas. They are prohibited by code from being used in operating rooms, intensive care units, and other sensitive areas. There are two basic types of fan coil unit systems—the two-pipe system and the four-pipe system. As the name implies, a two-pipe system has two water pipes from the central equipment to each of the fan coil units. This piping is set up to be either the cooling medium or the heating medium. The two-pipe system requires a seasonal changeover to supply either heating or cooling to the spaces. During the cooling season, chilled water is distributed throughout piping to the fan coils, and the units are thus able to cool the spaces. Sometime in the mid-to-late fall, the system is changed over to the heating mode and hot water is piped through the system to provide heating.

The four-pipe system uses two independent piping systems with supply and return lines to the fan, resulting in four branch lines to the fan coil. The four-pipe system allows for simultaneous heating and cooling functions depending on the space demands. The two-pipe system has an obvious disadvantage in that rarely does a building have a consistent demand for heating and cooling, especially in the intermediate seasons and thus determining when to change over the system is always a compromise. Some spaces will still want cooling after the system has been changed over to heating, and vice versa. Two-pipe systems are typically applied only to buildings where exact temperature control is not a necessity or where all spaces have a similar exposure.

A fan coil system has the advantage of being a relatively simple, low-cost system, but it does have its limitations.

For hospitals, the primary limitations are that fan coils are unable to provide high levels of filtration, room pressurization, or excessive quantities of outside air typically required for patient care and treatment areas, and they require the maintenance of filters, coils, and fans at many scattered, sometimes hard-to-access locations, instead of at one location as with a controlled all-air system.

Fan Coil System Operation

The fan coil system is a distributed system consisting of central cooling equipment, central heating equipment, and some type of supplemental fresh air system. The fan coil component of this system is used to control an individual or small group space. The unit fan is used to circulate warm or cool air through the space and therefore to either heat or cool the space. Once the air is introduced into the fan coil, it is either heated or cooled by the unit coil depending on the space requirements. There are several methods for controlling the unit, typically by a wall-mounted thermostat. For spaces requiring continuous air movement and filtration, as is the code-mandated case in hospitals, the fan must run continuously. The cooling and heating functions are then provided by control valves in the water line modulated by the room thermostat in response to the space requirements. This water is then circulated through the piping system, back to the central heating and cooling equipment to either reject the space heat to the atmosphere or be heated by the central heating equipment.

Fan coil systems often do not introduce code-required ventilation air into the space and therefore are not allowed for isolation rooms and other sensitive areas. Some fan coil systems employ fresh air connections directly to the outside at each unit. These are usually difficult to balance to even close to the desired amount of air, and the volume will change as the outside wind shifts direction and velocity. Other systems duct fresh air into the building. Depending on the fan coil unit configuration, the fresh air is introduced either directly into the room or through the fan coil unit if the unit location in relation to the fresh air supply is conducive to this type of arrangement.

Preferably, the fresh air will be tempered to meet the space conditions depending on the season, particularly when codes require this ventilation to be continuous, as is the case in hospitals. In summer, the primary air should be cooled and dehumidified, and in winter it should be warmed to avoid inhibiting the function of the fan coil unit.

The main drawbacks to a fan coil system are the relative inefficiency of the system and the maintenance required. A fan coil system requires as much maintenance of the central equipment as other systems, as well as maintenance of the individual fan coil units. As described previously, fan coils consist of fans, control components, an individual drain system, and low-grade filters that must be changed frequently to maintain system performance. In addition, maintenance of the fan coils typically requires that staff enter patient-occupied areas, causing disruption to the function of the hospital.

Because fan coil systems are not allowed in sensitive areas of the hospital, some centralized type of all-air system is required for that portion of the facility. As a result, the hospital engineer is required to maintain more than one type of system with the associated training, parts inventory, and duplication in periodic maintenance required.

Induction Units

Induction units are a somewhat dated design rarely used in current replacement or renovation projects. Induction systems were very popular in the early stages of HVAC development. Particularly in multistory structures, the system is composed of a high-pressure central station air-handling unit that supplies cooled and dehumidified air at a very high velocity to terminal units located in the spaces. Terminal units are either floor-mounted on an outside wall or concealed above the ceiling and ducted to a ceiling diffuser. As the term *induced air* implies, air is induced into the system by discharging the high-velocity cooled air from the central station unit through nozzles directed toward a discharge grille on the unit. The flow of this high-velocity air through the nozzles induces additional room air into the airstream and results in a flow of air approximately two to five times greater than the central supply air. The induced air is drawn in at the bottom or backside of the induction unit and passes through a lint screen and across a cooling coil or a heating coil before it mixes with the supply air and enters the space.

Like fan coils, induction units come in both two-pipe and four-pipe arrangements. As described previously, the two-pipe arrangement has severe limitations in that only one medium is available to the terminal unit at any given time. This means that the induction system has to be in either a heating mode or a cooling mode. This causes problems when spaces in the building have different exposures, particularly north and south. The northern exposure could require heat in the intermediate season, and the southern exposure could require cooling due to the solar gain. The four-pipe system alleviates this problem by providing both hot and chilled water to the terminal unit as required, depending on space and outside air requirements.

Induction units have an additional limitation in that they are very sensitive to a lack of regular cleaning of the lint screen and heating and cooling coils, as well as not-so-frequent cleaning of the unit nozzles. Because induction units do not have fans or any means of boosting the room airflow across the cooling coil and lint screen, any blockage has a severe impact on this system's ability to perform. Also, the cooling coil is not designed to condense moisture out of the room air. If the cold water circuit temperature is not accurately maintained, sweating on the unit coils will result.

In hospitals, induction units to patient rooms or administrative areas are limited due to their inability to provide large air quantities and/or high levels of filtration, and they are not allowed by code in sensitive areas.

Induction System Operation

Like fan coil systems, induction systems employ a central cooling plant, a central heating plant, and some form of piping distribution. Usually, they are limited to applications in perimeter spaces of buildings.

The induction unit is used for individual room temperature control, with a room thermostat modulating the water in the secondary coil to maintain the temperature. The primary air is constant flow and provides constant ventilation air into the space. It does an excellent job of providing a constant measured volume of pretreated fresh air to each space.

The disadvantages of an induction system are as follows:

- Induction units can be used only in limited areas of the hospital

- Required maintenance on both central and distributed components
- Maintenance personnel must enter patient care areas to maintain induction terminal units
- Somewhat dated design with limited suppliers
- Susceptibility to lint and dirt
- High installation cost (higher than fan coils or all-air systems)
- Relatively low energy efficiency

Water-to-Air Heat Pumps

Water-to-air heat pumps are another decentralized system that distributes the cooling system components to yet another level beyond that described for fan coil units and induction units. This further distribution means that the refrigeration component of the cooling system is moved to the terminal unit and only central equipment is limited to the heat rejection equipment. Thus, each terminal unit contains a fan, a filter, an evaporator coil, a condenser coil, and a compressor. These are all packaged in a casing that is suitable for mounting either above the ceiling of a room or, in the case of larger-capacity units, in a mechanical room.

The heat pump units are connected to a piping loop that is routed back to an evaporative heat rejection component and a central heating component, as well as the central pumping components.

Generally, water source heat pump terminal units (see Figure 5-8) range in capacity from three-quarters of a ton to almost 30 tons. As with most distributed-type cooling systems, water source heat pumps have two major advantages: The first is low cost, and the right application can be very cost effective from an operations standpoint. In addition, water source heat pumps are flexible systems that enable the addition of zones and system reconfiguration to be accomplished with minimal effect on the remainder of the system and usually in a very timely fashion. For this reason, water

Figure 5-8 Water Source Heat Pump Piping Schematic

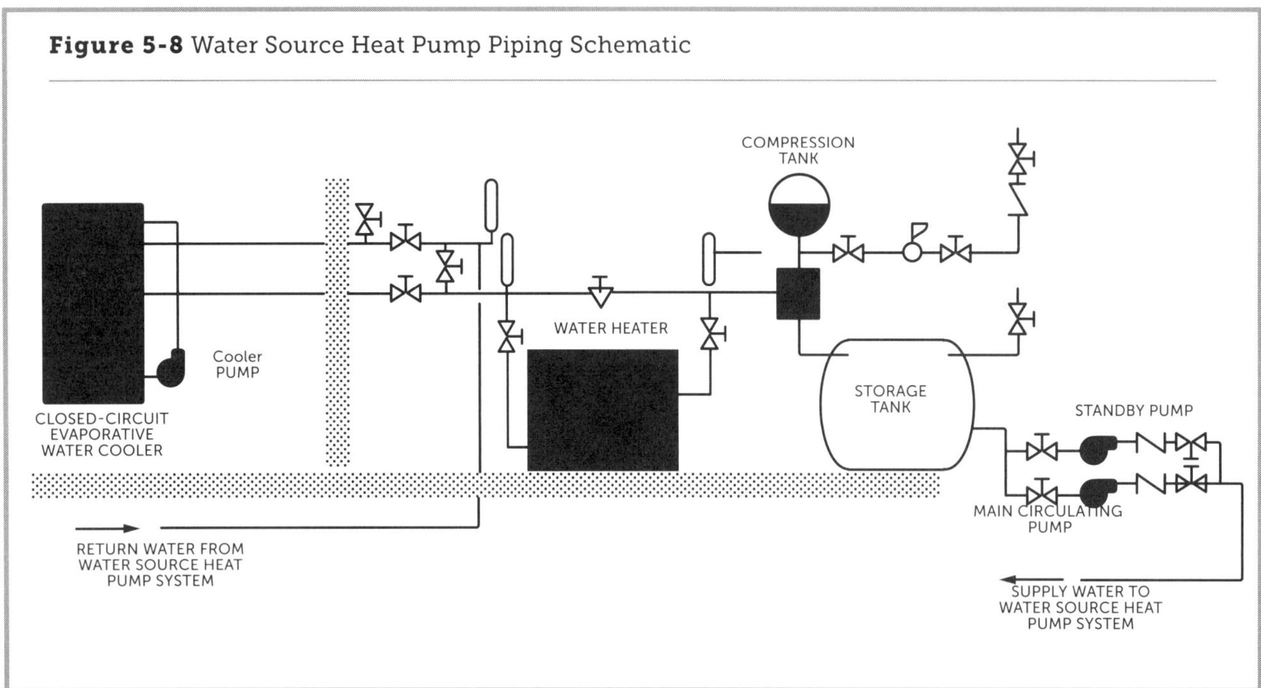

source heat pumps have typically been applied to office buildings and schools but, because of the disadvantages described below, they are rarely applied to acute care hospitals, except in administrative areas.

A disadvantage of water source heat pumps are that, compared to centralized system components, their components typically fall in the mid-range as far as the quality of construction, with reduced life expectancy. In addition, with the evaporator section, condenser section, supply air fan, and heat rejection piping concentrated within one enclosure, maintenance of the equipment is somewhat difficult. Most building operators who maintain a large quantity of water source heat pumps generally keep several spare whole units on hand. Thus, when a unit requires serious repair, a standby unit is put in place of the unit to be repaired, so that it can then be removed and taken to a maintenance area.

Water source heat pumps have a somewhat limited application in hospitals. Although it would be possible to use water source heat pumps for patient rooms or administrative areas, code does not allow their use in sensitive areas. Thus, this system would not be appropriate for diagnostic and treatment areas or other load or high-air circulation areas.

Often water source heat pumps are chosen for medical office buildings. Typically, these buildings are constructed without knowledge of the final tenant layouts, and from this standpoint, system flexibility is a significant advantage. Like fan coil units, water source heat pump units are not capable of handling much untreated fresh air. Consequently, to provide the ventilation air as required by code, a supplemental primary air system is needed to perform this function. Typically, this is in the form of a central 100 percent outside air–handling unit that tempers the outside air and distributes it to the room terminals. The tempering of outdoor air is important with the heat pump system, because the heat pump unit typically maintains space temperature by cycling the refrigeration component of the unit, and air that is too cold or too hot and humid for acceptable levels in occupied spaces is introduced into the space whenever the heat pump thermostat is satisfied.

One major disadvantage to the system is that maintenance (fan lubrication, compressor change-out, refrigerant charges, filter replacement) must be accomplished in areas of the hospital that are occupied by patients. Other disadvantages are as follows:

- Noisy terminal units
- Not easily accessible for performance of maintenance
- Poor humidity control
- High operating costs

Some of the advantages of water source heat pumps are as follows:

- Low first cost
- Minimal mechanical room space requirements
- Minimal central heating equipment size
- Requires cooling tower only, eliminating central cooling equipment
- Relatively simple equipment

All-Air Constant Volume Systems

The simplest type of all-air system is a single-zone constant volume unit where the air is tempered and supplied to one space or group of spaces and the unit is modulated by one thermostat. This type of unit can only be used if it also has a reheat coil, hot water, steam, or electric to ensure humidity control is maintained in the space. An energy-enhanced system can be accomplished by adding a VFD and controlling the system as a single-zone variable volume system. The control may also permit reset of the cooling coil leaving temperature as long as a space humidistat is incorporated to override the leaving air reset temperature and avoid space humidity from exceeding the set point. This system can be used in large, single-zone areas such as entrance lobbies, loading docks, and private dining areas.

A more common type of all-air system is a constant volume terminal reheat system (see Figure 5-9). This system employs a central air-handling unit supplying air through ductwork to individual

Figure 5-9 Constant Volume Terminal Reheat System

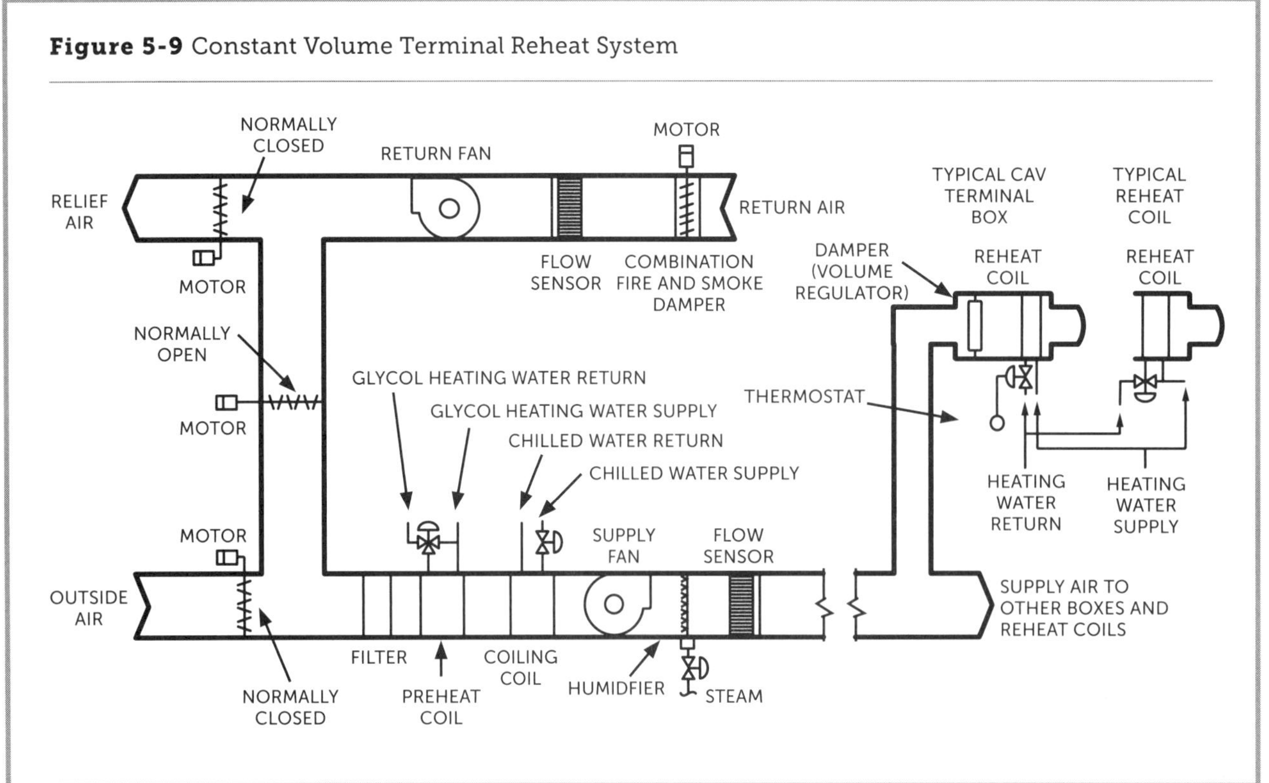

spaces. The individual space temperature control is maintained with a reheat coil and modulated by a room thermostat. Airflow to the space is constant and usually supplied at approximately 50 to 55°F. Hot water is piped through the reheat coil between 160 and 180°F, and a control valve modulates the water flow through the reheat coil to maintain room temperature.

The constant volume terminal reheat system shares with other all-air systems the advantage of being able to provide sensible and latent cooling, humidity control, air filtration, and ventilation and room pressurization prevalent in current hospital design. Maintenance on the central air unit is low relative to other systems in that there is only one fan, coil, and filter system to maintain, and it is typically located away from occupied spaces in a dedicated fan room. The main disadvantage of a terminal reheat system is that it is energy inefficient compared to a variable air volume system. Because the air is distributed at low pressure, the ductwork is much larger and requires much more space. ASHRAE 90.1 and other energy codes now prohibit and discourage the use of all-constant volume reheat systems.

Variable Air Volume Systems

Variable air volume (VAV) systems refer to the all-air systems that employ terminal units that vary the volume to individual spaces for temperature control (see Figure 5-10). VAV systems can be designed with or without some form of reheat. Typically, reheat is required where the space supplied by a VAV terminal has some heating load during the winter months or if the ventilation requirements are high enough that the air must be

Figure 5-10 Single-Duct Air Terminal

tempered before it enters the space to maintain the comfort levels required. The VAV system has the previously described advantages of all-air systems in that it addresses the ventilation, humidification, filtration, and dehumidification requirements typically found in a hospital and in that the single air-handling unit is located in a central mechanical room away from patient-occupied spaces.

VAV systems typically operate at higher velocities and relatively high pressures (greater than 2 inches water column) and therefore have somewhat smaller ductwork than constant volume systems. VAV systems are among the most energy efficient of all the air-conditioning systems. They also are among the most flexible and offer the greatest amount of zone control. VAV systems are capable of being coupled with constant volume systems using pressure-independent constant volume terminal units to supply spaces that require positive pressure, for example, surgery, isolation, or intensive care.

A VAV system consists of an air-handling unit distributing tempered air through medium-pressure ductwork to VAV terminals. The air at the central air-handling unit is cooled or heated by chilled water, hot water coils, or steam coils. Typically, cooling is provided from a central refrigeration plant and a central heating plant. Central cooling provides chilled water distributed with chilled water piping throughout the building to the various air-handling units. Hot water is pumped through the building to either the central air-handling units (if the mixed air condition so dictates) or the terminal reheats via hot water piping.

A VAV system has two coincidental functions. The primary function is temperature control. VAV terminals modulate space airflow in response to a thermostat to maintain the space temperature. As a result of varying the air quantity to a space, the total airflow provided by an air handler is reduced during off-peak times.

This reduction in airflow results in decreased fan energy. The reduction in fan energy is accomplished using variable frequency drives (VFD) to vary fan capacity based on maintain minimum duct static pressure. In the past, variable inlet vanes installed at the fan inlet reduce the airflow at the fan to the air quantity necessary. In many cases, it is advantageous to remove the vanes from an existing system or at least block them open and provide a fan capacity control. Variable frequency drives are electronic devices that modulate the fan motor speed to reduce the airflow to the necessary quantity.

One of the biggest concerns of the VAV system is maintaining the outside air required for ventilation of the building. The outside air quantity can be controlled in several ways, either by modulating the outside air damper, providing positive outside air by an outside air fan, or some type of airflow-measuring device that modulates the dampers to maintain correct outside air quantity.

The principal drawback of VAV systems is that, as the supply volume varies to meet the demand, the return volume must likewise be varied. Generally, this is done by tying the supply fan and the return control together so that, theoretically, the return fan tracks the supply fan, reducing or increasing the return air volume exactly to the same degree that the supply volume has changed. The problem is that the two fans do not often track exactly and the fresh air volume will change to make up the difference. This often results in too little fresh air being brought in and the building going negative in relation to the outside air pressure. The resulting increased infiltration causes drafts at entrances in the wintertime and excessive humidity in the summertime.

Dual-Duct System

The dual-duct system is an all-air system that derives its name from the fact that it has two independent supply air systems to each of the terminals supplying occupied spaces—a hot duct and a cold duct. The design of the system is such that heated and cooled air is supplied to the terminal units to be used as required by the space load demands. Dual-duct systems can operate as either constant volume or variable volume systems, with or without hot water reheat. A dual-duct terminal unit has a port for the hot side and a port for the cold side. As the thermostat in the cooling mode becomes satisfied, the cooling deck begins to close off. In a constant volume system, the hot side opens in proportion to the cold side, and in a VAV system the cold side closes down to some preset minimum before the hot side begins to open. In both systems, the ports are adjusted to fall within the range of the thermostat set-point and remain there until the thermostat requires either more cooling or more heating.

Dual-duct systems require central refrigeration equipment, central heating equipment, and their associated piping systems from the central plant to the mechanical equipment room, where the central air handler is located. Dual-duct systems typically operate on medium pressure and provide good zone control. However, because two-duct systems have to be installed as well as balanced and maintained, the installation and operating cost of a dual-duct system is relatively high. Dual-duct systems were fairly popular in hospitals in the mid-to-late 1970s and into the '80s but have since been displaced by more cost-effective and energy-efficient systems.

One strategy to improve the energy efficiency of traditional, single-fan, dual-duct systems is to replace the single-fan air-handling unit with a dual-fan. For systems requiring humidification, a netural deck should be provided. Refer to ASHRAE applications and ASHE's *Health Facility Commissioning Handbook* for a more complete explanation for saving energy with a dual-fan dual-duct air handling system.

Special Occupancies

Many areas of a hospital are required to have certain air flow rates and levels of filtration and to follow specific temperature and humidification guidelines. This information usually comes from two sources: the ASHRAE *Applications* Handbook (updated every four years, last published 1999) and the FGI *Guidelines*. Many state health licensing agencies refer to or have adopted the FGI *Guidelines*.

As well as listing specific indoor conditions to be maintained, the FGI *Guidelines* may restrict the type of air-conditioning system to be used. For example, recirculating room units are not allowed in operating rooms. These units would include fan coil units, induction units, and through-wall units. Where the term *central air-handling unit* is used, it means a unit composed of cooling coils, possibly heating coils, filters, and a supply fan that distributes air to many spaces. Typically, some sort of terminal box, with a reheat coil and volume damper, is used to temper the supply air from the central air-handling unit to maintain individual space temperature conditions.

Procedure Room (Class A surgery—minor surgical procedures performed under topical, local or regional anesthesia without preoperative sedation)

- Code requirements (FGI/ASHRAE) are for the rooms to be supplied with 3 air changes per hour of outside air and 15 total air changes per hour from a central air-handling unit with a single filter bank of MERV 13 filters.
- Indoor design conditions by code (FGI/ASHRAE) are 70 to 75° F/20 to 60 percent rh. These conditions can be obtained using standard 42° F chilled water supply to obtain 49° to 52° F supply air that is reheated to maintain space temperature. However, long gone are the days where 68 to 72°F/50 percent rh is a satisfactory design condition for operating rooms. For various reasons, most doctors and staff prefer the rooms be kept at 65°F or even lower. To maintain 65°F/50 percent rh requires supply air with a dew point below the room dew point of 45°F. This dew point cannot be provided with a chilled water supply temperature of 42°F. Conditioning the entire airstream to this low dew point temperature is very energy intensive because it increases the reheat energy. A better approach is to condition the ventilation, outside airstream with a DX/glycol, DOAS air-handling unit to a low dew point temperature and mix the conditioned outside air with the return air after it has been cooled to 48 to 50°F with a traditional chilled water coil with 42°F chilled water from the central plant. A glycol chiller is used in conjuction with the DOAS air handling to condition the outside air to 34 to 37°F. If room conditions of 62°F/50 percent rh (43.2°F dew point) are required, desiccant dehumidification is the most practical system choice. Central air-handling units are used for these rooms. Traditionally, at least one low return should be located in

the room in Class A surgeries, but Standard 170-2013 only requires low returns in Class B and Class C surgeries. When the space is occupied, a positive pressure relationship is required. Air supplied to Class A surgeries must use Group E, nonaspirating type diffusers per Table 6.7.2 of Standard 170-2013. Separate terminal boxes or fan coil units should be used for the equipment room that houses the computer equipment.

C/T Scan

These diagnostic rooms should have six air changes per hour, per FGI.

- Indoor design conditions should be 69 to 75°F/30 to 60 percent rh.
- The rooms can be served by central air-handling units with 90 percent final filters. Some state health regulations may allow the use of fan coil units.
- The equipment room housing the computer equipment should have a separate fan coil or terminal box. Equipment manufacturers' data should be reviewed for specific temperature and humidity requirements that must be maintained by the HVAC system.

Delivery/C-Section

FGI/ASHRAE requires 4 air changes per hour of outside air and 20 total air changes per hour from a central air-handling unit with two filter banks, MERV 7 and MERV 14.

- Indoor design conditions are 68 to 75°F/ 20 to 60 percent rh.
- As these rooms are similar to operating rooms, they should have two low returns and be maintained at a positive pressure.

Critical and Intensive Care

A central air handling unit with two filter banks, MERV 7 and MERV 14, is required by FGI/ASHRAE to provide 2 air changes per hour of outside air and 6 total air changes per hour. Indoor conditions are to be maintained at 70 to 75° F/30 to 60 percent rh.

There is no requirement (NR) for pressure relationship for CCU and ICU rooms.

Isolation Rooms

There are two types of isolation rooms: protective (PE, used for burn patients, for example, to protect the patient) and airborne infectious (AII, used to prevent the spread of an illness from the patient to others). PE rooms are maintained at a positive pressure, and infectious rooms are maintained at negative air balance. FGI/ASHRAE requires both AII and PE rooms to have 2 air changes per hour of outside air and a minimum of 12 total air changes per hour.

PE rooms are required to be supplied through HEPA filters. For AII rooms, all air must be exhausted directly to outside the building. Exhaust discharge should be 6 feet above the roof and backup exhaust fans are recommended. If AII exhaust can be reintrained into the building, the exhaust air must be HEPA filtered. In these cases, bag-in, bag-out filter housings are used to protect the maintenance staff during filter changes.

- Indoor design conditions are 70 to 75°F.
- Per Standard 170, in AII rooms exhaust grilles in the patient room shall be located directly above the patient bed on the ceiling or on the wall near the head of the bed. When an anteroom is provided, the pressure relationship shall be as follows: (1) the AII room shall be at a negative pressure with respect to the anteroom, and (2) the anteroom shall be at a negative pressure with respect to the corridor. These requirements are recent changes to the air distribution in AII rooms. Computational fluid dynamic models (CFD)

have indicated low exhaust grilles at the floor increases air turbulence and air mixing.

- For PE rooms, supply diffusers should be above the patient bed and the diffuser design shall limit air velocity at the patient bed to reduce patient discomfort. Return/exhaust grilles shall be located near the patient door.
- Air terminal units or venturi valves should be used on the supply and exhaust devices in the room to ensure the rooms are maintained at desired pressure relationships. Differenterial pressure between isolation rooms and adjunct spaces shall be a minimum of +0.01 inch wc. With ATUs or venturi valves, a common control strategy is volumetric offset between the supply and exhaust airflow. The airflows and required CFM are set up and commissioned to maintain the required +0.01 inch wc pressure differential. Exhaust fans serving AII rooms and adjoining anterooms must be dedicated and not serve other building functions (e.g., soiled utility rooms, public restrooms, toilets from other types of patient rooms).
- Protective rooms should have a positive air balance (i.e., more supply than return) and infectious rooms should be maintained at a negative pressure (more exhaust than supply).
- A room pressurization monitoring system is required to alert nursing and physical plant staff if the room air balance falls out of the desired function.

Laboratories

Labs require a single filter bed with MERV 13 filters.

- Indoor design conditions are 68 to 75°F.
- Labs are designed for 100 percent outside air and exhaust and should be maintained under a negative pressure. (Media transfer labs are maintained at a positive pressure.) Lab hoods should be served by a dedicated exhaust fan and not connected with other areas needing exhaust (toilets, soiled

utilities, etc). Infectious hood exhaust should have HEPA filters at the discharge of the exhaust system.

- One unique aspect of duct design for lab exhaust ducts from fume hoods or biological safety cabinets is that fire dampers should not be installed in these ducts. This necessitates that the ducts be enclosed in rated enclosures downstream of penetrating rated walls.

Linear Accelerators (Diagnostic and Treatment)

FGI/ASHRAE requires six total air changes in these treatment rooms.

- Indoor design conditions are 70 to 75°F/max 60 percent rh.
- Central air-handling units with two filter banks, MERV 7 and MERV 14, are required.
- The equipment rooms containing the computer systems should have a separate terminal box or fan coil unit. In addition, a packaged water chiller is usually required for the accelerator support equipment. The packaged water chiller may range from 2 to 5 tons and should be piped with a domestic water emergency bypass, to use domestic water for equipment cooling in case of chiller failure.
- Supply, return, and exhaust ductwork should be coordinated with the hospital's radiation physicist to maintain the wall shielding integrity.

MRI

FGI/ASHRAE requires six total air changes in these treatment rooms.

- Indoor design conditions are 70 to 75° F/30 to 60 percent rh.
- Central air-handling units with two filter banks, MERV 7 and MERV 14, are required.

- The equipment rooms containing the computer systems should have a separate terminal box or fan coil unit. Equipment data should be reviewed for specific temperature and humidity requirements that must be maintained by the HVAC system. In addition, a packaged water chiller is usually required for the magnet and support equipment. The packaged water chiller may range from 2 to 5 tons and should be piped with a domestic water emergency bypass, to use domestic water for equipment cooling in case of chiller failure.
- A cryogen vent is required, piped outside. The vent pipe should be copper, aluminum, or stainless steel inside the room; size the pipe per the manufacturer's recommendations.
- An emergency exhaust fan, to be used when there is a cryogen leak in the room, should be provided and sized for approximately 1200 cfm or 10 air changes, whichever is greater. The location of the magnetic shielding at the bottom of the structure in lieu of at the ceiling may require the use of nonferrous ductwork.

Nuclear Medicine

FGI/ASHRAE requires two air changes per hour of outside air and six total air changes per hour. (Heat gain inside the room may require additional air supply.) The rooms shall be supplied from a central air handling unit with two filter beds.

- Indoor design conditions are 72 to 78°F/max 60 percent rh.
- The nuclear medicine room and the adjacent hot lab should both be maintained at negative pressure and all air should be exhausted. The exhaust fan serving nuclear medicine should be dedicated to that room only and should be two speed: low speed for normal operation and high for Xenon spill evacuation. One low wall exhaust grille should be provided in the nuclear medicine room. The hot lab should be exhausted by a dedicated exhaust fan with a wall exhaust grille located over the sink backsplash or the room air should be exhausted through a hood. Exhaust fan discharge should

be carefully chosen to avoid recirculating back into the building air intake.

Nursery

Code requirements for this room are two air changes of outside air, six total air changes from a central air handling unit with two filter beds.

- Indoor design conditions are 72 to 78°F/max 60 percent rh.

Recovery/PACU

This room is similar to a nursery, with two outside air changes and six total air changes required from a central air-handling unit with two filter banks.

- Indoor design conditions are 75°F/45 to 55 percent rh.

Special Departmental HVAC Issues

Operating Rooms

Two principles for air-conditioning operating rooms are that air should be supplied at the ceiling, in a unidirectional or laminar air pattern, and that higher air change rates result in lower bacterial counts within the room. However, these principles are applied along a wide spectrum, and ongoing research is being conducted to optimize air distribution airflow patterns and quantities.

Standard 170 requires that air in an OR be introduced at the ceiling and exhausted at low wall grilles. A minimum of two low grilles, 8 inches above the floor, shall be provided. Research by Memarzadeh and Manning (2002) and Memarzadeh and Jiang (2004) has indicated appropriate air patterns even with some return/exhaust grilles placed high on the walls.

Laminar flow diffuser arrays are required because this minimizes any secondary air patterns or mixing of air currents within the room. The latest research in air flow patterns in ORs is for the average velocity of the diffusers to be 25 to 35 cfm/ft^2. The diffusers shall be concentrated to provide an airflow pattern over the patient and surgical team. The area of the primary supply diffuser array shall extend a minimum of 12 inches beyond the footprint of the surgical table on each side. No more than 30 percent of the primary supply diffuser array area shall be use for nondiffuser uses such as lights or gas columns. Because the greatest amount of the bacteria found in the OR comes from the surgical team and their activities during surgery, turbulent air patterns within an operating room are to be avoided. To provide a unidirectional air pattern, laminar flow diffuser arrays (Group E), sized to introduce air into the room at low velocities of maximum face velocities of 20 to 35 fpm, are used. The velocity is low enough to prevent secondary entrainment of room air into the supply pattern.

Two filter banks for air handling serving ORs are required. Filter bank number 1, MERV 7, is located prior to any cooling coils, while filter bank number 2, MERV 14, is located downstream of any fan, coil, or drain pan. All filter efficiencies shall be in accordance with ASHRAE Standard 52.2.

Current design practices for air distribution in operating rooms rely heavily on research by Memarzadeh and Manning. Early research in the late 1960s by Kenneth Goddard started the industry dialog about total air changes needed in operating rooms to minimize post-operative infection rates. Goddard experimentally derived curves that quantify the relationship between air change rates and bacterial count (see Figure 5-11). Note on the curves that increasing air changes per hour from 20 to 25 reduces bacteria colonies per cubic foot of room air from 3.8 to 2.5; increasing the air supply to 40 air changes per hour further reduces the bacterial colonies to 1.5 per cubic foot. However, the curves approach a limit, so that approximately 0.5 bacteria colonies per cubic foot is the lowest measured. These curves have been used as one reason for supplying up to 40 air changes per hour in heart and orthopedic operating rooms.

There have been conflicting opinions about the relative benefits of increasing airflow rate and the use of high air change, laminar flow in operating suites. Because of other variables, it is impossible

Figure 5-11 Bacteria Colonies/Cu. Ft. of Room Air

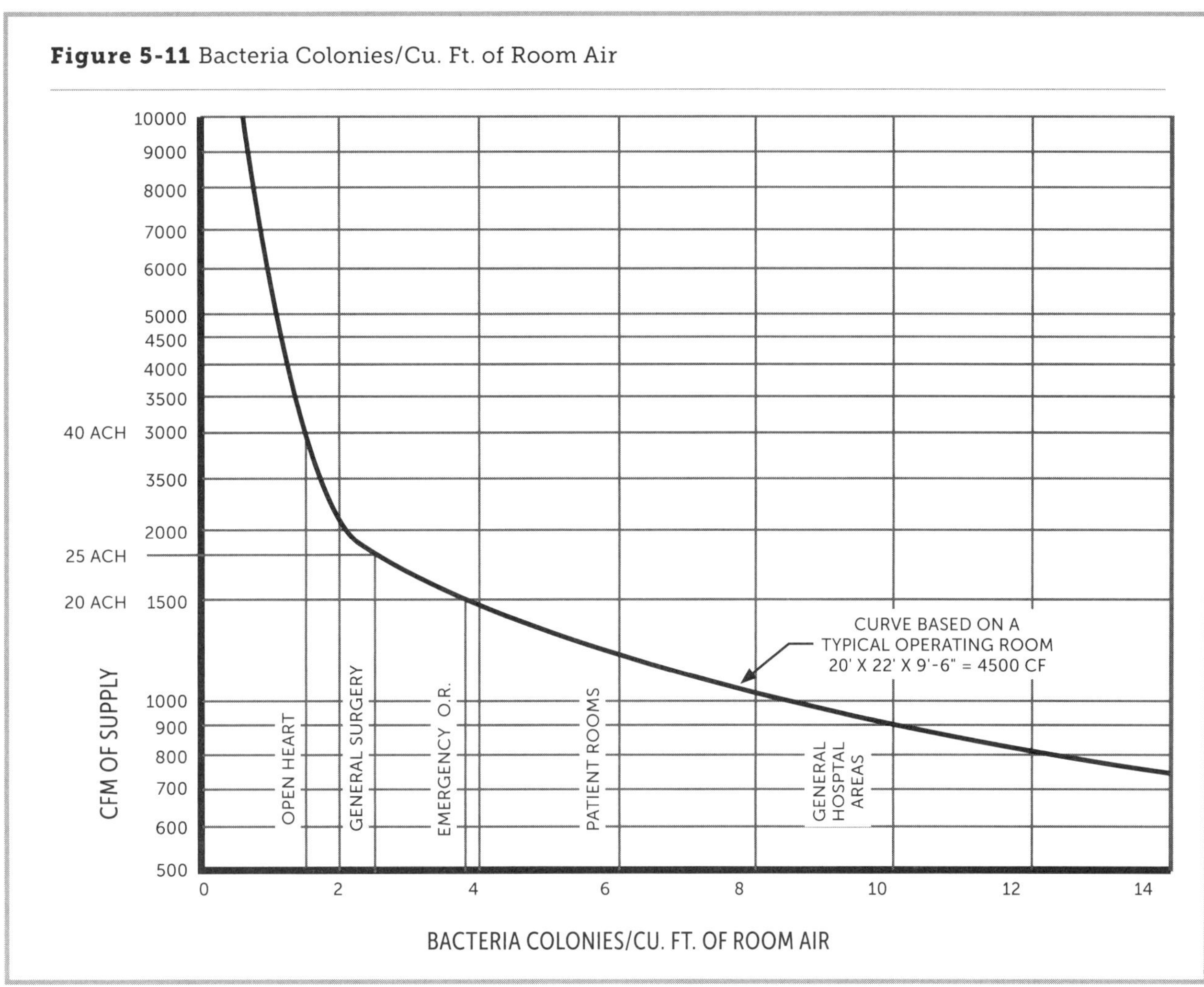

to directly correlate infection rates with total air changes or laminar flow. The latest guidelines allow 15 air changes in operating rooms. It has been found that the internal loads from people and equipment justify 20 to 25 air changes without regard to infection control. The curves produced by Kenneth Goddard show reduced bacteria at even higher (40 air changes) flow rates. Although the Goddard data is very dated, it is presented to indicate the early research for air distribution in operating rooms.

An air supply rate of 30 to 40 air changes per hour is about the maximum practical air supply available using a conventional hospital air-conditioning (A/C) system. However, some manufacturers offer packaged laminar flow modules, which are installed within a space and used to supplement the building A/C system, particularly if the building A/C system was not designed to provide either a unidirectional air pattern or a high air change rate. These manufactured units can be ceiling- or wall-mounted and usually consist of a large perforated face diffuser, a supply plenum, an internal circulating fan, and HEPA filters (sometimes a cooling coil is included). These units will recirculate air within the room, filter it, and discharge it at a low velocity in a laminar airflow pattern. In organ transplant and chemotherapy patient rooms, wall-mounted units are used to introduce air at the head of the bed and return it from the foot of the bed. In operating rooms, the units are either wall- or ceiling-mounted. Packaged laminar flow units are typically seen only in teaching hospitals or where directly requested by orthopedic or cardiac surgeons.

ASHRAE *Applications 2008* recommends MERV 17 HEPA filters in orthopedic ORs, bone marrow transplant ORs, and organ transplant ORs. While Standard 170 does not address these ORs, many feel HEPA filters are warranted. Placing terminal filters at grilles in series with HEPA filters at the air-handling unit is unnecessary and wastes fan energy while increasing maintenance. While standard ORs now require minimum of 20 ACHs total supply, high air quantities of 40 ACHs have historically been used in orthopedic and open heart ORs. Some still feel this is warranted; however, current research is still inconclusive on the effect higher air changes can have on reducing surgical site contamination. The current research on air velocity is based on the theory of a small thermal plume radiating up from an open surgical site. Ongoing ASHRAE research is investigating the effect of high air flow on the thermal plume in orthopedic surgery when the open wounds are at relatively low temperatures of 80°F. Many hospitals are installing ORs with built-in imaging equipment, such as CT or fluoroscope machines or, in some cases, even MRIs. These hybrid ORs can be as large as 1,000 ft^2, requiring high air flows. A 1,000 ft^2 room with a 10-foot ceiling requires 3,300 cfm to maintain 20 ACHs. This air quantity is more than sufficient to handle the increase in cooling load due to the imaging equipment.

Some manufacturers of air distribution equipment have tested and now recommend an alternate air distribution system for ORs. This method is an air curtain system consisting of a laminar array above the operating table with a four-sided linear slot diffuser outside the perimeter of the surgical area. Typically between 65 and 75 percent of the air is supplied through the perimeter slot diffusers; the remaining air is supplied through the laminar diffusers. This method of air distribution is particularly advantageous for the larger ORs with high air volumes necessary to maintain 20 ACHs.

Coordinating the large number of laminar flow diffusers required with other services in the ceiling of an operating room is a real challenge. Medical gas columns and hoses, imaging equipment, and surgical lights all compete for placement with the ceiling diffusers. Constructing the ceilings in the operating rooms is especially challenging. Air distribution manufacturers offer integrating ceilings to reduce total installed cost and the time to completely finish the ceiling in an operating room.

Figure 5-12 Relative Capacities Comparison of Using a Manufactured Laminar Airflow System vs. Supplying an Operating Room Directly from a Facility HVAC System

SYSTEM	FILTRATION AVAILABLE	DUCTWORK DISTANCE BETWEEN FILTER AND ROOM ②	TOTAL ROOM AIR CHANGE RATE (CHANGES/HOUR)	BACTERIA COLONIES FT^3 ①	OUTSIDE AIR CHANGE PROVIDED BY BUILDING A/C (CHANGES/HOUR)
1. Packaged laminar flow unit (make-up air supplied by building HVAC system(	HEPA	NONE – FILTERS ARE AT OUTLET	100 – 200	.5 – .7	4
2. Building A/C system designed to provide laminar flow air pattern in operating room	HEPA or 90%	± 100 FT.	40	1.5	10

① Based on Goddard's curves for the same room, supplied by the same system. varying only the air change rate.

② This distance can be eliminated by placing filters at the air supply outlet.

CHAPTER 6

Heating, Ventilation, and Air-Conditioning Controls

The automatic temperature control (ATC) system in a heating, ventilation, and air-conditioning (HVAC) system primarily modulates the system's capacity to maintain comfortable and stable environmental conditions in the hospital. Automatic controls can sequence equipment operation to meet load requirements and to provide safe operation using pneumatic, mechanical, electrical, electronic, and/or direct digital control (DDC) devices. The control system also may provide automatic redundancy in case of equipment failure, as well as automatic equipment shutdown to prevent damage to the equipment or the building in case of equipment malfunction. A properly designed and maintained control system will minimize energy consumption in the facility while maintaining comfortable conditions.

The hospital engineer should take an active role in the design and start-up of the control system in a new, renovated, or expanded facility. After becoming familiar with the operating characteristics of the facility, he or she may wish to modify the control logic to improve HVAC system effectiveness and reduce energy consumption.

Control Fundamentals

Automatic controls maintain a setpoint for a controlled variable such as temperature, pressure, humidity, or flow rate when changes occur to the process variable. There are two fundamental control schemes to control a process variable to maintain a desired setpoint. An *open-loop control system* is one in which there is no direct feedback to the controller. An example of this type of system is a perimeter fin tube radiation system that has hot water piped through convectors around the perimeter of the building, particularly under windows. This system is often controlled by the outside air temperature, and there is no direct feedback between the space temperature and the temperature of the hot water in the convection system. Another example of an open-loop control is controlling an air-handling system's return air fan directly from the same signal that controls the supply fan to maintain supply duct static pressure. This was common when VAV systems were introduced into hospitals. While the open-loop control of fin tube radiation is acceptable, open-loop control for return air fan control is not. Supply and return air fans in a hospital controlled in an open loop present a highly desirable retrofit opportunity to better maintain the design outside air quantity and to ensure the building is properly maintained.

A *closed-loop control system* senses the changes in the variable condition to be controlled and adjusts itself until the variable is brought to the desired condition. An example is a space thermostat, used to maintain space temperature. If the thermostat is controlling a variable volume box with a reheat coil, the box damper and hot water heating control valve will modulate according to the prescribed sequence. For example, the box damper modulates to 50 percent of maximum air flow before the hot water valve begins to open, until the space temperature reaches the setpoint on the thermostat. If the room temperature continues to fall, the control valve will open to allow more hot water to flow to the reheat coils until the space temperature rises to the thermostat setpoint.

Closed-loop control systems are usually classified by the type of action the controller takes to maintain the desired condition. To be effective, control loops must respond to the sensed conditions in a reasonable length of time and remain stable once they have reached the desired setpoint. The speed of response and the stability of the control loop are often contradictory because the faster the control loop responds to some deviation of temperature and pressure, the more likely it is to overshoot the desired setpoint and then continue to fluctuate above and below that setpoint as it continues to hunt for the desired setpoint.

A simple closed-loop control system is shown in Figure 6-1. In this figure, a reheat coil is used to control the space temperature in a patient room. The thermostat senses the temperature in the patient room and sends a signal to a hot water control valve to modulate flow in the heating coil to maintain the desired space temperature in the room. In this control loop, the thermostat contains a sensor that measures the room temperature or the variable desired.

Figure 6-1 Closed-Loop System

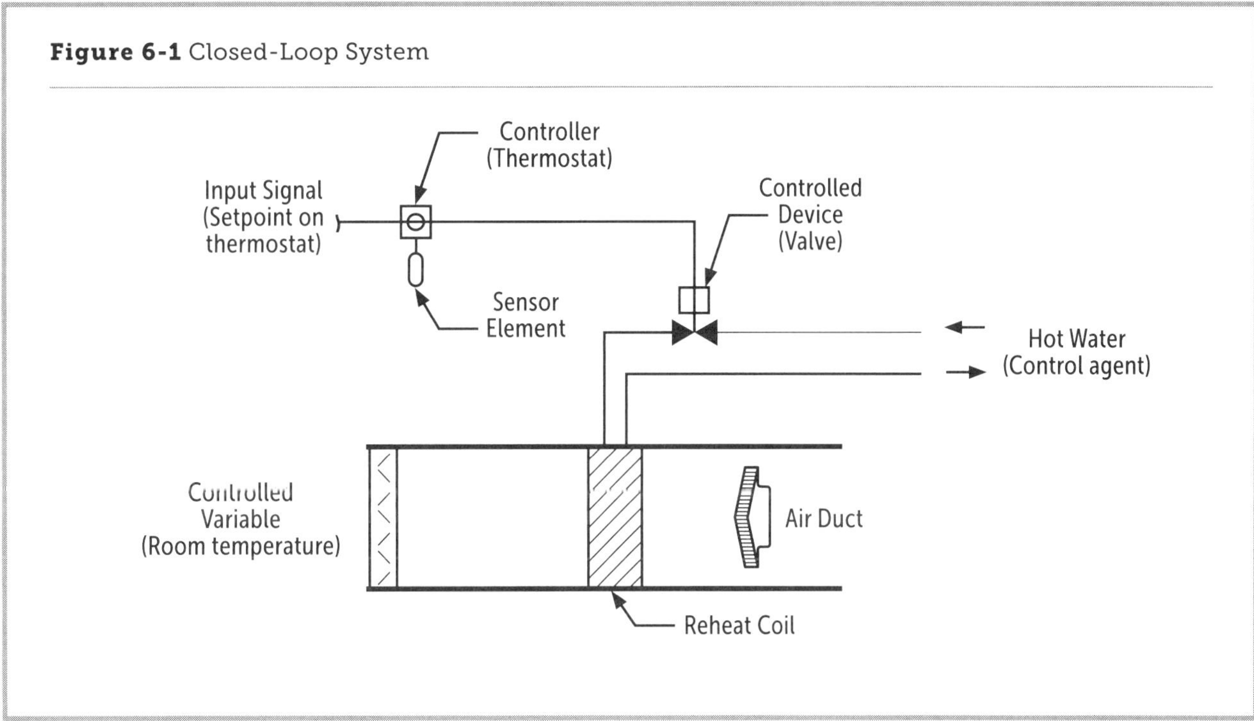

The thermostat is the *controller* that sends a signal to the reheat coil valve, and the reheat coil valve is the *control device*. Every control loop has a sensor, a controller, and a control device. The control device may be a valve, a damper, an inlet vane, a variable-frequency motor drive, or an electric relay; and the sensor may be used to sense temperature, humidity, air or water pressure, airflow, or water flow. These devices may be electric, electronic, or pneumatic. A combination of several of these types of systems may be used.

Figure 6-2 Two-Position Control

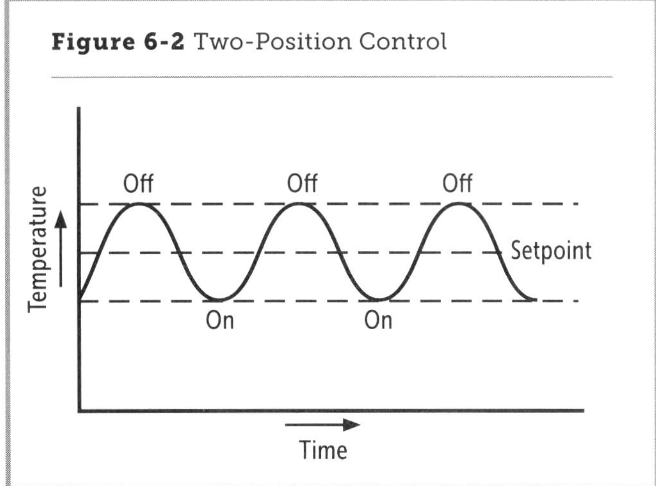

Two-position control systems (on or off) provide less stable conditions than do *modulating control systems*, which allow control settings over a wide range between fully open and fully closed. Some electric control valves in fan coil units are two-position valves that are either fully open or fully closed. Usually, these systems cause a three- or four-degree room temperature swing as the thermostat toggles the valve open and closed, to maintain the desired setpoint.

A modulating valve will usually settle out somewhere between fully open and fully closed, and the temperature variation will be less than plus or minus two degrees.

A minimum outside air damper on an air-handling unit that is fully open when the unit is running and fully closed when it is not is an example of a two-position control. The typical thermostat on a home heating furnace usually has an on or off position and is an example of this type of control. In Figure 6-2, the fluctuation above and below the setpoint can be shown graphically as the control is either fully open or fully closed.

The two-position action on a room thermostat is modified with a heat anticipator or a heating element within the thermostat that prematurely shortens the on-time to reduce the amount of fluctuation above and below the desired setpoint.

Types of Control Action

Proportional action or modulating controllers change the position of the control device in proportion to the amount of deviation from the desired setpoint that the sensor is receiving. The reheat coil and room thermostat in Figure 6-3 is a good example of this proportional action. As the room temperature falls below the setpoint, the controller sends a signal to open the hot water valve. The farther the room temperature falls below the setpoint, the more the hot water valve is opened to respond to the falling temperature. Figure 6-3 shows that the temperature in this case can drift off the setpoint, depending on the throttling range. Sometimes this throttling range can be adjusted for the variable being controlled.

Proportional plus integral (PI) control improves the proportional control by adding a time factor into the control logic that increases the controller output with time while the error or the difference between the actual condition and the setpoint exists. Most HVAC control loops are PI controlled. Figure 6-4 shows the improved accuracy over time of PI control.

Some controllers add a derivative (PID), which gives them an even faster response time with more stability. However, PID controls are very sensitive and PI control loops give very satisfactory results in HVAC control systems without getting too sensitive, which can be a problem in itself.

Figure 6-3 Proportional Control

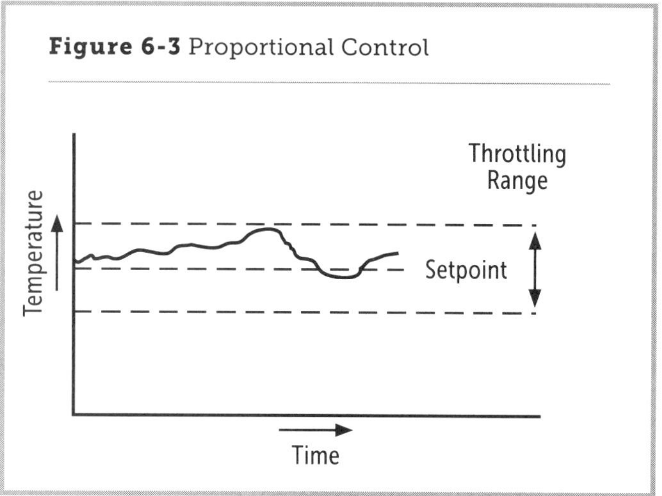

Figure 6-4 Proportional Integral (PI) Control

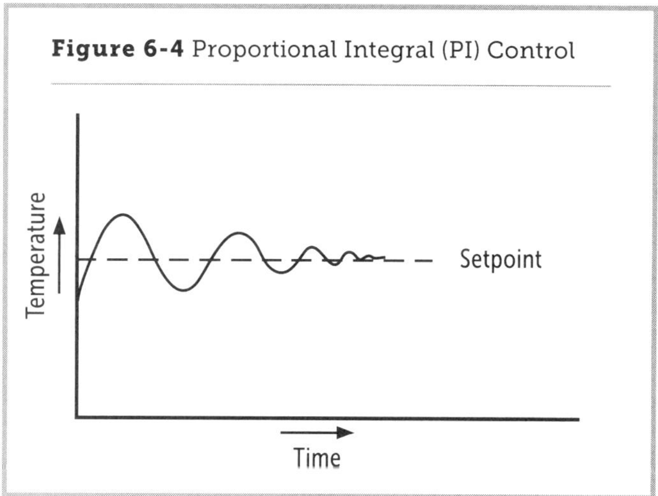

Selecting, Operating, and Maintaining Control Systems

Many existing hospitals have pneumatic control systems or a hybrid of direct-digital controls with pneumatic actuators for dampers and valves. Direct-digital controls with electric actuators are now the system of choice in all new construction, renovation, or control system upgrades. Hospitals are constantly upgrading control systems to provide improved comfort conditions, reduced energy consumption, and superior maintenance functionality and system troubleshooting.

A direct-digital control system (DDC) is the use of computers, microprocessors, and software in conjunction with sensors and actuators to provide closed-loop control. ASHRAE Guideline 13-2000: *Specifying Direct Digital Control Systems* provides a definition of direct digital control: "A DDC system is composed of both hardware and software combined to produce a seamless architecture that provides complete integration of a building's HVAC systems and may include control over or monitoring of lighting, security, and fire systems in the building. The DDC system can continuously monitor and automatically monitor and—through control of the HVAC mechanical and refrigeration systems—maintain desired ambient temperature, static pressure, relative humidity, indoor air quality, and energy management." ASHRAE widened the definition of a DDC to encompass the complete building automation system (BAS). A DDC system is not just one controller but a combination of distributed and other devices in the building. DDC microprocessors receive electronic signals from sensors and convert the signals to numbers. Software programs perform mathematical operations on these numbers, and the output from the computer is converted to a voltage or a pneumatic signal that can then be used to modulate the control device. DDC devices are more precise than pneumatic or electronic controllers, and they do not tend to drift out of calibration as pneumatic instruments will do. The control sequence also can be easily changed by rewriting the software at a central computing location. Direct digital control systems also have the advantage of being capable of bringing all of the control points and the sensor points to one central location on a double-twisted pair of wires. In this way, an operator sitting at a computer terminal in a central part of the building can check equipment and system operations throughout the building and change setpoints without leaving his or her workstation. In large facilities, this feature can greatly increase response time when troubleshooting problems and decrease personnel costs.

DDC components generically defined in ASHRAE Guideline 13 are as follows:

- Building controller (BC)
- Custom application controller (CAC)

- Application specific controller (ASC)
- Other communication devices
- Operator interface (OWS)
- Input/Output (I/O) devices

These distributed control components are connected on a BAS network to allow communication and data sharing with all of the devices. Each BAS vendor has its own proprietary communication network. This makes sharing information between vendors almost impossible.

Interoperability

Because of the limitations and noncompetitive environment created by vendor-specific communication protocols, owners created a demand for open protocol communication networks to allow any BAS manufacturer to work with another manufacturer's components. The three most common protocols are LON, BACnet, and an older industrial protocol, Modbus. LON has been developed and supported by Echelon, and a LONWorks industry consortium now regulates manufacturers choosing to use the LON protocol. LONWorks calls the communication packets on their network "standard network variable types" or SNVTs. ASHRAE developed its Standard 135: *A Data Communications Protocol for Building Automation and Control Networks.*

As technology has advanced, mechanical and electrical controllers have been replaced with DDC/BAS controllers. Digital controllers offer several advantages over the older types:

- Lower maintenance costs
- More accurate control sequences
- Faster response time
- More flexibility in control sequences

- Enhanced monitoring and data trending and archiving via local and wide area network communications with all of the DDC controllers, sensors, and actuators
- Enhanced energy management capabilities due to the availability of centralized control, scheduling, and control strategy optimization
- Enhanced troubleshooting capabilities along with remote alarms to allow the system operator to "see" what is going on throughout the mechanical systems at the central operator workstation
- Preset alarm limits to allow the operator to respond to equipment malfunction before the occupants of the building are aware of system problems
- Graphic user interfaces (GUI) and HVAC systems graphics to make the system user-friendly and facilitate training of new employees

For the hospital engineer to take advantage of the many features available on these DDC/BAS systems, he or she must have adequate working knowledge of the type of mechanical systems in the facility, as well as an understanding of how resetting one design parameter will affect other design parameters within the system. For example, raising the chilled water temperature in the main chiller loop can create significant energy savings by unloading the chillers. Although this may not significantly change the leaving air temperature at most air-handling units throughout the building, it may make enough change in critical systems, such as those serving the operating rooms, to cause them to lose their dehumidification capacity because higher leaving air temperatures off the air-handling unit reduce the amount of moisture that is removed from the air supply in these areas.

The rewards for fine-tuning and adjusting the control system can be significant. The hospital design engineer relies on mathematical models to size equipment and set up control sequences. Using the actual hospital conditions and equipment capacities, the hospital engineer can more accurately match the needs of the facility with the capacity and control sequences of the equipment.

The hospital engineer should be an integral part of the design process, working with the design engineer and the control systems designer. He or she should be involved in selecting the number and location of control and sensor points and knowledgeable regarding the intended operation sequence.

A design engineer uses schematic diagrams and block diagrams along with a written sequence of operation instructions to describe the control sequences and setpoints. The manufacturer's control system designer uses this information to select the hardware and software that will perform the functions described in the block diagrams and the written sequence of operation. The hospital facility engineer should require that adequate time be provided in the contract to start up and debug the control system, and to train engineering staff members in the system's operation and use. The start-up, debugging, and training are critical to the long-term successful operation of the mechanical systems in the facility. Too often, it is operated manually when hospital personnel cannot trust the system to perform stably and reliably. The problem may be improper design, improper programming, or lack of training. Often it is a combination of these. Ensuring that there are adequate start-up, debugging, and training, will ensure that the source of the problems is discovered and the problems corrected before the design and control personnel leave the facility.

A medium-pressure system serving a combination of constant volume reheat boxes and variable constant volume boxes with reheat is commonly used in sensitive areas of hospitals. Examination of the control sequence in this system will reveal the design engineer's intent, as well as opportunities for the hospital engineer to optimize the operation of the system once it is in operation. When the supply fan is started either manually or at the central console of the energy management system, there is a momentary delay to allow the smoke dampers in the system to open. This prevents the fan from starting from a closed-duct system. The ductwork may break at the seams if the fans were to start with all the dampers closed.

The smoke dampers and the minimum outside air damper open, and the return fan starts simultaneously with the supply fan.

A static pressure sensor in the supply duct controls the supply fan inlet vanes to maintain enough pressure in the supply duct to allow the constant volume and variable volume boxes to operate. (On fans larger than 25 horsepower, it may be more economical to use variable-frequency drives for the supply and return fans.) The static pressure sensor is located near the end of the supply ductwork system, at least two-thirds of the way toward the end of the supply fan. This sensor controls the inlet vanes of the variable-frequency drive of the supply fan. During start-up and balance, the optimum supply duct static pressure is determined based on the minimum amount of pressure needed to operate the constant and variable volume boxes at the end of the run. This sensor is set by trial-and-error experimentation because too much static pressure is a waste of supply fan energy and too little will cause an inadequate airflow at the end of the supply system.

The return fan VFDs are set up to track the supply fan so that the amount of air supply returned from the building is equal to the supply fan cfm less the exhausted air in the air-handling unit zone. It is a good idea to maintain an overall building positive static pressure to prevent infiltration of outside air through doors, windows, and other openings in the building envelope. The optimum settings for tracking the supply fan and return fan are determined during the test and balance and start-up to provide close tracking of the supply fan cfm with enough building positive pressure to prevent infiltration.

This system is set up on an economizer cycle that uses chilled water only when the outside air temperature is higher than 50°F. When the outside air temperature is higher than 50°F, the maximum outside air damper is closed, the return air damper is fully opened, and the relief air damper is closed. Minimum outside air is brought into the air-handling unit and the discharge air thermostat modulates the chilled water valve to maintain 50°F air leaving the cooling coil.

When the outside air temperature falls below 50°F, the chilled water valve is closed and the maximum outside air damper, the return damper, and the relief damper are modulated to use outside air to maintain 50°F discharge air. As the maximum outside air damper opens to admit more outside air, the return air damper closes, and the air that is returned from the building is relieved through the relief air damper. These three dampers operate in conjunction with each other, again with the intention of maintaining a slight positive pressure within the building. Depending on the actual outside air wintertime design conditions, a preheat coil may be required in front of the minimum outside air damper. This preheat coil is used to raise the temperature of the incoming outside air to prevent freezing the water in the chilled water coil.

A mixed air temperature sensor controls the hot water or steam valve to maintain the desired temperature in the unit.

An automatic reset freezestat, set at 40°F, is placed in front of the cooling coil. This is a safety device that, in the event of a preheat coil malfunction or a damper malfunction, will shut off the fan, which will start the chilled water pumps that will circulate water through the coil to prevent a freezing condition. A second freezestat, this one only manually resettable, set at 34°F, is located downstream of the cooling coil. It is an emergency control and is wired to shut off the fan. It is undesirable to have the fans for hospital air-handling units stop in an alarm condition when the fan serves a sensitive area, hence the reliance on the automatic resetting freezestat as the primary freeze protection device. Starting the chilled water pumps allows the fan to continue running while protecting the coil from freezing, and gives maintenance personnel time to determine why the freeze condition is occurring and to correct the problem. The low-limit freezestat protects the unit in case all else fails.

A steam humidifier located in the supply duct downstream of the final filters is controlled by three humidistats. One humidistat is in occupied space and is set for 50 percent relative humidity. Two high-limit humidistats set at 90 percent relative humidity are located in the ductwork downstream of the humidistat to shut off the humidifier in the event the air duct becomes saturated due to a humidifier valve malfunction.

The prefilter bank and the final filter bank have static pressure sensors with remote readout to the central station computer terminal. Based on the filter manufacturer's recommended pressure drops, these readouts tell the facility engineer when the filters are loaded and need to be changed. Duct-mounted smoke detectors in the supply and return of the unit stop the supply and return fan, which in turn shuts off the smoke dampers in the system and closes the outside air dampers.

Room-mounted thermostats control the constant volume reheat boxes and the variable volume reheat boxes. The constant volume boxes have only reheat valve control and the room thermostat opens the reheat valve upon a drop in room temperature. The variable volume boxes with reheat first reduce airflow by closing a variable volume damper to a preset limit (usually 50 or 60 percent). If the room temperature continues to fall, the reheat valve opens to warm the air leaving the terminal box.

CHAPTER 7

Code Compliance Checklist

This chapter provides the health care facility staff with an overview of the codes and standards that apply to the installation, operation, and maintenance of heating, ventilation, and air-conditioning (HVAC) systems. The HVAC system is an integral part of the hospital's life safety system. In the event of a fire, HVAC systems provide either active or passive smoke control between smoke compartments and each floor of the facility. In high-rise facilities, stairwells and exit corridors are pressurized to provide smoke-free exits from the building. Fire and smoke dampers in the duct system prevent smoke and fire migration throughout the building, and smoke detection devices in ducts and air-handling devices start or stop equipment to contain smoke and allow safe exit.

The HVAC system also is a key component of infection control in the facility. Ventilation rates, filtration requirements, and pressure relationships between various areas of the facility act together to control the spread of infection and to prevent staff and patients from exposure to potentially harmful substances.

Health Facility Codes

Many states have adopted health care facility codes that are based on national codes discussed in these chapters. Although most of the provisions are the same or similar to those in the national codes, some provisions are unique and may be open to interpretation. States also adopt different editions of the National Fire Protection Association (NFPA) codes and the Life Safety Code (NFPA 101), which further complicates the issue of code compliance. Finally, because most codes are updated at least every three years (and some annually), the target of code compliance moves continually.

The following are national codes and standards that apply to hospital HVAC systems.

- 2014 FGI *Guidelines for Design and Construction of Hospitals and Outpatient Facilities*
  - Pressure relationships, filtration, ventilation rates, exhaust requirements, and environmental conditions for various spaces in hospitals
  - Air intakes and standby heating
- ASHRAE Standard 170-2013: *Ventilation of Health Care Facilities*
  - Integral with FGI-2014 Guidelines, Part 4, to define ventilation system design requirements that provide environmental control for comfort, asepsis, and odor in healthcare facilities
- ASHRAE Standard 62.1-2010: *Ventilation for Acceptable Indoor Air Quality*
  - Ventilation requirements and standards for spaces not specifically listed in ASHRAE 170
  - Previous editions of NFPA 99 required smoke purge in anesthetizing locations such as operating rooms, but this requirement has been deleted; however, CMS has not recognized the omission. Prior to design or construction of new anesthetizing locations, check with local and state AHJs and CMS for requirements regarding smoke control.
- NFPA 101: *Life Safety Code*, Sections 7-2 and 7-3

  - Smoke control, HVAC systems, and fire alarm interlock

- NFPA 99
  - Ventilation requirements in laboratories, including fume hood installation and operation

- NFPA 90A: *Installation of Air-Conditioning and Ventilation Systems*
  - HVAC system fire dampers (inspection and test every two years)
  - Inspection and cleaning of ductwork coils, plenums, motors, and fans
  - Annual testing of shutdown devices

- NFPA 96: *Removal of Grease-Laden Vapors from Commercial Cooking Equipment*
  - Hood and duct construction, clearance, and duct access for cleaning
  - Airflow at hood and ductwork; makeup air to hood
  - Fire-extinguishing equipment and fire interlocks with source of fuel and fire alarm
  - Procedures for operating and maintaining cooking exhaust systems and fire protection system (inspections every six months)

- NFPA 31: *Fuel Storage Tanks*
  - Fuel storage tanks, piping, and leak detection

- NFPA 85: *Boilers and Furnaces*
  - Boiler construction, installation, fuel supply, and maintenance

The publication of the FGI *Guidelines for Design and Construction of Hospital and Outpatient Facilities* is the latest in a long history of consensus guidelines for design and construction standards for health care facilities. These guidelines provide the basic code requirements for HVAC systems that have been adopted either entirely or with modifications by most states. This document specifies ventilation rates, filtration requirements, and pressure relationships between spaces.

Although the design engineer and the building contractor have responsibility for ensuring that the installed HVAC system meets these standards, it is the hospital maintenance staff who have ongoing responsibility for maintaining those conditions.

Pressure relationships can be affected by a buildup of lint in return and exhaust systems. Lint can collect at grilles, turning vanes in ductwork, airflow measuring stations, and fire/smoke dampers, reducing airflow and changing pressure relationships between rooms. These ducts should be inspected at least every two years and more often in spaces where linens are stored and used. Lint also may build up on return and exhaust fan wheels, which can reduce their capacity. Dampers at outside air intakes and return air controls should be checked annually for proper settings and operation.

Filter maintenance not only affects the quality of air entering patient care spaces, but also the quantity. As filters load up with dirt, resistance increases. Medium-pressure systems with constant static pressure controls will compensate for this buildup, as long as the capacity of the fan is not exceeded. Low-velocity systems will not compensate, and airflow will vary depending on the condition of the filters. Almost 90 percent of final filters have a recommended final static pressure of between 1 inch water column and 1.2 inches water column. System parameters may require that the filters be changed more often to provide the airflow necessary to meet the required air changes and pressure relationships. The installation of filters in the filter racks also is critical because any air leakage around the filters effectively reduces filter efficiency.

Variable volume systems have been common in hospitals since the mid-1970s, and FGI/ASHRAE encourages use of variable volume systems as long as pressure relationships in spaces identified in Standard 170 are maintained.

The following issues must be addressed in the design and operation of variable air volume systems:

- Unless the return duct system is designed with venturi valves or air terminals, variable volume systems do not track the supply and return at each space, so there is no way to guarantee that the pressure relationship will not change as the supply air volume varies; therefore, spaces requiring positive pressure relationship must be designed with constant volume terminals. Spaces such as operating rooms or AII or PE isolation rooms must be designed to specifically maintain the required pressure relationship.
- Unless the design incorporates a method to maintain constant outside air, the amount of outside air introduced into the building could change as the total air volume changes on space temperature load. Control strategies to maintain outside air at setpoint include supply and return fan synchronization, mixed air constant pressure control, or direct measurement and control of outside air.

Critical spaces have remained constant volume through the years, but today even operating rooms can be designed to maintain pressure relationships while reducing air volumes during unoccupied periods.

A simple procedure for testing pressure relationships in critical areas such as isolation rooms and operating room suites is opening the door to a space about one inch and holding a tissue in front of the gap between the door and the door frame. Air movement into or out of the space will be apparent, and the supply or return volume can be adjusted, if necessary, to get air to move into or out of the space as required. Critical spaces require room pressure monitors to continuously monitor the pressure relationship in these spaces. The pressure monitors can be interfaced with the BAS/DDC system to record the data, or they may just indicate a local alarm if the pressure relationship is not maintained at the desired setpoint.

Testing for outside air-ventilation rates and room air changes can be accomplished with flow hoods, velometers, and pitot tubes (see

Chapter 9). This procedure may require the services of a test and balance contractor. Many small renovation projects within a hospital are often done without testing and rebalancing the existing air-handling system that serves these areas. After repeated changes and renovations, systems are often in critical need of testing and balancing by certified personnel to ensure that ventilation rates and pressure relationships are maintained.

Large hospitals may be able to afford the equipment and personnel to do this work. In any event, it should not be left out because a renovation project is small with a tight budget. The infection control issue is too important to overlook the impact of changed ductwork in a remodeled area and how it may affect other areas in the same system.

Chapter 7 of the *Guidelines for Design and Construction of Hospitals and Outpatient Facilities* provides mechanical standards for HVAC systems in hospitals. In it, Table 3 provides standards for air filtration in various areas of the hospital, and Table 2 provides pressure relationships, total and outside air-ventilation rates, and temperature and humidity ranges for most spaces in a hospital. Spaces that are allowed to recirculate air in room-conditioning units, and rooms that must have all air exhausted also are listed. The standard provides that air movement should be, as much as possible, from clean to less clean areas to prevent the spread of infection. For a complete understanding of these tables and other requirements, maintenance staff should have access to the FGI *Guidelines* and Standard 170.

CHAPTER 8

HVAC Energy Management Opportunities

The hospital environment presents unique challenges to the implementation of energy cost-reduction programs. Patient care is the number one priority in health care facilities. Energy management opportunities are mission and philosophy secondary priorities. Hospitals are different from most other structures in that they operate 24 hours a day and require redundancy in all major systems. Scheduled maintenance and equipment breakdown must not interfere with facility operation. These reasons or justifications are why many hospitals have virtually ignored energy management or energy conservation. These are excuses. Because of the intense energy consumption in health care facilities, energy management is even more important than in other buildings. Energy conservation does not need to conflict with the prime directive of patient care.

Cooking, cleaning, and laundry areas are energy-intensive operations, and large amounts of outside air are needed to dilute odors and control the spread of bacteria. High outside air rates are indeed one reason for high energy costs, but many energy saving methods can compensate for these requirements. In recent years, outside air quantities for hospitals are being clarified. Previous engineering design practices to continuously increase outside air are being challenged and changed. One example of this is the methods described in Standard 170 for determining the outside air rates for a central handling system.

The energy manager's war cry of "Turn it off when not in use" does not apply well to the health care facility because much of the facility is occupied 24 hours a day, 365 days per year. Even when critical spaces are not in use, ventilation is still required to maintain pressure relationships and control the spread of infection (or infectious bacteria). However, even though systems must operate 24/7, many opportunities remain to turn down or set back the temperatures and air flows during periods of reduced use and occupancy.

History

Originally, the U.S. Green Building Council's LEED rating system was developed to encourage sustainable design; promote energy-saving practices in schools, office buildings, and shopping centers; and increase environmental consciousness. Today, the LEED-HC (LEED for Healthcare) standard encourages the health care industry to be more environmentally responsible. The rating system continues to gain acceptance. Many hospitals have received LEED certification, proving that high-performance, sustainable facilities are appropriate goals in health care. Hospitals have found that being green can actually improve patient outcomes and recovery.

The 80/20 rule applies to energy management as well as to other areas of business. The first 80 percent of the energy-saving opportunities can be obtained by spending only 20 percent of the first-cost dollars. The energy management checklist in this chapter covers energy management opportunities over a wide range, from the simple and obvious to the more complex and expensive. Cogeneration and thermal storage (see Chapter 8) are perhaps the most complex and expensive first-cost modifications to consider.

The decision whether to implement an energy management opportunity in the final analysis is a financial one. It usually comes down to "What is the bottom line?" Several methods are used to determine the relative merits of energy-saving investments. Often with energy management opportunities, simple or discounted payback is the only measurement required. Sometimes present worth analysis is used in the decision-making process, and some financial managers use the internal rate of return to judge the relative merits of an investment in building or system modifications.

In all of these analyses, estimates of the following must be determined:

- First cost of the modification
- Annual savings
- Inflation rate estimate
- Cost of money or interest rate
- Changes in maintenance cost over the life of the equipment or the facility

The first two are determined by the hospital engineer or with the help of an outside engineering consultant. The labor for maintenance also can be determined by the hospital engineer. Estimates of interest and inflation can be determined by a Nobel Prize–winning economist or a monkey throwing darts at a wall. All these numbers are estimates, and the cost-benefit analysis is a soft number.

Occupancy patterns, weather patterns, and part-load system efficiencies are all estimates at best, and therefore using the simplest calculations appropriate to the energy management opportunity being analyzed is the most appropriate response.

Simple payback is the initial cost of the energy management opportunity divided by the estimated annual savings (payback = first cost/annual net savings). For example, assuming that installation of a heat recovery wheel on a patient room air-handling system will cost $10,000 and will save $1,500 per year in energy costs, the simple payback will be $10,000 divided by 1,500, or 6.7 years.

The simple payback method has several disadvantages in that it does not consider either cash flows beyond the payback period or the opportunity cost of capital or the discount rate. A more accurate way to calculate the payback period would be to use the discounted payback period. This formula takes into account the discount rate, or the time value of money. The equation for the discounted payback period is:

$$N = \frac{\log\left(1 + \frac{ic}{S}\right)}{\log(1 + i)}$$

In this formula, N equals break-even number of years, S equals yearly net savings, c equals initial investment cost, and i equals discount rate (or interest rate).

Using the previous example with a 6 percent discount rate, the payback period is:

$$N = \frac{\log\left(1 + \frac{.06(10{,}000)}{}\right)}{\log(1 + 0.06)}$$

$$N = \frac{\log(1 + 0.4)}{\log(1.06)}$$

$$N = \frac{0.146}{0.0253}$$

$$N = 5.7 \text{ years}$$

An even more comprehensive method of evaluating energy investments is to use the present-worth method, or the net-present-value method. The equation for calculating the net present value is as follows:

present worth = savings × present-worth escalation factor at year *n* (PWEF),

$$\text{where PWEF} = \frac{[(1+j)/(1+j)] - 1}{1-(1+i)/(1+j)}$$

In this formula, i equals the discount rate of interest, j equals the escalation rate for energy and other costs, and n equals the payback period. As an example, assuming that a \$10,000 investment in a heat recovery device will yield a \$1,500 energy savings in the first year, the interest rate will be 6 percent and the energy escalation is expected to be 8 percent. The payback period is when the present worth of the investment and the sum of the savings are equal. Then

$$N = \frac{[(1.08/1.06)^n - 1]}{1 - (1.06/1.08)} \times 1{,}500$$

$$10{,}000 = 1{,}500^{\,(1.0189n)}$$

$$0.1233 = 1018^n - 1$$

$$1.1233 = \frac{1.0189^n}{.0185}$$

$$n = \frac{\ln 1.1233}{\ln 1.0189} = \frac{.1162}{.01872} = 6.2 \text{ years}$$

The internal-rate-of-return method calculates the rate of return the investment is expected to yield. The internal-rate-of-return method expresses each investment alternative in terms of a greater return or a compound interest rate. The internal rate of return is calculated by process of trial and error, where the net cash flow is computed for various discount rates until its value is reduced to zero. A set of discount tables is used to determine, by visual inspection, the internal rate of return, which will set the net present value at zero. This internal rate of return is compared to the expected rate of return that the hospital might receive from an alternative investment.

Each of these methods has advantages and disadvantages, and usually it is best to calculate the benefit using several formulas to ensure the economic viability of an energy investment. Chapter 3 of the National Bureau of Standards Handbook No. 121, *Waste Heat Management Guidebook*, gives a thorough explanation of investment analysis for heat recovery.

There are interactive financial computer programs for personal computers that will perform calculations for discounted payback, present worth, and life cycle cost analysis. With these tools, the hospital engineer can make effective presentations of energy management opportunities without having to rely on outside consultants or vendors to determine economic feasibility.

HVAC Energy Checklists

Building Envelope

Assuming the building envelope meets current standards, energy losses throughout the building represent a relatively small portion of HVAC operating costs. A hospital has significant internal-load generation, and envelope losses are not nearly as significant compared to the total building energy use as in most other facilities. This is true as long as there are no major building envelope issues, such as vapor barrier failures, leaky windows, roof damage, or outside walls not sealed at beam penetration or above eaves, soffits, or canopies. Therefore, a survey of the building envelope, particularly in older buildings, is worthwhile. The survey should include the following steps:

1. Look for cracks and missing caulking around windows and doors.
2. Add vestibules at main entrances, ER entrances, and employee entrances to eliminate infiltration through heavy traffic areas. Vestibules must be large enough to prevent inside and outside doors from opening at the same time.
3. Check elevator shaft vents. Older designs required the vents to be fully opened. Today's codes allow a smoke damper in the shaft vent that remains closed unless smoke is detected in the elevator shaft.
4. If the building is old, consider replacing steel sash windows. Note: The replacement of windows with double-pane reflective glass creates significant energy reduction, although paybacks are typically long (possibly 7 to 12 years).
5. On southern or western exposure glass, consider reflective film or other shading devices, particularly where the existing glass is single pane and clear.

6. Provide interlocks between exhaust fans and laboratories and kitchens with outside dampers to balance makeup air and exhaust air. Significant savings can be achieved by shutting down exhaust hoods when not in use, with a corresponding reduction in outside makeup air.
7. Provide untempered air to kitchen range hood exhaust to prevent conditioned air from being exhausted from other spaces in the building through the kitchen.
8. Rework 100 percent outside air systems to return air to the air-handling unit. If this is unfeasible, consider a heat wheel to recover both sensible and latent heat if the exhaust and supply ducts are in close proximity to each other. If this is not feasible, consider runaround loops to exchange heat from the exhaust stream to the supply stream to pick up sensible heat only (see the heat recovery options).
9. Reset discharge air temperatures on air-handling units to raise the discharge air temperature. This should only be incorporated with override humidistats to prevent loss of humidity control.
10. On air-handling systems equipped with outside air economizer, use enthalpy controllers rather than providing changeover at designated outside air temperature. Enthalpy controllers measure humidity and temperature of return air and outside air and changeover based on total energy content rather than temperature alone. There are issues with enthalpy changeover control strategies.
11. On systems not equipped with air-side economizer cycles, use a water-side economizer with plate frame heat exchanger to produce chilled water from cooling tower water during cold weather. This is particularly appropriate with fan coil systems and small air-handling units that serve interior spaces.
12. On double-duct systems serving noncritical areas, modify double-duct boxes to provide variable volume airflow. This can be an expensive retrofit, and a full LCCA should be consider to see if the change is economically viable.

Lighting

To reduce internal lighting loads and HVAC loads:

- Change incandescent lights to fluorescent.
- Replace existing lighting with LED fixtures during any remodel.
- Replace traditional ballasts and tubes with high-efficiency ballasts and tubes.
- Disconnect one ballast and two tubes in four-lamp fixtures in areas where reduced lighting levels will not have an adverse effect, such as in corridors and storage rooms.
- Add occupancy sensors to turn off lights when space is unoccupied in all public areas, office areas, etc.
- Add photo cells in lobbies, dining rooms, and other spaces with large glass areas to turn off lights when there is sufficient daylight in the space.

Powerhouse

In the powerhouse, consider:

- Resetting air fuel ratios on boiler burners and recalibrating boiler controls on a regular basis.
- Running one boiler fully loaded rather than two boilers at partial load. Boiler efficiency drops dramatically at part load.
- Inspecting and cleaning internal tubes annually for soot and water deposit buildup to increase heat transfer efficiency.
- Inspecting steam traps for proper operation on a regular basis. A proactive steam trap maintenance program is an absolute necessity to reduce energy use of steam distribution systems.
- Resetting hot water heating converters and hot water boilers to track outside air temperature.

- Reducing boiler operating pressure to the minimum necessary to operate building equipment.
- Using the flue gas heat recovery system to preheat domestic hot water.
- Adding a chiller optimization control system. This is an adaptive supervisory system that will direct the DDC system to make setpoint adjustments in the control sequence to optimize chiller, pumps, and cooling tower operation.
- Maintaining water treatment in cooling towers and cleaning condenser tubes annually to enhance heat transfer.
- Changing to induced-draft cooling towers with propeller fans rather than forced draft centrifugal towers. Induced-draft cooling towers have approximately half the horsepower requirement of centrifugal forced-draft towers.
- Adding VFDs to vary speed of cooling tower fans to maintain condenser water temperature at setpoint.
- Resetting chilled water temperature during intermediate seasons to reduce chiller energy consumption.
- Adding dedicated chillers for operating rooms and delivery rooms. Often chilled water temperatures are set at 40°F to maintain humidity control in these areas. By using a dedicated chiller for these areas, the main chillers could be set for a higher leaving chilled water temperature without affecting the temperature needs of the operating and delivery suites.
- Using double-bundle heat exchangers for new chillers to preheat domestic hot water or to provide reheat hot water during intermediate and summer seasons.
- Recalibrating controls and checking operation of damper and valve motors on a regular basis.
- Using a waste heat recovery boiler for the infectious waste incinerator.

- Installing two-way valves on air-handling unit cooling coils and providing variable-frequency drives for secondary pumps to decrease the pumping horsepower required and increase chilled water flow available to remote units.

Laundry

In the hospital laundry area, consider:

- Reclaiming energy from the wastewater to preheat incoming domestic water using plate frame (cleanable) heat exchangers.
- Recovering exhaust air off flatwork ironers to preheat makeup air to the laundry.
- After additions and expansions, rebalancing air flow and water flow on all affected systems.
- Cleaning heating and cooling coils, particularly in older facilities, to increase heat transfer and reduce air pressure drop. Also consider replacing coils that show internal or external corrosion.

Heat Recovery Options

The large amounts of ventilation air required in a hospital make air-side heat recovery a viable option worth analyzing in many health care facilities. This energy conservation measure transfers energy from air being exhausted from a building to the outside air being introduced into the building.

Heat recovery devices fall into two main categories—total heat devices and sensible heat devices. *Total heat devices* can transfer both sensible heat and latent heat (or moisture) from one airstream to another. The most common total heat recovery heat exchanger is the rotary wheel, or heat wheel as it is often called. This device has a large disk made out of metal or ceramic. The axis of the wheel is on the partition between the two ducts, and as the wheel slowly rotates, it transfers energy from one airstream to the other. The wheel is porous, and the pores trap not only sensible heat but also moisture that can be transferred from one airstream to another.

Heat wheels have a disadvantage in transferring contaminated exhaust air used because the pores can transfer undesirable contamination between the exhaust air and the supply air. A purge section can be added to heat wheels to reduce the possibility of contamination. In the hospital environment, it is recommended that the heat wheel be used only for uncontaminated exhaust airstreams that would normally be returned to the air-handling unit. Thus the heat wheel is best applied under the following circumstances:

- In 100 percent outside air units such as those serving operating rooms and delivery rooms, where the air could be returned to the unit and filtered under existing codes and good engineering practice
- Where the airstreams run in close proximity to each other, in fact side by side
- Where the supply and exhaust fan are capable of developing an additional 0.75 to 1.25 inches of static pressure to overcome the resistance of the filters necessary for air entering the heat wheel and the wheel itself
- In exhaust and supply airstreams of over 10,000 cfm, in which heat wheels have increasing economies of scale

The second category of heat recovery devices is *sensible heat devices*. Fixed-plate heat exchangers, heat pipes, and runaround coils are all sensible heat devices. A fixed-plate device consists of alternate passages of exhaust and supply airstreams separated by a thin metal wall.

Sensible heat is transferred from one airstream to the other through the metal wall. These devices prevent all possibility of cross-contamination because the airstreams are totally separated and, like the heat wheel, they require the exhaust and supply ducts to be side by side to accomplish transfer. There are no moving parts, and they can achieve efficiencies in the range of 50 percent. Fixed-plate heat exchangers do not require filters, which reduces the static pressure needed to accomplish the heat transfer.

Thermosiphon or heat pipe exchangers rely on a phase change of the fluid in the pipe to create circulation from one airstream to another. As warm air passes through one side of the heat exchanger, the fluid (usually a refrigerant) is evaporated and transferred to the colder side, where it is cooled and condensed. The continuous evaporation and condensation process causes circulation from one side of the heat exchanger to the other. This device has the advantage of no moving parts, and several exhaust and supply ducts can be piped together on one system by looping heat pipe coil loops together. Filters are required because the heat pipe coils resemble any normal HVAC fin tube-type heating or cooling coil.

Runaround coil heat exchangers use standard HVAC heating and cooling coils in the exhaust and supply airstream. Water or an ethylene glycol solution for freeze protection is circulated between the two coils. This system has a significant advantage in that the loop piping can connect coils on exhaust systems and supply systems that are separated by great distance. Also, if multiple small-exhaust ducts are located in various equipment rooms, all these exhaust streams can be interconnected and taken to a central supply air intake. The interloop piping requires a pump expansion tank and control valve just as in any hot or chilled water circulation system. Filters also are required to maintain the heat transfer effectiveness of the coils. Typically, these systems can operate in the neighborhood of 50 percent efficiency, and maintenance is required for the circulation pump control valve and damper operators. The thermal transfer fluid must be replaced periodically because ethylene glycol solutions break down with gradual use.

CHAPTER 9

Alternative Energy-Saving Strategies: Cogeneration and Thermal Energy Storage

Cogeneration and thermal storage may be attractive strategies for larger hospital facilities seeking to reduce energy costs. Because emergency power generation is required, designers have considered peak shaving and cogeneration as possible additional uses for the capital cost invested by standby power. Thermal storage helps to level the cooling peaks and takes advantage of time-of-day rates offered by some utilities.

Cogeneration

As many health care facility managers continue their efforts to reduce their institutions' energy costs and improve their building systems' efficiency, cogeneration often is one of the more glamorous options they explore. Cogeneration is exactly that—the cogeneration of useful heat and electrical energy at the same time from the same fuel.

When applied to health care institutions, cogeneration usually means running a gas-fired reciprocating engine or a gas turbine to turn an electric generator, and then recovering the heat from the engine to produce steam and/or hot water. Benefits of using cogeneration include the following:

- Reduced electrical energy costs, that is, lowering the total number of kilowatt hours (kWh) used
- Reduced monthly electrical kilowatt demand costs
- Reduced boiler steam costs
- Increased reliability and equipment redundancy

But these benefits must be evaluated against the technique's drawbacks: high up-front installation costs, increased reliance on natural gas, and greater engine maintenance costs.

Of course, opinions about the benefits and drawbacks of cogeneration vary considerably. Gas utilities and engine manufacturers like it a lot; electric utilities, unless they are hurting for capacity, do not like it at all.

In the midst of the local gas company's incentives to use cogeneration and the electric utility's dire warnings against it, how can it be decided whether cogeneration makes economic sense for the health care facility?

Hospitals present an excellent scenario for combined heat and power (CHP) applications because they have high electric demands, high thermal requirements, and extended building occupancy. Hospitals must have generator backup, because power outages are often unexpected and unpredictable and lives are at risk. Furthermore, hospitals must comply with regulations set forth by the National Fire Protection Agency (NFPA) and the Joint Commission. These two agencies require hospitals to test and exercise on-site standby generators as well as address the issue of generator sizing. A 30-minute test is typically conducted once a month in compliance with NFPA regulations. The most commonly used generators for backup or commercial power uses are CHP (natural gas) and diesel-fueled combustion engines. Hospitals require at least 8 hours of backup time, ideally 24 hours. As long as there is no interruption to the natural gas service, CHP-based backup systems can offer even longer runtimes and can be coupled with onsite fuel storage (liquefied natural or petroleum gas—LNG or LPG) in parallel with the pipeline gas for additional reliability.

What Are Microturbines?

Microturbines such as the Capstone units are compact turbine generators that deliver electricity onsite or close to the point where it is needed. Microturbines are suitable for applications ranging from remote locations to city centers, delivering clean, high-quality power from a wide variety of fuels with excellent safety and low emissions. Other features include maintenance-free air bearings, the lowest emissions of any noncatalyzed fossil fuel combustion, and digital power conversion. Microturbines are typically in the 40 to 200 kilowatt size range but are often ganged together for larger applications of up to 1 to 3 megawatt.

The Three-Point Spread

One rule of thumb regarding cogeneration is often referred to as the three-point spread. This rule advises that if the facility's electrical energy usage rate (in cents per kWh) is three numbers higher than its gas rate (in dollars per thousand cubic feet), cogenerating for 18 hours per day will result in enough cost savings to pay for the extra equipment in three years.

Note, however, that this return is not guaranteed: The three-point spread assumes the health care facility maintains such a utility rate difference for 18 hours per day *and* that the institution *always* will be able to use *all* of the steam and electricity produced.

Many other factors will determine the actual savings for the health care facility. For example, a greater spread in local utility rates will help.

Some year-round use for the steam is necessary, too, such as a laundry, an absorption chiller, or a long heating season. Domestic hot water systems and process-steam systems (sterilizers, kitchen equipment, and so on) are typically not able to use all of the thermal output from a cogeneration system.

A large monthly electrical demand charge (in dollars per kilowatt for the highest-peak electrical demand in a billing month) makes cogeneration more practical, especially if the facility's electrical rate schedule contains a demand ratchet, under which it is billed for the highest kilowatt demand during the past 11 or 12 months.

When the facility cogenerates, it reduces its electrical demand—and the resultant demand charge—from its electric bill.

Three System Types

As a point of reference, cogeneration systems in hospitals use either gas-fired reciprocating engines or gas turbines as prime movers—the driving force of the generator. Heat can be recovered from reciprocating engines in the exhaust gas and in the jacket-cooling system.

The exhaust gas, heated to between 800°F and 1,000°F, can produce low- or high-pressure (125 psig) saturated steam by passing the gas through a heat recovery boiler. The jacket-cooling water, at 250°F, can be routed through a heat exchanger to produce hot water.

Alternately, an ebulliently cooled engine is configured so that the engine-cooling jacket produces low-pressure (15 psig) steam; feed water continually replaces steam produced. Note that because the engine is acting as a low-pressure boiler, treatment of the makeup water must be on a level equal to that of the boiler system.

Reciprocating engines will provide approximately 1.2 pounds of steam from exhaust gas heat recovery per kilowatt of generator size, plus about 3,500 Btu per hour of hot water per kilowatt from the engine jacket-cooling system.

When gas turbines are used to drive the generator, all heat is recovered from the exhaust gases in a heat recovery boiler. Because the gas turbine is less efficient mechanically than a reciprocating engine, more waste heat is available per kilowatt of electricity produced.

Gas turbines will provide approximately 6 pounds of steam per kilowatt of generator size; this heat is from the exhaust gas. Note that gas turbines need supply gas pressures above 150 psig, which typically require a gas compressor.

When either type of prime mover is used, exhaust gases are cooled to approximately 400°F (but not lower) to prevent the condensation of acids on the heat-recovery boiler tubes.

A third method of cogenerating steam and electricity involves using boilers to produce steam, which is then sent through a steam turbine to turn the generator. However, this cycle only becomes cost-efficient when boiler steam pressures exceed 600 psi, and health care institutions do not typically maintain steam systems in that range.

Sizing the System

A health care facility's cogeneration system should be selected and sized so that all of its capacity can be used during the institution's hours of operation. This depends on the thermal and electrical usage profiles for the facility and on the local electric utility's rate structure.

A small percentage of the total number of cogeneration systems installed in U.S. health care institutions has been sized not only to provide electrical power to the facility itself but also to sell excess power back to the local electric utility.

The utility is obligated to buy this power under federal law but has to pay only the avoided cost, that is, the minimum cost that the utility would have had to pay to produce the power on its own. This price is significantly less than the retail price of electricity, which covers not only the cost of producing electricity, but also costs related to its distribution and expenses generated by the utility company's operations.

Because the utility's avoided cost is so low, it generally makes no economic sense for a health care facility to size its new cogeneration system so that it can sell excess electricity back to the local utility, unless the utility is actively soliciting capacity for its system.

A utility's rates may be structured so that during on-peak hours (typically during the day), it will be economically attractive for the health care facility to cogenerate, whereas during off-peak hours (usually during the night), the institution would be better served by buying power from the utility. In such a case, the cogeneration system would have to be sized for the base load (the minimum constant load) during on-peak hours.

However, if off-peak rates are expensive and round-the-clock cogeneration would save money, several system sizes should be investigated to determine which one would provide the shortest payback rate. For example, Urban University Medical Center maintains a minimum base-load demand of 2,500 kilowatts, which usually climbs to 3,200 kilowatts for a few hours during the day. The medical center pays $3 per million cubic feet for gas and 7 cents per kilowatt-hour for electricity around the clock. These relatively flat charges and demand rates would indicate sizing for the medical center's 2,500-kilowatt base load.

On the other hand, St. Suburban Hospital maintains a minimum base load of 750 kilowatts at night but, with a large medical office building and an ambulatory surgery center attached, the demand shoots up to 1,600 kilowatts during much of the day. The hospital's electric utility charges 9 cents per kilowatt-hour during the day, but only 4 cents per kilowatt-hour between 8 p.m. and 8 a.m. With a gas price of $3.80 per million cubic feet, it would be best to size St. Suburban's cogeneration system to accommodate daytime demand but not to run during cheaper off-peak hours.

How Much Will It Cost?

To provide, install, and start a cogeneration system costs $900 to $1,200 per kilowatt, depending on equipment type and size, local construction rates, and site. This cost range includes the engine or turbine, the generator, the waste-heat recovery boiler, the steam separator, the electrical switching gear and control panels, and the piping that is required for connection to the existing systems (assuming the new cogeneration system is installed reasonably close to the existing boilers and electrical switching gear). This cost range does *not* include any new buildings that may be required, any absorption chillers that would use the steam in the summer, and so on.

Economies of scale dictate that smaller (500 kW) systems will cost more per kilowatt than will larger (1,200 kW) systems. A monthly expense of 0.8 cents to 1.2 cents per kilowatt-hour should be factored in to cover scheduled maintenance and overhauls.

Thermal Energy Storage

Introduction

Thermal energy storage (TES), often called off-peak cooling, is the process of producing cooling capacity during one period of time and storing it for use during a later period of time. TES is not a new concept; it has been in existence since the 1940s. However, it has enjoyed a resurgence spawned by the electric utility industry's need to curtail peaking conditions in their systems and yet maintain energy consumption revenues.

In conventional TES systems, cooling capacity is produced during utility off-peak periods using electric refrigeration equipment and stored for use during on-peak periods. Thus, the electric utility maintains energy consumption (kWh) revenues, while reducing on-peak demand (kW). The end user of TES benefits by taking advantage of off-peak electric rates and avoiding on-peak electric demand charges. In addition, the size of the refrigeration plant can also be reduced because the leveling of on-peak capacity requirements results in savings in the initial investment of central cooling equipment.

Most major electric utilities offer up-front cash rebates, usually expressed in dollars per projected kilowatt of on-peak demand offset, to provide additional financial incentive for prospective TES end users. Often the opportunity exists for the end user to negotiate the level of these rebates to obtain the rate of return necessary to make the project attractive.

The Types of TES Systems Available

All commercially available thermal storage systems (TESs) are similar in concept and configuration. The primary difference between systems is the storage medium. Although a number of mediums are available, the most common are chilled water, ice, and phase change materials.

Prior to 1980, water typically was chosen as the storage medium. Since 1980, phase change materials have grown in popularity and are now used in a majority of applications. In a temperature change, one pound of water stores one Btu for every degree Fahrenheit of temperature change.

In a phase change, one pound of water stores 144 Btu in changing from one pound of liquid at 32°F to a solid. Chilled water storage is traditionally designed around a 20-degree temperature rise, which equates to approximately 10 cubic feet of water per ton-hour. This compares to approximately 9.1 cubic feet of ice per ton-hour (water weighs 62.4 pounds per cubic foot, whereas ice weighs approximately 57 pounds per cubic foot).

In the common chilled water storage system, the refrigeration system chills water during off-peak periods to take advantage of the lower rates, then pumps it into the storage tanks for later use. When chilled water is required for cooling, it is pumped out of the storage tank to cooling coils and then returned. Because of the problems encountered when mixing masses of different temperatures, such as in a chilled water system, thermal gradients may exist within the tank. Antiblending techniques, such as flexible membranes, baffles, or multiple tanks, are all effective to varying degrees but are costly, require a great deal of space, and are inherently problematic. Leakage of cold supply water into the return water can occur at a variety of locations in the system (such as a leaking control valve). Incorrect design of the storage tank can allow return water to bypass cool supply water, or return water can mix with supply water while still in the tank, lessening its cooling potential. Designs to minimize these problems are often difficult and costly.

Ice storage has a definite advantage over chilled water storage due to the latent heat of fusion of water, which is 144 Btu per pound. Each pound of water frozen into ice can provide 144 Btu of cooling (compared to 1 Btu per lb for chilled water). Ice can reduce the storage volume by as much as a factor of five. Ice also reduces the weight of the storage system. Typically, a chilled water system weighs as much as 700 pounds per ton-hour of storage, whereas an ice system weighs as little as 90 pounds per ton-hour. The lighter weight of ice storage systems allows them to be placed almost anywhere in the building or, with some systems, to be installed underground. A manufactured ice storage system can deliver specific performance, eliminating the complicated design and possible misapplication with chilled water storage.

There are a variety of systems for generating and storing ice in a thermal storage system. Some of the recognized systems are ice builders, ice tanks, and ice harvesters.

The ice builder uses a larger, open, insulated steel tank containing serpentined steel piping to form a coil. Ice is formed on the outside of the pipe while refrigerant (usually R22) is circulated through the pipe. The ice thickness varies from 1 to 2½ inches. It is melted by circulating water through the tank. Separation between the cylinders of ice is maintained by the pipe spacing coil design and water turbulence. Agitation promotes ice melting and prevents bridging between pipes during freezing. The spacing of the pipes requires half the tank volume to remain as water, even when the storage system is fully charged. This excess water significantly increases the volume and weight of the ice builder system. Because of their weight, these open ice tanks usually are located at lower levels or at grade. Because the tanks are open, an additional heat exchanger is required to isolate the tanks from the static head of the chilled water system.

Ice tanks are modular insulated polyethylene tanks approximately 10 feet in diameter and 8 feet in height. Each tank contains a circular coil construction of ⅝-inch polyethylene tubing. A glycol solution cooled to approximately 24°F is circulated through the tubing, freezing approximately 17,000 pounds of water in the tank. This is a total freeze-up system, meaning when the ice-building cycle is complete, the tanks are frozen solid. The water remains in the tank with no need for agitation. Ice is melted by circulating the same glycol through the tubing. An external or accessory heat exchanger to isolate this system from the main chilled water system is not necessarily required. The open tanks remain at atmospheric pressure; however, the polyethylene coil is a closed system. The coil is suitable for the operating pressures associated with a standard chilled water system. Ice tanks of this type are designed for glycol solutions only. A solution of 25 percent ethylene glycol and 75 percent water by weight is most commonly used. This necessitates a separate feeding and monitoring system to maintain the proper proportions of water to glycol in the solution at all times.

The ice harvester system is unlike the previously discussed systems in that ice is produced on plates above the tanks and stored in an open tank below the ice maker. Hot gas defrost is used to release or shuck the ice from the plates. The palm-sized plates of ice then fall into the tank below. Warm return water is sprayed over this tank of ice plates, which simultaneously cools the water and melts the ice. The ice water at the bottom of the tank is then pumped to the cooling supply. The cooling supply water leaving the tank is approximately 32 to 33°F, signifying a need for an intermediate heat exchanger to maintain a 40 to 42°F supply water for a normal cooling system. The ice harvester system can be purchased as a complete skid-mounted unit including the plate ice maker, compressor, water filtering and deionizing system, heat exchanger, and evaporative condenser. The volume of such a system represents a significant construction cost and would require careful evaluation concerning its placement.

Eutectic salt describes a mixture or compound usually fused at a relatively high temperature. The eutectic salt used in thermal storage applications is a salt hydrate that fuses at 47°F. In a crystalline form, the salt fuses with several water molecules. Energy, in the form of heat, must be added to the hydrate to cause the disassociation. The heat of fusion of this salt hydrate is 41 Btu per pound, compared to 144 Btu per pound heat of fusion for water, or a sensible heat gain of 20 Btu per pound for chilled water storage. Eutectic salts can be used to store heat at a higher temperature than ice and a lower volume than water. The salt and water is packaged in plastic containers (approximately 8 × 24 × 1¾ inches). The container, or tray, is constructed with internal weight-bearing supports and spacers to maintain vertical separation between the trays.

The tank design for a eutectic salt system must provide for uniform entrance velocity to the trays. The slow laminar flow into the tray section requires additional space for headers and supply diffusers. Because the eutectic salt composition fuses at 47°F, chilled water to this system is required at 42°F, which is substantially higher than the 28°F supply temperature required with an ice tank system. This allows for greater flexibility of chiller selection in that lower kilowatt per ton application for normal chilled water use can be applied. The eutectic salts allow greater flexibility in that a special low-suction temperature chiller rated at a much higher kilowatt per ton is not necessary as with the ice-tank-type storage systems.

Partial Storage versus Full Storage

A full-storage system is designed to generate all of the on-peak cooling capacity for a facility. Full storage is best suited for cooling applications where the length of the required cooling cycle is short in comparison to the thermal storage charge cycle. Depending on the magnitude of the ratio between cooling and charged cycles, a reduction in the size of the refrigeration equipment may be possible. Because a full-storage system must handle the entire on-peak cooling load, the comparatively large storage capacity required may limit its practicality in many comfort cooling applications. However, if the relative cost of on-peak consumption is high or if excessive demand charges exist, full storage can be a viable alternative.

In a partial-storage system, the storage provides part of the cooling capacity and operation of the refrigeration system provides the remaining capacity. Because the refrigeration system may operate 24 hours a day to meet either the cooling load or charged storage tank, smaller and less costly installations for both the refrigeration and storage systems are possible in a partial-storage design. Installed cost can be comparable to a conventional chilled water system that provides cooling as it is needed. Because the refrigeration equipment is allowed to run during on-peak periods with a partial-storage system, the on-peak savings are less than those for a full-storage system.

Economic Analysis

To evaluate the annual cost savings, hourly load profiles for chilled water systems' electric kilowatt demand are prepared for typical winter, fall/spring, and summer days. The electric kilowatt demand includes the chiller plus chilled water and condenser water circuiting pumps brake horsepower and cooling tower fan motor brake horsepower.

Once the daily load profiles are established, the applicable time periods of on-peak usage are overlaid to help determine the amount of electric demand and usage that would be shifted by discharging the thermal storage system (and the resulting savings); the profiles also show the extra electric demand and usage that was added during off-peak times (and the resulting costs) to charge the thermal storage system. The net savings are calculated for the typical day for each season and then totaled into annual savings.

Savings from TES systems are derived by shifting energy usage and lowering peak demands, using two different strategies:

1. *Leveling the demand curve.* In this approach, the chiller load is constant 24 hours a day (see Figure 9-1).
2. *Eliminating chiller usage during on-peak demand periods.* In this approach, the chiller must run at a higher load (and thus higher demand) because it will not run at all during on-peak times (see Figure 9-2).

Demand charge savings and any incremental usage savings are then evaluated against the premium installation costs for the TES system and a brine chiller (if applicable) to determine a payback. Brine chillers typically cost 25 percent more than a water chiller of equal tonnage.

Ice tank systems are approximately $80 per ton-hour, installed. A eutectic salt storage system costs $130 per ton-hour, installed. Ice builders can cost $400 to $500 per ton-hour. An economic feasibility study tailored for a specific hospital's demand profiles and electric rates will determine which strategy produces the highest energy cost savings.

Figure 9-1"Leveling" the Demand Profile

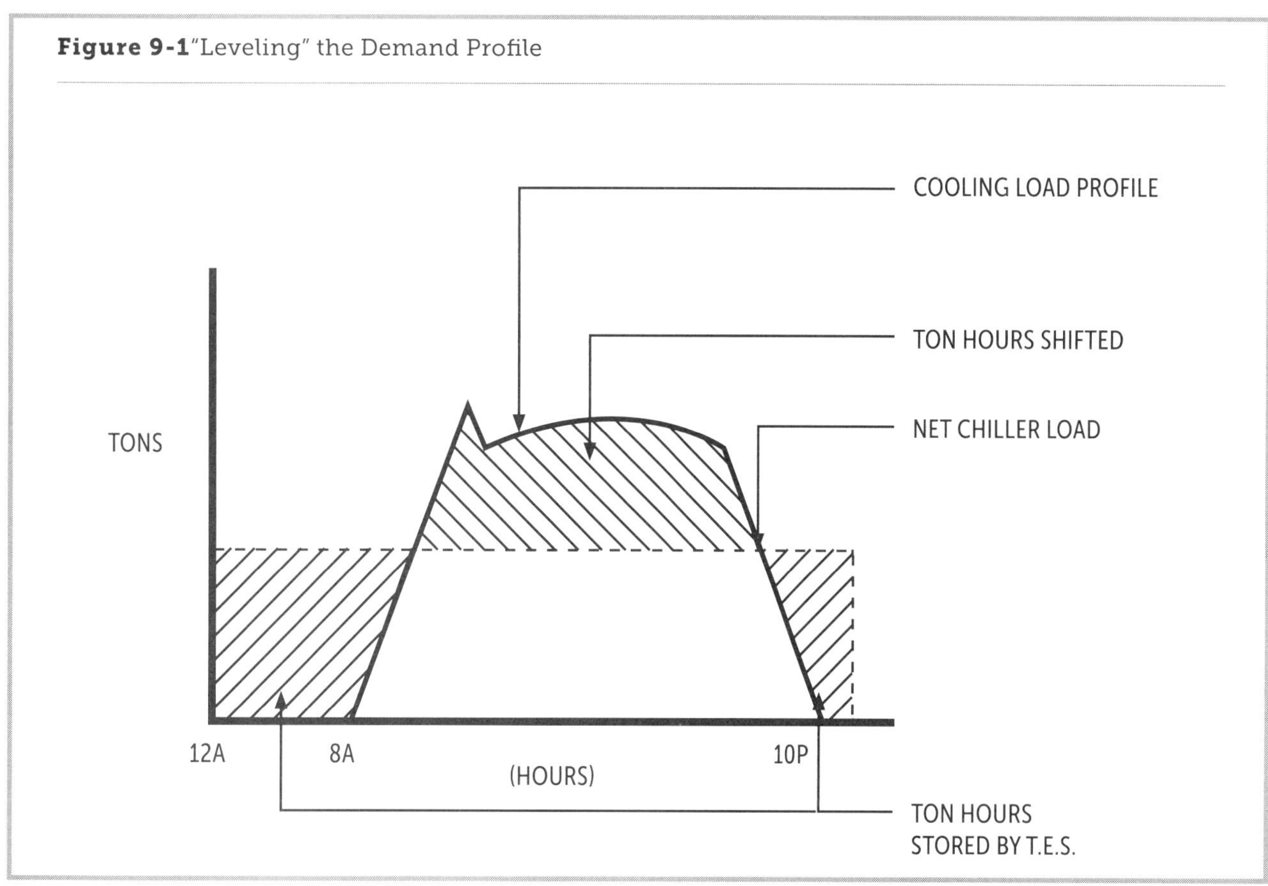

Figure 9-2 Eliminating Chiller Usage During On-Peak Time

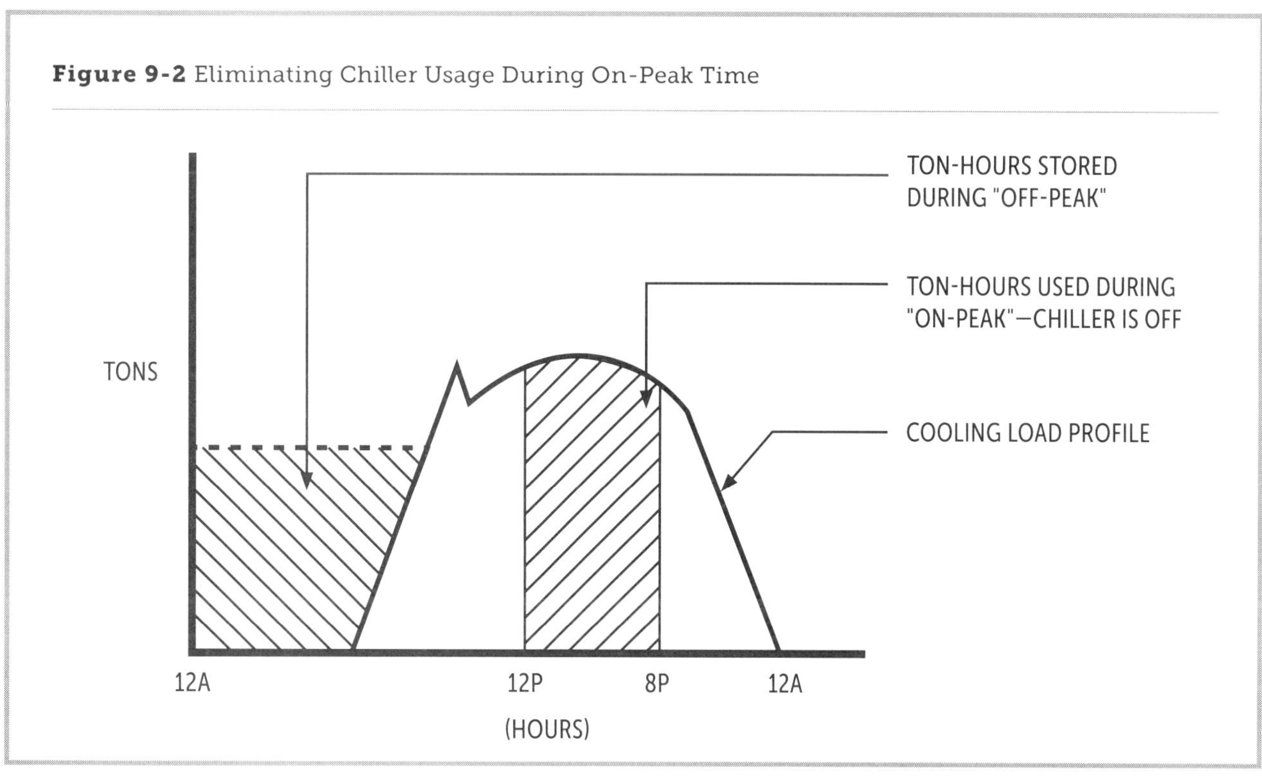

What makes thermal storage economically attractive? The biggest requirement is a time period when there is a high demand charge. Second, the range of electric rates between on- and off-peak must be significant. Most applications of thermal storage take advantage of electric rates that have $8 to $15 per kilowatt difference in demand rates, as well as off-peak usage rates that are less than half the on-peak costs. Third, there must be help from the electric utility for up-front costs; typical utility rebates range from $200 to $300 per on-peak kilowatt shifted. Usually, this up-front rebate helps pay for about one-third of the installation costs of the thermal storage tanks (not including the costs of glycol chillers, piping, and so on).

CHAPTER 10

Testing, Balancing, and Adjusting Heating, Ventilation, and Air-Conditioning Systems

The testing, balancing, and adjustment of heating, ventilation, and air-conditioning (HVAC) systems is critically important in health care facilities. Not only does this process attempt to ensure that comfortable conditions exist, but the code-required ventilation rates and pressure relationships necessary to reduce infection risk depend on the successful completion of this work.

This process should be accomplished by a certified test and balance contractor at the completion of all hospital construction projects, regardless of size, if the HVAC system is modified during construction. In many cases, it is a good idea to test existing systems before a renovation or expansion project is undertaken. This gives the design team better information regarding decisions to reuse or replace equipment and indicates problem areas that should be addressed during the project.

Contractor Certification

Many mechanical contractors offer cost savings for performing this work by their own personnel rather than an independent testing and balancing firm. It is important to ask for certifications regarding test and balance training and personnel before accepting these proposals. The National Environmental Balancing Bureau (NEBB) and the Associated Air Balance Council (AABC) have established guidelines and training procedures. They also certify contractors who have demonstrated qualifications in testing and balancing procedures.

In-House Troubleshooting

Hospitals often undertake small remodeling projects or change the use of space without regard to changes in heating/cooling loads due to equipment and personnel relocation. These projects are often so small that they do not seem to warrant a test and balance contractor. This work may be accomplished by qualified in-house personnel. Personnel with a basic knowledge of test and balance procedures can also improve the ability of staff to troubleshoot HVAC systems and locate the sources of problems.

For in-house testing and troubleshooting, the following instruments would be required:

- A vertical/inclined combination manometer reading from 0" to 10" water column
- Pitot tubes (various sizes from 2' to 4' long)
- Deflecting vane anemometer
- Dial, glass, and digital thermometer
- Centrifugal tachometer
- Clamp-on amp meter
- Alnor velometer set
- Flow measuring hood (optional)
- Hydronic pressure gauges in three ranges:
  - 30"–30 psi
  - 30"–60 psi
  - 0–200 psi

These instruments allow most of the measurements necessary to accomplish testing and balancing and adjusting for very small in-house projects and, troubleshooting specific problem areas.

Basic Procedures

Following are procedures for taking basic airflow and water flow measurements. These measurements allow in-house personnel to determine system operating conditions to within plus or minus 10 percent. Many troubleshooting opportunities can be diagnosed with these test and balance procedures.

Readings at return and exhaust grilles. These readings may be taken using the deflecting vane anemometer at the face of the grilles. Traverse readings are taken across the face of the grille to determine average velocity. The average velocity is multiplied by the free area of the grille (from manufacturers' data) to determine air flow in cfm.

Readings at supply diffusers. These readings may be measured directly using an airflow hood, or an Alnor velometer may be used to determine average velocity. The average velocity is multiplied by the K factor (from manufacturers' data) to determine airflow.

Determining water flow across pumps. The flow rate through a pump can be determined by using the pump curve, a pressure gauge, and a wattmeter or amp meter. Using the same gauge (for accuracy), the entering and leaving pressure can be measured at the pump to determine the total head, then the balancing cock or discharged piping valve can be closed to determine the shutoff head of the pump. If the shutoff head does not fall on the manufacturer's pump curve, a new curve should be plotted parallel to the design curve. The total head pressure at full flow can then be plotted on the pump curve to approximate the system flow. The motor power draw should be checked to ensure that the motor does not overload at full flow. The horsepower draw should be used as a check against the operating point on the curve and could indicate cavitation or air in the system.

Determining water flow across system components. The manufacturers of chillers, hot water boilers, coils, and heat exchangers publish certified pressure-drop tables or curves. The tables or curves can be used to determine flow rates through the devices by determining the actual entering and leaving pressures and plotting these points on the curves.

Determining outside air quantities at air-handling units. The outside air being introduced into the air-handling system can be fairly accurately determined by using thermometers to measure the outside air temperature, the return air temperature, and the mixed air temperature downstream of the prefilters. These readings are taken while the unit is set on minimum outside air (economizer cycle off).

The percentage of outside air can be determined using the formula:

$T_{ma} = T_{oa}(I\text{-}X)+T_{ra}(X)$ where

T_{ma} = Temperature of mixed air

T_{ra} = Temperature of return air

T_{oa} = Temperature of outside air

X = Fraction of return air

Different systems tolerate system flow problems better than others. Hot water heat exchangers provide nearly 90 percent of the design capacity at only 50 percent of the design flow rate. Chilled water coils provide about 75 percent of the sensible capacity at 50 percent flow rate, but only 30 percent of the latent cooling capacity will remain. The severe latent-capacity reduction makes chilled water flow problems more readily apparent to building occupants as humidity control is lost very quickly with flow or water temperature problems.

Airflow reduction produces a nearly linear capacity reduction, so that a 50 percent airflow reduction will produce a 50 percent reduction in heating or cooling capacity.

Generally Accepted Test and Balance Procedures

The sequencing of balancing an HVAC system is important because the air and water systems are interdependent and changes in one system may affect another. It is generally accepted in the industry that air balancing should be done before water balancing. Many systems will require several passes to bring all the flows to within design specifications.

The ASHRAE *Systems Handbook* provides generalized procedures for air distribution systems addressed specifically to those who do not need detailed information but require a conceptual understanding of the testing and balancing process. Following are excerpts from this section. This information describes the testing procedures a qualified test and balance contractor should follow to balance a system.

Preliminary Procedure for Air Balancing

Before putting the system in operation, perform these steps:

1. Obtain design drawings and specifications and become thoroughly acquainted with the design intent.
2. Obtain copies of approved shop drawings of all air-handling equipment, outlets (supply, return, and exhaust), and temperature control diagrams.
3. Compare design to installed equipment and field installation.
4. Walk the system from the air-handling equipment to terminal units to determine variations of installation from design.
5. Check filters, dampers (both volume and fire) for correct and locked position, and temperature control for completeness of installation before starting fans.
6. Prepare report test sheets for both fans and outlets.
7. Obtain manufacturer's outlet factors and recommended procedure of testing. Summation of required outlet volumes permits a cross-check with required fan volumes.
8. Determine best locations in main and branch ductwork for most accurate duct traverses.
9. Place all outlet dampers in the open position.
10. Prepare schematic diagrams of system as-built ductwork

and piping layouts to facilitate reporting.

Equipment and System Check

Place all fans (supply, return, and exhaust) in operation, and immediately check the following items:

1. Motor amperage and voltage to guard against possible overload.
2. Fan rotation.
3. Automatic dampers for proper position.
4. Air and water resets operating to deliver required temperatures.
5. Check for air leaks in the casing and in the scarfing around the coils and filter frames by moving a light source along the outside of the joint while observations are made in the darkened interior of the casing. Caulk any leaks. Make particular note of points where piping enters the casing to be sure that the escutcheons are tight. Do not rely on pipe insulation to seal these openings because, in time, the insulation may shrink. In prefabricated units, check that all panel fastening holes are filled to prevent whistling.

Traverse the main supply ductwork whenever possible. All main branches should also be traversed where duct arrangement permits. Selection of traverse points and method of traverse should be as follows:

1. Each main or branch should be traversed after the longest possible straight run for the duct involved.
2. Note temperature and barometric pressure to determine if correction is necessary to obtain standard air quantity. Normally, these corrections are insignificant; however, abnormal conditions where very accurate results are desirable would justify the corrections.
3. After establishing the total air being delivered, it may be necessary to adjust the fan speed to obtain excess air to allow for normal leakage and additional static pressure

imposed by balancing requirements. Check power and speed to ensure that motor power and critical fan speed have not been exceeded.

4. Adjust branch dampers until the proper air volume is obtained in each.
5. With all the dampers and registers in the system open and with the supply, return, and exhaust blowers operating at or near design speed, set the minimum outdoor and return air ratio. This can be conveniently done with thermometers in the return air, outdoor air louver, and the filter section, measuring the mixed temperature.

Report Information

To be of value to the consulting engineer and owner's maintenance department, the air-handling system report should consist of at least the following items:

Design

- Air quantity to be delivered
- Fan static pressure
- Motor power
- Percent of outside air under minimum conditions
- Fan rpm
- Power required to obtain this air quantity at the design static pressure

Installed

- Equipment manufacturer
- Size unit installed
- Arrangement of the air-handling unit
- Class fan

- Nameplate horsepower (kW), nameplate voltage, phase, cycles, and full-load amperes of the motor installed
- Tested voltage and corrected full-load amperes for this voltage
- No-load amperes on all three-phase motors and single-phase 0.5 horsepower (0.373 kW) and up

Field Tests

- Fan rpm
- Power readings (voltage, amperes of all legs at motor terminals)
- Calculated approximate brake horsepower (kW)
- Total suction pressure
- Static discharge pressure
- Fan static pressure

It is very important to establish the initial static pressures accurately for the air treatment equipment and the duct system, so that the variation in air quantity due to filter loading may be calculated. It enables the designer to ensure that the total fan quantity is never less than the minimum requirements. It also serves as a check to establish the contribution of dirt loading in coils, because the design air quantity for peak loading of the filters has been calculated.

Terminal Outlets

1. Properly locate outlet by room designation and position.
2. Report outlet manufacture and type.
3. Indicate outlet size. (Use manufacturer's designation to ensure proper factor.)
4. Indicate neck area for diffusers and core area for grilles.
5. Insert the manufacturer's outlet factor. (Where no factors are available, or where field tests indicate that the listed

factors are incorrect, it becomes necessary to determine a factor by the traverse of a duct leading to a single outlet in the field.)

6. Indicate the design air quantity and the required velocity in fpm (m/s) to obtain this cfm (l/s).
7. Indicate the test velocities and resulting air quantity.
8. Indicate the adjustment pattern for every air terminal.
9. List induction unit manufacturer and size. List required air quantity and plenum pressures for each unit. Test plenum pressures and resulting primary air delivery from the manufacturer's listed curves.

The following additional information is desirable under applicable circumstances:

- Air-handling units
  - Belt number and size
  - Drive and driven sheave size
  - Belt position on adjusted drive sheaves (bottom, middle, and top)
  - Motor speed under full load
  - Motor heater size
  - Filter type and static pressure at initial use and full load (time to replace)
  - Variations of velocity at various points across the face of the coil
  - Existence of vortex or discharge dampers, or both
- Distribution system
  - Unusual duct arrangements
  - Branch duct static readings in double-duct and induction system

- Relationship of building to outdoor pressure under both minimum and maximum outdoor air

Report all equipment nameplates not visible and easily readable.

GLOSSARY

Absolute humidity: The weight of water vapor per unit volume.

Absolute pressure: The pressure of a perfect vacuum. It is the sum of gauge pressure and atmospheric pressure.

Absorption: A process whereby a material extracts one or more substances present in an atmosphere or mixture of gases or liquids accompanied by the material's physical and chemical changes.

Absorption chiller: A refrigeration machine using heat as the power input to generate chilled water.

Acceptable indoor air quality: Air in which there are no known contaminants at harmful concentrations as determined by cognizant authorities and with which a substantial majority (80 percent or more) of the people exposed do not express dissatisfaction. (ASHRAE 62-2001)

Air changes: A method of expressing the amount of air leakage into or out of a building or room in terms of the number of building volumes or room volumes exchanged.

Algae: Minute fresh water plant growth that forms a scum on the surfaces of recirculated water apparatus, interfering with fluid flow and heat transfer.

Ambient air: Generally speaking, the air surrounding an object.

Amps (A): Amperes, units of electrical flow.

Anemometer: An instrument for measuring the velocity of a fluid.

Apparatus dew point: The temperature that would result if the psychrometric process occurring in a dehumidifier, humidifier, or surface-cooler were carried to the saturation condition of the leaving air while maintaining the same ratio of sensible-to-total heat load in the process.

Approach: In an evaporative cooling device, the difference between the average temperature of the circulating water leaving the device and the average wet-bulb temperature of the entering air. In a conduction heat exchanger device, the temperature difference between the leaving treated fluid and the entering working fluid.

Atmospheric pressure: The pressure indicated by a barometer. Standard atmosphere is the pressure equivalent to 14.696 psi, or 29.291 in. of mercury at 32°F.

Barometer: An instrument for measuring atmospheric pressure.

British thermal unit (Btu): A heat unit equal to the amount of heat required to raise one pound of water one degree Fahrenheit.

British thermal unit per hour (Btuh): A heat unit equal to the amount of heat required to raise one pound of water one degree Fahrenheit per hour.

Building envelope: All external surfaces that are subject to climatic impact; for example, doors, walls, windows, and roofs.

Building-related illness: Diagnosable illness whose symptoms can be identified and whose cause can be attributed to airborne building pollutants (e.g., Legionnaire's disease).

Celsius (formerly Centigrade): A thermometric scale in which the freezing point of water is 0 degrees and its boiling point 100 degrees at normal atmospheric pressure (14.696 psi).

Chillers (centrifugal): A refrigeration machine using mechanical energy input to drive a centrifugal compressor to generate chilled water.

Condensate: The liquid formed by condensation of a vapor. In steam heating, water condensed from steam; in air-conditioning, water extracted from air, as by condensation on the cooling coil of a refrigeration machine.

Condensation: The liquid formed by extracting heat. Condensation of steam or water vapor is affected in either steam condensers or dehumidifying coils, and the resulting water is called condensate.

Condenser: A heat exchanger that removes heat from a vapor, changing it to its liquid state; in refrigeration systems, the component that rejects heat.

Connection in parallel: A system whereby flow is divided among two or more channels from a common starting point or header.

Connection in series: A system whereby flow through two or more channels is in a single path entering each succeeding channel only after leaving the first or previous channel.

Control: Any device for regulation of a system or component, manual or automatic.

Convection: Transfer of heat by movement of fluid.

Cooling tower: A device that cools water directly by evaporation.

Counterflow: In heat exchange between fluids, opposite direction of flow, coldest portion of one meeting coldest portion of the other.

Cubic feet per minute (cfm): Volume rate of airflow.

Damper: A device used to vary the volume of air passing through an air outlet, inlet, or duct.

Degree day: The difference between 65°F and the outdoor mean daily temperature.

Dehumidification: The condensation of water vapor from air by cooling below the dew point, or removal of water vapor from air by chemical or physical methods.

Double-bundle condenser: Condenser (usually in refrigeration machine) that contains two separate tube bundles, allowing the option of rejecting heat to either the cooling tower or another building system requiring heat input.

Dry air: Air without contained water vapor; air only.

Dry-bulb temperature: The measure of the sensible temperature of air.

Dust: An air suspension (aerosol) or particles of any solid material, usually with particle size less than 100 microns.

Dynamic or total head: In flowing fluid, the sum of the static and velocity heads at the point of measurement.

Economizer cycle: A method of operating a ventilation system to reduce refrigeration load. When the outdoor air conditions are more favorable (lower heat content) than return air conditions, outdoor air quantity is increased.

Enthalpy: For the purpose of air-conditioning, enthalpy is the total heat content of air and is expressed in Btu/lb. It is the sum of sensible and latent heat and ignores internal energy changes due to pressure change.

Entropy: The ratio of the heat added to a substance to the absolute temperature at which it is added.

Evaporative cooling: Involves the adiabatic exchange of heat between air and water spray or wetted surface. The water assumes the wet-bulb temperature of the air, which remains constant during its traverse of the exchanger.

Evaporator: A heat exchanger that adds heat to a liquid, changing it to a gaseous state; in a refrigeration system, it is the component that absorbs heat.

Face area: The total plane area of the portion of a grille, coil, or other items bounded by a line tangent to the outer edges of the openings through which air can pass.

Face velocity: The velocity obtained by dividing the air quantity by the component face area.

Fan, centrifugal: A fan rotor or wheel within a scroll-type housing and including driving mechanism supports for either belt drive or direct connection.

Fan, tube-axial: A propeller or disc-type wheel within a cylinder and including driving mechanism supports for either belt drive or direct connection.

Feet per minute (fpm): Velocity rate of air flow.

Free area: The total minimum area of the openings in an air inlet or outlet (or the net area of the opening in system components) through which air can pass.

Grains of moisture: The unit of measurement of actual moisture contained in a sample of air (7,000 grains = one pound of water).

Heat pump: A refrigeration machine capable of reversing the flow so that its output can be either heating or cooling. When used for heating, it extracts heat from a low-temperature source to the point where it can be used.

Heat pump coefficient of performance (COP): The ratio of the compressor heating effect (heat pump) to the rate of energy input to the shaft of the compressor, in consistent units, in a complete heat pump, under designated operating conditions.

Heat, sensible: Heat that results in a temperature change but no change in state.

Horsepower (hp): Unit of work.

Humidifier: A device that adds moisture to air.

Humidifying effect: The latent heat of vaporization of water at the average evaporating temperature times the weight of water evaporated per unit of time.

Infiltration: The process by which outdoor air leaks into a building by natural forces through cracks around doors, windows, and so on.

Kilowatt (kW): 1,000 watts.

Latent heat: The quantity of heat required to effect a change in state.

Laws of thermodynamics: Two laws on which the classical theory of thermodynamics rests. These laws have been stated in many different but equivalent ways.

The First Law

1. When work is expended in generating heat, the quantity of heat produced is proportional to the

work expended; conversely, when heat is employed in the performance of work, the quantity of heat that disappears is proportional to the work done.

2. If a system is caused to change from an initial state to a final state by adiabatic means only, the work done is the same for all adiabatic paths connecting the two states.
3. In any power cycle or refrigeration cycle, the net heat absorbed by the working substance is exactly equal to the net work done.

The Second Law

1. It is impossible for a self-acting machine, unaided by any external agency, to convey heat from a body of lower temperature to one of higher temperature.
2. It is impossible to derive mechanical work from heat taken from a body unless there is available a body of lower temperature into which the residue not so used may be discharged.
3. It is impossible to construct an engine that, operating in a cycle, will produce no effect other than the extraction of heat from a reservoir and the performance of an equivalent amount of work.

Life cycle cost: The cost of the equipment over its entire life, including operating and maintenance costs.

Load profile: Time distribution of building heating, cooling, and electrical load.

Load shedding: Controlled shutdown of nonessential equipment and services to avoid peak electrical loads.

Makeup air: Air taken from outside the building to replace relieved or exhausted air.

Manometer: An instrument for measuring pressures; essentially a U-tube partially filled with a liquid, usually water, mercury, or a light oil, so constructed that the amount of displacement of the liquid indicates the pressure being exerted on the instrument.

Micron: A unit of length; the thousandth part of 1 mm or a millionth of a meter.

Nosocomial infection: An infection acquired while being treated in a hospital.

Orifice plate: A device inserted in a pipe or duct that causes a pressure drop across it. Depending on orifice size, it can be used to restrict flow or form part of a measuring device.

Overall coefficient of heat transfer (thermal transmittance): The time rate of heat flow through a body per unit area, under steady conditions, for a unit temperature difference between the fluids on the two sides of the body.

Pressure: The normal force exerted by a homogeneous liquid or gas, per unit of area, on the wall of its container.

Psychrometer: An instrument for ascertaining the humidity or hygrometric state of the atmosphere.

Psychrometric chart: A graphical representation of the thermodynamic properties of moist air.

Relative humidity: A measurement indicating moisture content of air as a percentage of the amount of moisture that would completely saturate the air.

Revolutions per minute (rpm): Turning speed.

R-value: The resistance to heat flow.

Saturated air: Moist air in which the partial pressure of the water vapor is equal to the vapor pressure of water at the existing temperature. This occurs when dry air and saturated water vapor coexist at the same dry-bulb temperature.

Sick building syndrome: Condition in which building occupants experience acute health and comfort effects while spending time within a particular building, but no specific illness or cause can be identified. The complaints may be localized within a particular room or zone, or spread throughout the building.

Static head: The static pressure of fluid expressed in terms of the height of a column of the fluid, or of some manometric fluid, which it would support.

Thermal conductivity: The time rate of heat flow through unit area and unit thickness of a homogeneous material under steady conditions when a unit temperature gradient is maintained in the direction perpendicular to area. Materials are considered homogeneous when the value of the thermal conductivity is not affected by variation in thickness or in size of sample within the range normally used in construction.

Thermal transmittance (U factor): The time rate of heat flow per unit area under steady conditions from the fluid on the warm side of a barrier to the fluid on the cold side, per unit temperature difference between the two fluids.

Thermocouple: A device for measuring temperature using the electromotive force generated whenever two junctions of two dissimilar metals in an electric circuit are at different temperature levels.

Thermodynamics: The science of heat energy and its transformations to and from other forms of energy.

Ton of refrigeration: A means of expressing cooling capacity—1 ton = 12,000 Btu/hour cooling.

U value: A coefficient expressing the thermal conductance of a composite structure in Btu per square foot, hour, or F° temperature difference.

Vapor barrier: A moisture-impervious layer designed to prevent moisture migration.

Velocity head: In a flowing fluid, the height of the fluid or of some manometric fluid equivalent to its velocity pressure.

Volt (v): Unit of electrical pressure.

Watt (W): Electrical work measure.

Wet-bulb temperature: The lowest temperature attainable by evaporating water in the air without the addition or subtraction of energy.

Δ (delta): Differential.

Economic Terms

Base year: The year to which all future and past costs are converted.

Compound interest: Interest paid on the principal and on any accumulated interest.

Constant dollars: Values expressed in terms of the general purchasing power of the dollar in the base year. Constant dollars do not reflect price inflation.

Construction cost: The "as-built" cost of construction based on bid price, including cost escalation.

Cost-effective: Estimated benefits (savings) from an energy conservation investment project are equal to or exceed the costs of the investment where both are assessed over the life of the project.

Current dollars: Values expressed in terms of actual prices of each year; current dollars reflect inflation.

Differential cost: The difference in total cost between two alternatives.

Discount rate: The rate of interest reflecting the time value of money that is used to convert benefits and costs occurring at different times to a common time. OMB Circular A-94 specifies that the discount rate for evaluating government projects is 10 percent. This 10 percent represents the rate of interest after inflation is removed.

Discounted payback period: The time required for the annual net benefits derived from an investment to pay back the investment, considering the time value of money.

Economic life: The period over which an investment is considered to be the lowest-cost alternative for satisfying a particular need.

Interest: Payment for the use of money.

Interest period: The time period for which the interest rate is applied.

Interest rate: The ratio, usually expressed as a percentage, of the amount paid at the end of a period of time and the amount of money owed at the start of the period.

Life cycle costing (LCC): A method of economic evaluation of alternatives that considers all relevant costs associated with each alternative activity or project during the time it is in use. For buildings, life cycle costs include all costs of owning, operating, and maintaining a building over its economic life, including its energy costs.

Net present value of savings: The present value of energy savings minus (or plus) the present value of the increase (or decrease) in all future nonenergy costs.

Operating cost: The expenses incurred during the normal operation of a building or a building system, component, or equipment, including costs of manpower, fuel, power, water, and so on.

Payback period: The length of time required for the stream of net cash proceeds or cost savings produced by an investment to equal the original cash outlay required by the investment; see *discounted payback period.*

Present value: Past and future costs or benefits expressed as a time-equivalent amount as of the present time, taking into account the time value of money.

Principal: The amount of money outstanding at the start of an interest period.

Recurring costs: Those costs that recur on a periodic basis throughout the life of a project.

Residual (salvage) value: The net sum to be realized from disposal of an asset at the end of its economic life or at the end of the study period.

Simple interest: Where money is borrowed for a number of periods, interest is paid only on the amount of the original principal. Interest is not paid on accumulated interest. This type of interest rate is rarely used.

Time value of money: The difference between the value of a dollar today and its value at some future time if invested today at a stated rate of interest.

References

American Conference of Governmental Industrial Hygienists (ACGIH). 1992. *Industrial Ventilation.* 21st ed. Cincinnati: ACGIH.

American Industrial Hygiene Association (AIHA). 2003. *American National Standard for Laboratory Ventilation (ANSI/AIHA Z9.5-2003).* Fairfax, VA: AIHA.

American Institute of Architects (AIA) Committee on Architecture of Health and the U.S. Department of Health and Human Services. 2001. *Guidelines for Construction of Equipment of Hospitals and Medical Facilities.* Washington, DC: AIA Press.

American Society of Heating, Refrigerating and Air Conditioning Engineers (ASHRAE). 2013a. ASHRAE *Fundamentals Handbook.* Atlanta: ASHRAE.

———. 2013b. ASHRAE Standard 62.1-2013: *Ventilation for Acceptable Indoor Air Quality*. Atlanta: ASHRAE.

———. 2013c. ASHRAE Standard 90.1: *Energy Conservation in New Building Design.* New York: ASHRAE.

———. 2012. ASHRAE *Equipment Handbook.* Atlanta: ASHRAE

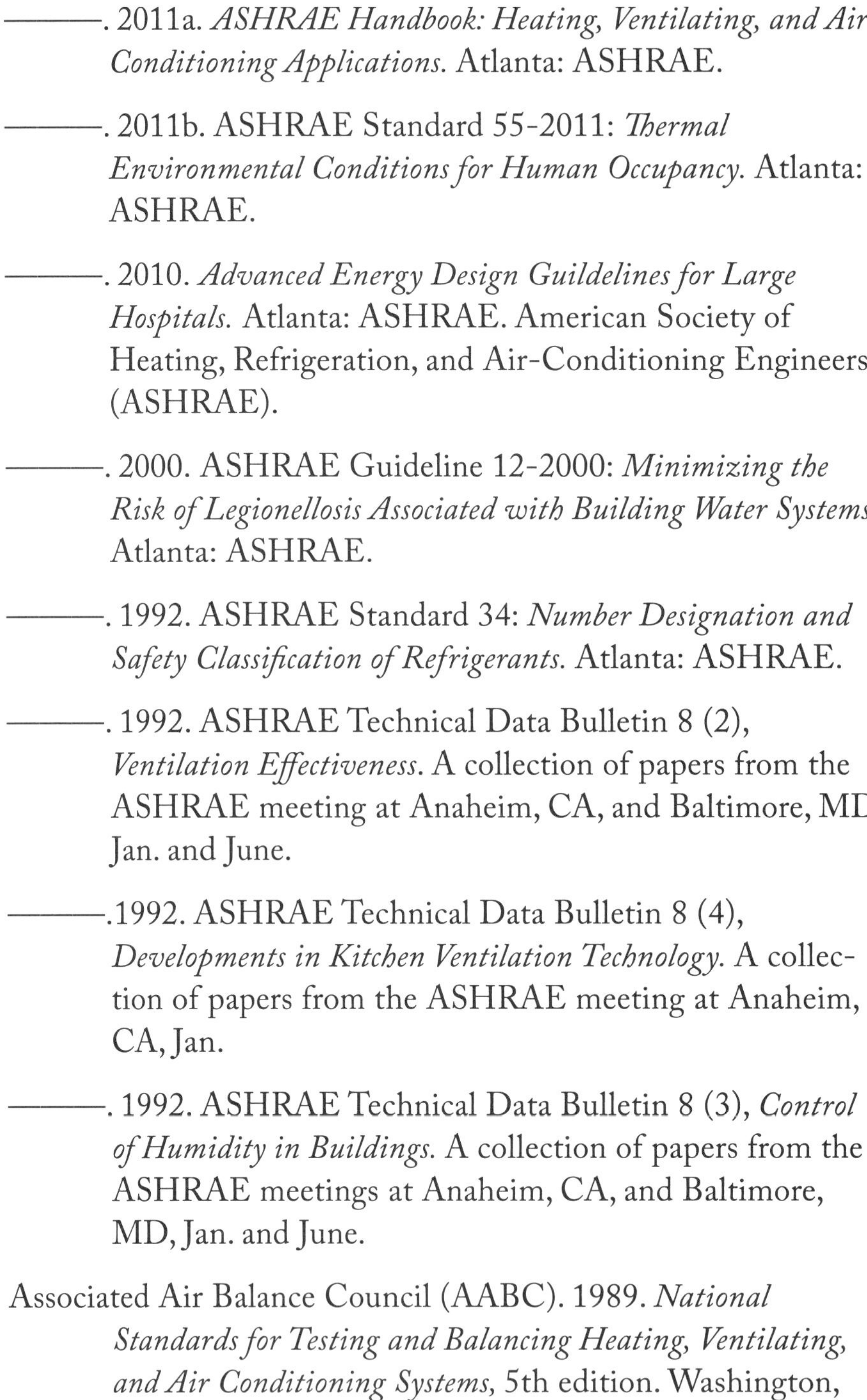

———. 2011a. *ASHRAE Handbook: Heating, Ventilating, and Air-Conditioning Applications.* Atlanta: ASHRAE.

———. 2011b. ASHRAE Standard 55-2011: *Thermal Environmental Conditions for Human Occupancy.* Atlanta: ASHRAE.

———. 2010. *Advanced Energy Design Guildelines for Large Hospitals.* Atlanta: ASHRAE. American Society of Heating, Refrigeration, and Air-Conditioning Engineers (ASHRAE).

———. 2000. ASHRAE Guideline 12-2000: *Minimizing the Risk of Legionellosis Associated with Building Water Systems.* Atlanta: ASHRAE.

———. 1992. ASHRAE Standard 34: *Number Designation and Safety Classification of Refrigerants.* Atlanta: ASHRAE.

———. 1992. ASHRAE Technical Data Bulletin 8 (2), *Ventilation Effectiveness.* A collection of papers from the ASHRAE meeting at Anaheim, CA, and Baltimore, MD, Jan. and June.

———.1992. ASHRAE Technical Data Bulletin 8 (4), *Developments in Kitchen Ventilation Technology.* A collection of papers from the ASHRAE meeting at Anaheim, CA, Jan.

———. 1992. ASHRAE Technical Data Bulletin 8 (3), *Control of Humidity in Buildings.* A collection of papers from the ASHRAE meetings at Anaheim, CA, and Baltimore, MD, Jan. and June.

Associated Air Balance Council (AABC). 1989. *National Standards for Testing and Balancing Heating, Ventilating, and Air Conditioning Systems,* 5th edition. Washington, DC: AABC.

Associated Air Balance Council. (AABC) Test and Balance Forms.

Blake, R. T. 1980. *Water Treatment for HVAC and Potable Water Systems.* New York: McGraw-Hill.

Burton, D. Jeff. 2000. *IAQ and HVAC Workbook.* Bountiful, Utah: IVE, Inc.

Carrier Corporation. 1972. *Carrier Corporation System Design Manual.* Syracuse, NY: The Carrier Corporation.

Centers for Disease Control and Prevention (CDC). 2003. *Guidelines for Environmental Infection Control in Healthcare Facilities.* Atlanta: CDC.

Environmental Protection Agency (EPA) and National Institute for Occupational Safety and Health (NIOSH). 1991. *Building Air Quality: A Guide for Building Owners and Facility Managers.* Washington, DC: EPA.

Hensley, J. C., ed. 1985. *Cooling Tower Fundamentals.* Mission, KS: Marley Cooling Tower Company.

Honeywell, Inc. 1988. *Honeywell Engineering Manual of Automatic Control for Commercial Buildings, Heating Ventilating, Air Conditioning.* Minneapolis: Honeywell, Inc.

Hunt, V. D. 1983. *Energy Conservation in Healthcare Facilities.* Atlanta: The Fairmont Press, Inc.

Indoor Air Quality Association (IAQA), Inc. 2000. *IAQA 01-2000 Recommended Guidelines for Indoor Environments.* Kensington, MD: IAQA.

International Code Council (ICC). 2012. *International Building Code.*Washington, DC: ICC

Joint Commission. 1990. *Accreditation Manual for Hospitals* Oakbrook Terrace, IL: Joint Commission.

———. 1989. *Accreditation Manual for Hospitals.* Oakbrook Terrace, IL: Joint Commission.

———. 1989. *The Kips Survey Guide.* Oakbrook Terrace, IL: Joint Commission.

Kendrick, L. 1986. *Design Manual for Heating, Ventilation, and Air Conditioning Systems with Coordinated Details,* 4th ed. Arlington, VA: Frank M. Trent & Associates, Inc.

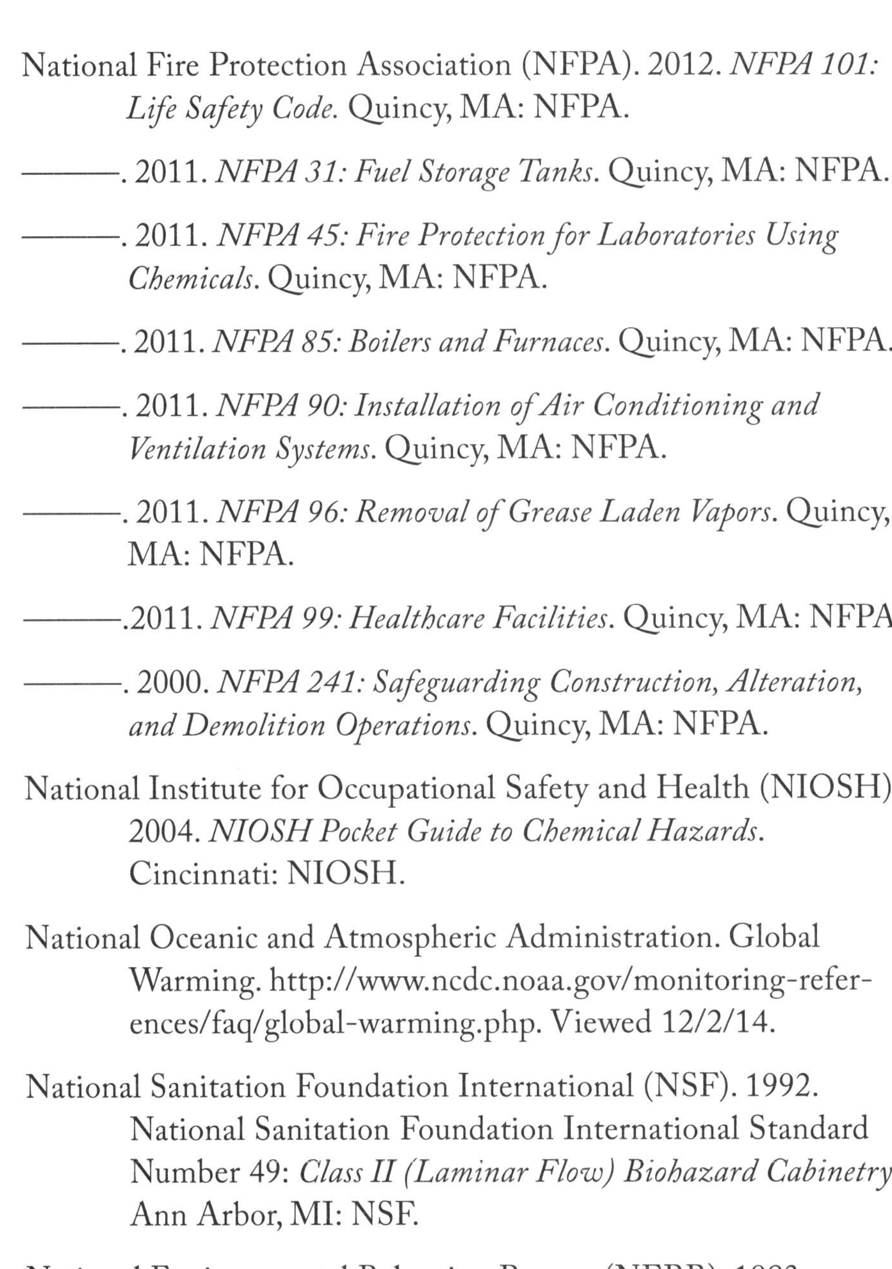

National Fire Protection Association (NFPA). 2012. *NFPA 101: Life Safety Code.* Quincy, MA: NFPA.

———. 2011. *NFPA 31: Fuel Storage Tanks.* Quincy, MA: NFPA.

———. 2011. *NFPA 45: Fire Protection for Laboratories Using Chemicals.* Quincy, MA: NFPA.

———. 2011. *NFPA 85: Boilers and Furnaces.* Quincy, MA: NFPA.

———. 2011. *NFPA 90: Installation of Air Conditioning and Ventilation Systems.* Quincy, MA: NFPA.

———. 2011. *NFPA 96: Removal of Grease Laden Vapors.* Quincy, MA: NFPA.

———.2011. *NFPA 99: Healthcare Facilities.* Quincy, MA: NFPA.

———. 2000. *NFPA 241: Safeguarding Construction, Alteration, and Demolition Operations.* Quincy, MA: NFPA.

National Institute for Occupational Safety and Health (NIOSH). 2004. *NIOSH Pocket Guide to Chemical Hazards.* Cincinnati: NIOSH.

National Oceanic and Atmospheric Administration. Global Warming. http://www.ncdc.noaa.gov/monitoring-references/faq/global-warming.php. Viewed 12/2/14.

National Sanitation Foundation International (NSF). 1992. National Sanitation Foundation International Standard Number 49: *Class II (Laminar Flow) Biohazard Cabinetry.* Ann Arbor, MI: NSF.

National Environmental Balancing Bureau (NEBB). 1983. *Procedural Standards for Testing, Adjusting, Balancing of Environmental Systems.* Vienna, VA: NEBB.

Sheet Metal and Air Conditioning Contractors' National Association, Inc. (SMACCNA). 1997. *HVAC Duct Construction Standards, Metal and Flexible,* 2nd ed. Chantilly, VA: SMACCNA.

———. 1995. *IAQ Guidelines for Occupied Buildings Under Construction.* Chantilly, VA: SMACCNA.

———. 1994. *HVAC Systems Commissioning Manual.* Chantilly, VA: SMACCNA.

———. 1993. *Indoor Air Quality*, 2nd ed. Chantilly, VA: SMACCNA.

———. 1992. *Fire, Smoke and Radiation Damper Installation Guide for HVAC Systems*, 4th ed. Chantilly, VA: SMACCNA.

———. 1982. *Flexible Duct Performance Standards and Flexible Duct Installation Standards.* Vienna, VA: SMACCNA.

———. 1979. *Energy Recovery Equipment and Systems.* Arlington, VA: SMACCNA.

———. 1975. *Duct Liner Application Standard.* Vienna, VA: SMACCNA.

———. 1973. *Manual for Balancing and Adjustment of Air Distribution Systems.* Arlington, VA: SMACCNA.

Occupational Safety and Health Administration (OSHA). 1999. *OSHA Technical Manual.* Published January 20. https://www.osha.gov/dts/osta/otm/otm_toc.html.

Swift, J. M., Jr., and T. Lawrence. 2011. *ASHRAE Green Guide: The Design, Construction, and Operation of Sustainable Buildings*, 3rd ed. Atlanta: ASHRAE.

U.S. Department of Health and Human Services, Public Health Service. 1987. *Control of Legionella In Cooling Towers, Summary Guidelines.* Section of Acute and Communicable Disease Epidemiology, Bureau of Community Health and Prevention, Division of Health, Wisconsin Department of Health and Social Services, Aug.

Westaway, C. R., and A. W. Loomis.1981. *Cameron Hydraulic Data*, 16th ed. Woodcliff Lake, NJ: Intersoll-Rand.

Wood, R. H., Jr. 1990. "Will Cogeneration Payoff for Your Health Facility?" *Health Facilities Management* 3(9): 28–30.

Appendix A-1

Front End Project Report for Code and Utility

Survey/Project Report Date: ___/___/___

Project Name: ______________________________

Location: ______________________________

Architect: ______________________________

Owner's Representative: ______________________________

New or Renovation: ______________________________

Number of Floors Now: ______________________________

Future Floors: ______________________________

Number of Patient Beds Now: ______________________________

New Patient Beds: ______________________________

Approx. Square Feet of Project: ______________________________

Located in City: ______________________________

County: ______________________________

Construction Type: ______________________________

Occupancy Classification: ______________________________

Report Prepared By: ______________________________

At SSR Job #: ______________________________

Items Needing Attention Back to City, State, or Utility Companies

1. Gas Company
   a. Site plan locating building and gas meter ( )
   b. Estimated gas demand in CFH ( ) CFD ( )
   c. Forms requesting service ( )
2. Power Company
   a. Site plan locating building and transformer ( )
   b. Estimated connected load ( )
   c. Forms requesting service ( )
3. Water Company
   a. Site plan showing point of entry to building ( )
   b. Approx. meter location ( )
   c. Approx. domestic water use: GPD ( )
   d. Estimated fire water use: GPM ( )
   e. Forms requesting service ( )
4. Sewer Company
   a. Site plan locating building and point sewer leaves building ( )
   b. I.E. of sewer at property line ( )
   c. Estimated sewer use: GPD ( )
   d. Forms requesting service ( )

5. Fire Department

    a. Site plan showing building and paving to locate fire hydrants (   )

6. Others:

Building Inspector Questions

Date: ____/____/____

Answers by: ________________________________

General Questions

1. Are auto closures required on patient room corridor doors? (   )

2. Plan submittal:

   a. Who do we submit plans to? ______________________
   ____

   b. Who reviews plans for building permit?______________
   ____

   c. Do we also have to submit plans to?________________
   ____

   1. State Health (   )
   2. State Fire (   )
   3. Electrical Inspector (   )
   4. Plumbing Inspector (   )
   5. Fire Chief (   )
   6. Any other? ______________________________
   7. At what stage do you want to review drawings? _____

3. Renovation ______________________________

How much of the building do we have to bring up to current codes for this renovation?____

____

____

____

Fire Department

Date: ______/______/______

Fire Department

Local: ____

Fire Official

State: ____

Address: ____

Phone: ____

Fax: ____

1. Automatic Sprinklers:

   a. Can alarm be connected to local fire department, and how? ____________________________

   b. Is building required to have A/S in every room? ________

   c. Type zoning for A/S system:

      1. Zone per 52,000: ____________________________

      2. Zone per floor: ____________________________

   d. Is P.I.V. required outside or is OS&Y inside OK? ______

   e. Are A/S required over dock areas?____________________

      Under canopies? ____________________________

   f. If building area is over 52,000 square feet per floor, can we bring in one entrance to building and split to two control valves inside at entrance to building? __________

   g. What agency approves A/S drawings? ________________

   h. Is it OK to have A/S drawn by contractor? ____________

   i. Is a registered engineer's seal required? ________________

j. Does the contractor have to be licensed by city and state? ______________________

k. Mounting height of floor (zone) control valves? ________

l. Control valve accessibility? ______________________

m. Do sprinkler zones have to match fire alarm zones?

____

2. Standpipe System

a. Where are standpipes and 2½" valves to be located?

____

b. Type and number of 2½" outlets required on roof ______

c. Are rollouts to 2½" valves on first floor considered standpipes and need cutoff valves? ______________

d. Is fire pump sized by number of standpipes in largest fire area? ______________________

e. Does fire pump have to be in its own room? __________

f. Does fire pump room require a wall rating? __________

g. Are 1½" hoses required on standpipe system? _________
Fire pump:

3. How is electricity supplied to pump?

a. Served directly from utility transformer ahead of main breaker for building? ______________________

____

b. Is fire pump required to be on emergency power?_______

c. Are there special requirements not in NFPA 20? _______

4. Outside Fire Protection

a. What spacing is required on fire hydrants? ___________

b. Is a fire loop required around building? ______________
How far from siamese to pumper hydrant? ___________

5. Fire Misc.

a. Is a fire control room required in building? ___________

b. Is an outside electrical shutoff or annunciator required? _

c. Are smoke detectors required in corridors 30' on center? _

d. What happens to A/C system on fire alarm activation? _

shut system down in that zone (   )

shut down entire building (   )

leave systems on (   ).

e. Type of fire extinguishers required in: corridors (   ), elect. rooms (   ), storage rooms (   ), mech. rooms (   ), kitchen hood (   ), kitchen hood port (   ).

f. Describe required operation of range hood fire extinguishing system ______________________________

HVAC Survey

Date: _____/_______/______

Local Building Official

Address: ____

Phone: ____

Fax: ____

Local Fire Inspector

Address: ____

Phone: ____

Fax: ____

Mechanical:

1. Fire and smoke damper requirements for sheet metal ducts passing through the following walls:

	Fire Damper	Smoke Damper
2-hour fire wall		
2-hour fire and smoke		
1-hour smoke wall		
1-hour fire wall		
Corridor wall		
Floor penetrations		
NFPA 101 hazardous		
Storage rooms		
Janitor's closet		
Other		

Are separate smoke and fire damper assemblies OK where both are required at one wall ( )? Are there other areas or walls requiring fire or smoke dampers?

2. Is it OK to undercut doors for exhaust from:

    a. Patient room to patient toilet? ( )

    b. Corridor to janitor closet or toilet? ( )

    c. Is there a max. size room? ( )

3. Is smoke venting or smoke evacuation required? ( )
4. Is supply and return/exhaust required in every room in building? ( )
5. Can fan room be used as a plenum? ( )
6. Can several hazardous areas (powerhouse) be all enclosed by one 2-hour wall and fire damper that wall only? ( )
7. Are boilers required to be in a separate room? ( )
8. Are chillers required to be in a separate room? ( )
9. Can building be built over boilers? ( )
10. Is a smoke-proof stair tower required? ( )
11. For projects under the 1997 edition of the Uniform Building Code and Uniform Mechanical Code:

    a. Are duct-mounted smoke detectors required at each fire/smoke damper and smoke damper? ( ) Code reference: ______________________________

    b. Are duct-mounted smoke detectors required only in the supply and return ducts for each unit if the air handling unit is shut down and all fire/smoke and smoke dampers are closed when the unit is shut down? ( )

    c. Are corridors required to be served by dedicated air handling units not serving other areas? ( ) Code reference: ______________________________

    d. Can air from patient rooms be returned to an air-handling unit? ( )

e. Must air from patient rooms be exhausted? (   )

f. What constitutes a "patient room?" ________________

g. Can variable volume air systems be used?____________

h. What are specific conditions for use? ______________

Site Sanitary Sewer Survey

Date: ______/______/______

Name of Sewer Company ______________________________

Address: ______________________________

Phone: ______________________________

Fax: ______________________________

1. Location and size and I.E. of city sewer: ______________
2. Approval to connect this project to city sewer and point we connect ______________________________
   by ______________________________
3. Will there be a charge to bring sewer to site? (   )
4. Sewer tap fee ______________________________
5. Can we have a copy of area map on sewers? ______________
6. Is a comminutor required? ______________________
   a. Min. size of connection to city sewer ______________
   b. Is a lift station required? ______________________
7. Min. slope (   ) Max. slope (   ) of outside sewer pipe
8. Type pipe allowed outside:
   a. Cast iron (   )
   b. PVC (   )
   c. Clay (   )
   d. Concrete (   )
   e. Transite (   )
9. Is there a city standard for manholes? (   ) Can we have a copy? (   )
10. Are profiles required for sewer on our property? (   )
11. Max. distance in 8" sewers manhole can be apart (   )

12. Items needed by city from SSR ______________________
13. Above was done by______________________________
    on ____

Costs to Owner _________________________________

____

____

____

____

____

Diagram of Sewer Tie-in

Items Needed from Sewer Company

1. I.E. of sewer at tie-in pt.
2. Copy of area map of sewers
3. Standard manhole detail

Water Department Survey

Date: ______/______/______

Name of Water Company ______________________________

Address: ______________________________

Phone: ______________________________

Fax: ______________________________

1. Approval to connect this project to city water and location of tie-in (   ) by ______________________________
2. Location and size of city water main ______________________________
3. Will there be a charge to bring water to site? ______________
4. Water tap fee ______________________________
5. Who pays for connection to city main? ______________
6. Is it OK to have unmetered water on our property? (   )
   a. City to own line? (   ) ______________________
   b. Easement required (   ) ______________________
   c. OK for meter to be outside of building? (   ) ______
7. City water entrance, what is required?
   a. Tapping sleeve and valve (   ) Who does, who pays?______________________________
   b. City water meter:______________________________
      Who pays for meter? (   ) Who sets meter? (   ) Who pays to set meter? (   )
   c. R.P.B.P. (   ) One or two required? (   )
   d. Who sizes the city water meter? (   )
   e. Can water not going to sewer be metered and not pay sewer charge? (   )
8. Fire entrance, what is required?______________________________

a. T.S.&V. ( ) Who does?______________________
   Who pays? __________________________________

b. Fire meter ( )

c. Detector check ( )

d. Double check valves ( )

e. R.P.B.P. above ground ( )

f. P.I.V. outside ( ) or OS& Y inside ( )

g. Types of pipe required if loop around building ________

9. Depth required for loop______________________________
   Pressure test required_____________________________psi
   Action required back to city

10. Site plan showing building and meter location ( )
    a. Estimated GPD use ( ) Estimated GPM ( )

Items Needed from Water Company

11. Static pressure ( )

12. Residual Press____________________________________
    PSI @____
    GPM

13. Total hardness in CA CO 3__________________________
    PPM/17.1 =______________________________________
    GPG

14. Copy of area map of water lines _______________________

15. City water meter details______________________________

Costs to Owner: _______________________________________

Diagram of Water Piping to Building

Plumbing Survey

Date: ______/______/______

Answers by:

1. It is OK to put the following into the sanitary sewer:
   a. Dishwash 180°F water (   )
   b. Boiler blowdown (   )
   c. Drain at dumpster (   )
   d. A/C condensate (   )
2. Grease interceptor required inside or outside (   )
   a. Does grease trap require venting? ____________________
   b. Does city have sizing criteria for grease trap? __________
3. Where does swimming pool discharge go? ________________
   a. Elevator sump pumps:
   b. Connect to sanitary or storm sewer? ________________
   c. Connect indirectly to hub drain or direct with check valve?____
4. Can OVC/DWV Schedule 40 pipe material be used for storm water? (   ) Waste and vent? (   ) Above floor? (   ) Below floor? (   )

Electrical Utility Survey

Date: _____/_____/_____

Name of Power Company

Address: ______________________________

Phone: ______________________________

Fax: ______________________________

Cost Items to Owner

1. Are two feeds available from separate substations? (   )
   a. If yes, is auto or manual transfer available? __________
2. Will there be a charge to bring power to the site? (   )
   ____
3. Transformer
   a. Is service through a pad mount OK? (   ) ________
   b. Who furnishes pad mount? ____________________
      Who pays? ______________________________
   c. Is there a max. available pad mount you furnish
      (   ) If so, what size? ____________________
   d. Is 480/277 volt grounded wye service available?
      (   ) ______________________________
   e. Who pours pad for pad mount? ____________________
      Who pays? ______________________________
   f. Are there clearance restrictions on locating transformer? _
4. Primary Conductors
   a. Is conduit necessary? (   )
      Who furnishes? ______________________________
      Who pays? ______________________________
      Who installs? ______________________________

Size and # required ______________________

If owner furnishes, can we have a copy of standard detail?
(   )

b. How is conduit to be terminated at the pole property line? ______________________

c. Who furnishes primary conductors? ____________
Who pays? ______________________

5. Secondary conductors

   a. Who furnishes secondary conductors? ____________
   Who pays? ______________________
   Who installs? ______________________

   b. Does the utility limit the max. conductors per phase on secondary? ______________________

6. Metering

   a. Who furnishes? ______________________

   b. Where is meter located? ______________________

   c. Is metering conduit required? ______________________

7. Obtain copy of applicable rate schedules ____________
8. Do any special codes apply? ______________________
9. Who is the phone company in the area? ____________
10. Are there local requirements on lighting levels, heights, etc. outside? ______________________
11. Are closed transition transfer switches permitted? (Closed transition switches synchronize and parallel the standby generators(s) with the electric system for approximately 100 milliseconds when transferring.)
12. In the case of multi-tenant buildings, is it permissible to meter each tenant separately? ______________________
    Does the utility require hot or cold sequences metering? (Hot sequence indicates the meter before any disconnecting means; cold sequence has a disconnect prior to the meter.)

Electrical Inspector Survey

Date: ______/______/______

Answers by:

1. Are smoke detectors required in corridors 30'0" O.C. ? (   ) Patient/sleeping rooms? (   ) Electrical rooms? (   ) Mechanical room? (   )
2. What color exit lights required? Red OK (   ) Green OK (   )
3. Is an outside electrical shutoff or command station required? (   )
4. What activates a smoke damper?
   a. Detectors in corridors? (   )
   b. Detectors in S & R at A/C unit? (   )
   c. Does detector have to be in duct at damper? (   )
   d. Fire alarm in that zone? (   )
   e. Any fire alarm in building? (   )
5. Are diversified electrical loads accepted for:
   a. Emergency generator? (   )
   b. Wiring, panels, etc.? (   )
6. Is low voltage wiring above ceiling required to be in conduit if:
   a. Area is used as a return air plenum? (   )
   b. Area is not used as a return air plenum? (   )
7. Is electrical switchboard required to be in a separate room? (   )
8. Where is a remote annunciator panel required and what readouts are required? ______________________________

   ____
9. Fire pump:

a. How is electricity supplied to pump?

1. Served directly from utility transformer ahead of main breaker for building________________________

2. Served from main switch board ahead of main breaker ________________________

b. Is fire pump required to be on emergency power? ______

c. Are there special requirements not in NFPA 20?_______

10. Will utility company require proposed site plan prints? ______

a. Connected load summary to utility company? _________

Natural Gas Utility Survey

Date: _____/_____/_____

Name of Gas Company

Address: ______________________________

Phone: ______________________________

Fax: ______________________________

Gas is available and we have approval to connect to gas for this project (   ) by ______________________________

1. Is gas available on firm rate? (   )
   a. If yes, is there a max. amount available? (   ) ____
2. What pressure of gas is available to site?____
3. Will there be a charge to bring gas to the site? (   ) __
4. Will there be a connection fee to use gas? (   ).
5. High pressure line:
   a. Who installs?
6. Open ditch ____
7. Install pipe ____
8. Covers ditch ___
9. Cost to owner for above _____
10. Who sets meter? _____
    a. Is there a charge to set meter? (   )
    b. Is a concrete pad required for meter? (   )
    c. Is gravel required under meter? (   )
11. Distance from meter (in feet) to:
    a. Building (   )

b. Opening in building ( )

c. Fuel tank above ground ( ) Below ground ( )

d. Oxygen park ( )

12. Action required back to gas company:

a. Site plan showing meter location ( )

b. Estimated gas demand in CFH ( )

13. Who completes this at SSR? ____________________________

14. Report completed by_________________________date ______

Appendix A-2

Blank Psychometric Chart

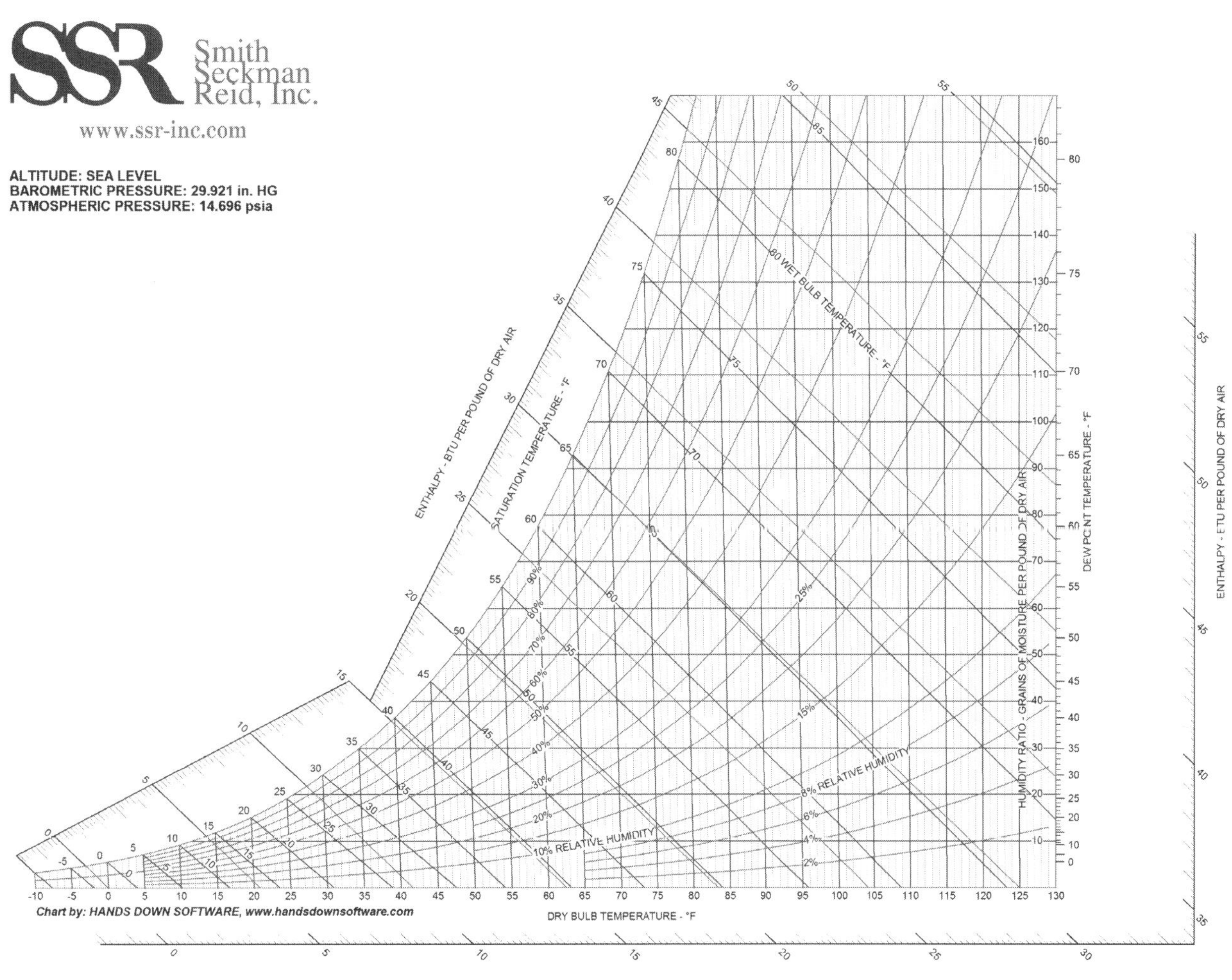

Appendix A-3

How to use the Psychrometric Chart

Figure 1

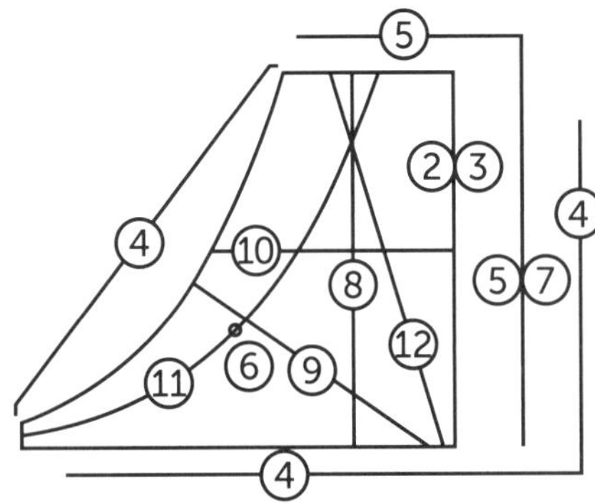

Lines and Scales

1. Dry Bulb Temperature Scale
2. Humidity Ratio Scale
3. Humidity Ratio Scale
4. Enthalpy Scale
5. Sensible Heat Ratio Index
6. Sensible Heat Ratio Index Origin
7. Vapor Pressure Scale
8. Dry Bulb Temperature Line
9. Wet Bilb Temperature Line
10. Humidity Ratio Line
11. Relative Humidity Line
12. Specific Volume Line

Figure 2

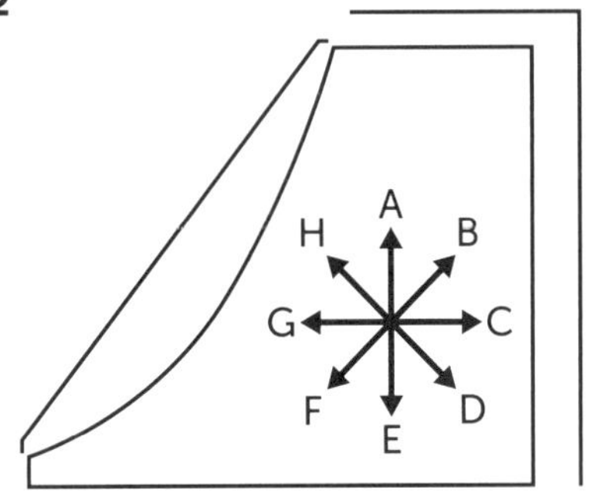

Processes

A. Humidify Only
B. Heat & Humidify
C. Sensible Heat Only
D. Chemical Dehumidify
E. Dehumidify Only
F. Cool & Dehumidify
G. Sensible Cool Only
H. Evaporative Cool

Commonly Used Sea Level Rules of Thumb:

Qtotal = CFM x (hi-hf) x 4.5 Btuh
Qsensible = CFM x (ti-tf) x 1.085 Btuh
Qlatent = CFM x (Gri - Grf) x .68 Btuh
Humidification = CFM x (Grf - Gri) / 1,555 lbs/hr

Problem 1

Return Air (RA) of 7500 cfm at 80°F dry bulb and 67°F wet bulb is mixed with Outside Air (OA) of 2500 cfm at 95°F dry bulb and 78°F wet bulb.
Using the psychrometric chart, determine the Mixed Air (M) condition.

Figure 3

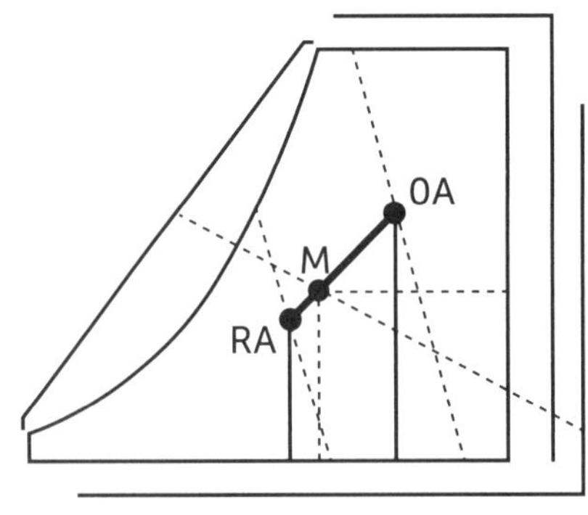

Solution

Locate the Outside Air and Return Air points on the chart. Connect the points using a straight line. Record the specific volumes for each point.

OA = 14.4 cu.ft./lba
RA = 13.8 cu.ft./lba

Convert the airflow from cfm to lbs/min for each point by dividing the airflow cfm by the specific volume:

OA: 2500 / 14.4 = 173.6 lba/min.
RA: 7500 / 13.8 = 543.5 lba/min.
Total = 717.1 lba/min.

Mixed Air (M) dry bulb temperature =

95 x 173.6 / 717.1 = 23.0
80 x 543.5 / 717.1 = 60.6
Mixed Air (M) dry bulb = 83.6°F

Read other properties at the intersection of the dry bulb line and the line between the RA & OA points;

Wet bulb = 69.9°F, Enthalpy = 33.9 Btu/lba
Humidity Ration = 88 gr/lba

Problem 2

Qutside Air (OA) of 5000 cfm is at 35°F and 60% relative humidity and is to be heated to 95°F (2)
Using the psychrometric chart, determine the final relative humidity, wet bulb and amount of sensible heat energy needed.

Figure 4

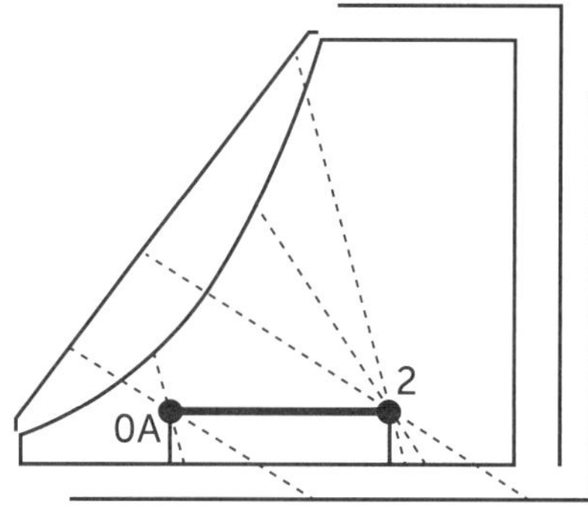

Solution

Locate the Outside Air point on the chart. Draw a horizontal line to the 95°F dry bulb line. The final point is the intersection of the horizontal line and the 95°F dry bulb line. Record the relative humidity, wet bulb and enthalpy for the point 2.

Point 2:
Web Bulb Temperature - 59.1°F
Relative Humidity = 7.3%
Enthalpy = 25.6 Btu/lba

Record the enthalpy and specific volume for the Outside Air (OA) point.

OA:
Enthalpy = 11.2 Btu/lba

The required sensible heat energy is given by the following equation:
Q = (h2 - h1) x (cfm x 60) / specfic vol.

Q = (25.6 - 11.2) x (5000 x 60) / 12.5
Q = 345,600 Btu/hr

Problem 3

Entering Air (EA) of 6000 cfm at 82°F and 50% RH goes through a cooling coil with Leaving Air (LA) at 55°F and 98% RH. Determine the total heat removed., moisture removed (dehumidification) and sensible heat ration (SHR).

Figure 5

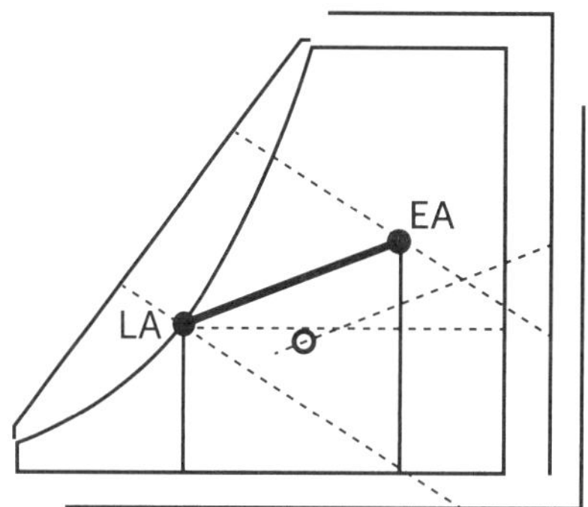

Solution

Locate the Entering Air (EA) and Leaving Air (LA) on the chart. Record the enthalpy and large unit humidity ratio (lB/lb) for both points. Also record the specific volume for the Entering Air (EA).

EA Enthalpy = 32.5 Btu/lba
EA humidity Ration = .0117 lbw/lba
EA Specific Volume = 13.9 cu.ft./lba
LA Enthalpy = 23 Btu/lba
LA Humidity Ration = .009 lbw/lba

the total heat removed is given by:
Q = (h2 - h1) x (cfm x 60) / specific vol.

Q = (23 - 32.5) x (6000 x 60) / 13.9
Q = 246,043 Btu/hr

The moisture removed is given by:
dW = (W2 - W1) x (cfm x 60) / specific vol.

dW = (.009 - .0117 lbw) x (6000 x 60) / 13.9
dW = - 69.9 lbw/hr

The SHR is determined by drawing a parallel line from the SHR index to the SHR scale and reading the value.

SHR = .691

Appendix A-4

Building Commissioning

As the complexity of health care facilities, systems, and equipment increases, building commissioning is becoming predominant in new and existing facilities. The idea that every health care facility should perform commissioning on new and existing projects and continue with ongoing commissioning to maintain energy-efficiency operations is becoming more common. Without commissioning, too many facilities fail to meet their performance goals. The business case or justification for health care commissioning has been proven in many facilities. Commissioning saves money, improves system performance, and increases building comfort.

Many industry resources are available on building and systems commissioning, including those from ASHRAE, PECI, AABC, NEBB, and ASHE. ASHE has developed and published *The Health Facility Commissioning Handbook and Health Facility Commissioning Guidelines.* These publications explain all aspects of the commissioning processes for hospitals and other health care facilities.

The commissioning process includes the observation of building performance during normal operation of peak and partial loads and during emergency and alarm conditions. The process provides short and long term benefits that include the following:

- Ensuring that the building operates as intended from day one

- Ensuring integration among the various systems and pieces of equipment within the building
- Verifying that controls and alarms are working as intended
- Increasing the energy efficiency of the building
- Ensuring that the operations and maintenance staff are knowledgeable about the systems and equipment installed

The traditional definition of commissioning is a process that ensures the performance of systems meets the owner's original intent and expectations. Commissioning is a team effort and should begin early in every project. Commissioning should be led by a commissioning agent or authority that reports directly to the owner. This agent must be able to provide an independent and objective view of commissioning activities and should not be the contractor, although the contractor will assist in many of the verification procedures. The process will identify corrective actions in a timely manner to the persons responsible for correcting deficiencies.

In addition to construction commissioning for new or renovation projects, types of commissioning include the following:

- Recommissioning: This is type of commissioning is performed on projects that were originally commissioned at turnover but for any of a number of possible reasons the process needs to be repeated.
- Retrocommissioining: This type is applied to facilities or specific systems that have been operating for some time but were never commissioned.

These types of commissioning are common in the industry and the processes are well documented in many available sources.

An additional type of commissioning, called Continuous Commissioning® (CC) by Energy Systems Laboratory at Texas A&M University (http://esl.tamu.edu/continuous-commissioning), is an ongoing process to resolve operating problems, improve comfort, and optimize energy use for existing commercial and institutional buildings and central plant facilities. CC incorporates and extends existing building commissioning practices. The Energy Systems

Laboratory has developed the CC process to improve comfort and performance using cost-effective measures. CC incorporates the most effective retrocommissioning techniques into a process that has achieved superior performance in over 300 buildings around the globe. The objective of CC is to produce a rapid payback while providing sustained improvement to building performance based on the facility's actual use.

Index

A

B

D

E

U

V

W